The School Counselor's
MENTAL HEALTH SOURCEBOOK

The School Counselor's
MENTAL HEALTH SOURCEBOOK

Strategies to Help Students Succeed

RICK AUGER

CORWIN
A SAGE Company

For information:

Corwin
A SAGE Company
2455 Teller Road
Thousand Oaks, California 91320
(800) 233-9936
Fax: (800) 417-2466
www.corwin.com

SAGE India Pvt. Ltd.
B 1/I 1 Mohan Cooperative
   Industrial Area
Mathura Road, New Delhi 110 044
India

SAGE Ltd.
1 Oliver's Yard
55 City Road
London EC1Y 1SP
United Kingdom

SAGE Asia-Pacific Pte. Ltd.
33 Pekin Street #02-01
Far East Square
Singapore 048763

Library of Congress Cataloging-in-Publication Data

Auger, Rick.
The school counselor's mental health sourcebook:strategies to help students succeed/Rick Auger.
    p. cm.
Includes bibliographical references and index.
ISBN 978-1-4129-7273-4 (pbk.)
   1. School mental health services—Handbooks, manuals, etc. 2. Children—Mental health—Handbooks, manuals, etc. I. Title.

LB3430.A94 2011
371.7'13—dc22   2010045947

11   12   13   14   15   10   9   8   7   6   5   4   3   2   1

Acquisitions Editor:	Jessica Allan
Associate Editor:	Allison Scott
Editorial Assistant:	Lisa Whitney
Production Editor:	Amy Schroller
Copy Editor:	Cynthia Long
Typesetter:	C&M Digitals (P) Ltd.
Proofreader:	Victoria Reed-Castro
Indexer:	Judy Hunt
Cover Designer:	Scott Van Atta
Permissions Editor:	Karen Ehrmann

Contents

Preface

During my first year as an enthusiastic but raw school psychologist, I was having trouble figuring out how best to help a very unmotivated and low-energy eighth grader. The student's strong test scores belied his poor classroom performance, and even though he just sat in his desk doing virtually nothing in class, he seemed to care about his grades. I was muddling around trying to find the right set of rewards and academic interventions that would light a fire under him, and I was not having much success.

What finally turned things around and led to an approach that was more useful was a conversation I had with the school counselor, who had just met with the student. "I think he's depressed," she stated. "I wonder if all the rest of his school issues revolve around that." That made very good sense, and jointly we worked with the student's teachers and parents to devise some appropriate interventions to better support the boy. This case was an early and tremendously valuable lesson on the importance of recognizing and appreciating the mental health needs of students—and of the critical role school counselors can play in providing appropriate support to students with mental health needs.

While this book is primarily intended to be read by school counselors, the true beneficiaries are the thousands of students in schools across the country who have mental health needs that interfere with their school success and their well-being. School counselors are in a unique position to assist students by helping teachers create better classroom environments for students with mental health needs, by providing supportive individual and group counseling services, and by working together with families to make appropriate referrals and create networks of support. The intent of this book is to provide school counselors with a foundation of information about mental health disorders, as well as an array of intervention tools and strategies, to help students with mental health needs be more successful in school.

Some administrators and parents—and even some school counselors—may question whether it is a proper role of the school counselor to become involved with students with mental health problems. After all, students with mental health needs often have complex and very challenging problems. In my view, the intricacy and gravity of the problems *is all the more reason for school counselors to be involved.* The American School Counselor Association, in its position statement on the role of school counselors vis-à-vis students with mental health needs, notes that unmet mental health needs can serve as substantial barriers to the personal, social, academic, and career development of students and states that school counselors are committed to helping *all* students, including students with mental health needs, achieve their potential (American School Counselor Association, 2009). The position statement outlines a number of ways school counselors can assist students with mental health needs, including providing appropriate referrals to out-of-school resources, advocating in the school and community for access to appropriate mental health services, and providing short-term crisis intervention and counseling. The ensuing chapters in this book provide a number of ideas and strategies to help school counselors carry out these tasks.

It is important to note that school counselors should not be expected to serve as the sole providers of counseling services for students with mental health needs or to function as mental health counselors. Ideally, school counselors should work in tandem with community mental health counselors to provide services. Even in the absence of involvement from community mental health counselors, however, school counselors cannot be expected to provide in-depth, intense individual counseling services to any student. Neither is it a good idea for school counselors to take the view that they have nothing to offer students with mental health needs. These are students who need all the help they can get—and school counselors have much to offer them. In the absence of school counselor involvement, teachers and other school personnel are left to manage students with mental health needs on their own, with much less training in the area of children's mental health than school counselors receive. My hope is that this book can provide school counselors with ideas and tools to help them better serve students with mental health needs.

Acknowledgments

Corwin gratefully acknowledges the contributions of the following reviewers:

Carol Cox
Guidance Counselor
Willis Elementary
Willis, Virginia

Katie DeHope
Sixth- and Seventh-Grade Counselor
Malibu High School
Malibu, California

Steve Hutton
Educational Consultant
Elementary School Principal
Area Coordinator of the Highly Skilled Educator Program
Kentucky Department of Education
Villa Hills, Kentucky

Marian White-Hood
Principal (Retired)
Ernest Just Middle School
Mitchellville, Maryland

About the Author

**Rick Auger, PhD,** has been involved in the field of children's mental health for over 25 years. Auger was a school psychologist in an urban school district for 14 years, working with hundreds of students with mental health problems. He also worked as a predoctoral intern in several outpatient mental health clinics, providing mental health services to children, adults, and families. Since 2000, Auger has been a faculty member in the Department of Counseling and Student Personnel at Minnesota State University, Mankato, where he specializes in children's mental health and the training of school counselors. Auger is a frequent presenter at state, regional, and national conferences and has published articles in a number of national journals. He is also involved in research centering on children's mental health, children's career development, and school counseling issues. Auger has served as editor of *Professional School Counseling,* the flagship journal of the American School Counselor Association, and has served on the editorial boards of several counseling-related journals.

This book is dedicated to the two sets of people who bookend my life: my parents, John and Martha Auger, and my sons, Jamie and Alex. To my parents, for providing me with unconditional support and encouragement, and to my boys, for providing joy and pride.

1

Mental Health, Children, and Schools: A Call to Action

Ask virtually any teacher, school counselor, or principal to describe the challenges that interfere with students' ability to succeed in school, and high on the list will be the increasing number of diagnosed and undiagnosed mental health disorders impacting students. This is more than just a perception: Research indicates that substantial numbers of children and adolescents are experiencing mental health problems. Indeed, national studies show that almost one in five youth aged 9 to 17 has a diagnosable mental disorder with at least minimal impairment, with about one in twenty youth having mental disorders with extreme impairment (U.S. Department of Health and Human Services, 1999). A recent household survey of over 9,000 homes reveals that about half of all Americans will meet diagnostic criteria for a mental disorder at some point in their lifetime, with the age of onset usually occurring during childhood or adolescence (Kessler, Berglund, Demler, Jin, & Walters, 2005). If we project the prevalence rates among youth for mental disorders associated with at least mild impairment of functioning (Shaffer et al., 1996) onto a middle school or high school with 1,000 students, on average that school would have around 130 students with an anxiety disorder, about 100 students with a disruptive behavior disorder, and over 60 students with a mood disorder. This does not even count students with less-prevalent disorders such as

Asperger syndrome or early-onset personality disorders. No wonder school counselors, teachers, and other school personnel are so concerned about students' mental health needs!

While the overall prevalence rates tell us that a significant segment of the K–12 student population is dealing with mental health disorders, the picture becomes even more concerning when the rates of mental health disorders among certain subgroups are examined. For example, as many as 70% of youth in the juvenile justice system have been found to display some level of mental health concerns (Osterlind, Koller, & Morris, 2007). Other subgroups of children and adolescents exhibiting elevated levels of mental health problems include youth in substance-abuse treatment facilities (Chan, Dennis, & Funk, 2008), youth exposed to mass violence and large-scale disasters (Endo, Shiori, Someya, Toyabe, & Akazawa, 2007; Hoven et al., 2005; Murthy, 2007), youth experiencing victimization (Turner, Finkelhor, & Ormrod, 2006), and even students who have been suspended from school (Stanley, Canham, & Cureton, 2006).

Adding to these alarming facts is the reality that large numbers of children and adolescents have undiagnosed mental disorders, and many of those youth whose disorders are properly diagnosed do not receive appropriate treatment. Studies of both urban (Mennen & Trickett, 2007) and rural (Angold et al., 2002) populations indicate that less than half of children and adolescents with mental health needs receive mental health services. For example, in a study of rural African American and White youth aged 9 to 17, researchers found that only one in three youth with a psychiatric diagnosis had received mental health care in the previous three months, and less than 15% had received specialty mental health care during that time (Angold et al.). Youth with depressive disorders seem particularly at risk for not receiving appropriate mental health services; a large-scale epidemiological study found that children and adolescents with disruptive disorders were about three times more likely than youth with depressive disorders to receive mental health services (Wu et al., 1999). Furthermore, while mental health services are often unavailable to youth in need of those services, at times mental health services are directed to youth who do not seem to be in high need. A study of urban youth found not only that over half of the youth with clinical levels of mental health symptoms did not receive services, but also that some of the children who did *not* display clinical-level symptoms *did* receive services (Mennen & Trickett). All in all, the research indicates that mental health services are frequently unavailable or misdirected, leading to a situation where children and adolescents with mental health needs are routinely not receiving the services they need.

IT'S NOT JUST ABOUT DIAGNOSES

While the overt focus of this book is on students with diagnosable mental disorders such as attention-deficit/hyperactivity disorder (ADHD) and

Asperger disorder, it is important to understand that many students have significant mental health needs even though their social, emotional, or behavioral difficulties may not fit in a formal diagnostic category. A student may be highly impulsive and distractible but not meet diagnostic criteria for ADHD, or a student may be plagued by persistent sadness and low self-esteem but not meet diagnostic criteria for a depressive disorder. We can look at surveys that ask youth to offer simple, basic descriptions of their behavior and mood to gain an understanding of the numbers of youth who are struggling. For example, a well-designed survey of over 130,000 sixth-, ninth-, and twelfth-grade students in the state of Minnesota found that about 10% of the students reported that they are often irritable and angry; 15% reported that they often have trouble concentrating; and around 8% reported that they are often unhappy, depressed, or tearful (Minnesota Department of Health, 2007). The Minnesota survey results present a revealing picture, indicating that there is a substantial segment of students who experience pervasive sadness, discouragement, and hopelessness, often accompanied by thoughts of suicide. There is also a significant percentage of both boys and girls who report physically assaulting others, often multiple times. This is not unique to Minnesota. National surveys indicate that 13% of adolescents reported having at least one major depressive episode in their lifetime (Substance Abuse and Mental Health Services Administration [SAMHSA], 2007). (A *major depressive episode* is defined as two weeks or longer during which there is either depressed mood or loss of interest or pleasure and at least four other symptoms that reflect a change in functioning, such as problems with sleep, eating, energy, concentration, and self-image; SAMHSA.) Furthermore, 28% of high school students report experiencing at least a two-week period in the past year during which they felt so sad or hopeless almost every day that they stopped engaging in usual activities, and 8% of high school students have attempted suicide (Centers for Disease Control and Prevention, 2006).

It is important not to lose sight of the fact that this discussion of survey results has been a glass-half-empty discussion, as the focus has been on those students reporting troubling emotions and antisocial behaviors. While it is necessary to examine these negative responses to understand the numbers of struggling students in our schools, it is also important to recognize the positive aspects the surveys reveal: Most students are *not* pervasively unhappy, most do *not* feel crushed by discouragement, and most do *not* assault others. The sky is not falling. Neither, however, is it a rare occurrence for a student to be aggressive, anxious, or miserable. The numbers do not lie. But the numbers tell just part of the story.

IT'S NOT JUST ABOUT NUMBERS

While the numbers of youth with diagnosed and undiagnosed mental health problems are alarming, the true impact of the numbers is fully understood only when one considers the multiple layers of negative consequences experienced by children and adolescents with mental health problems. Mental health problems generally interfere with school functioning, including academic achievement and relationships with teachers. Some mental health disorders (oppositional defiant disorder, for example) are by their very nature accompanied by resistance to rules and authority at school and tend to elicit strong negative reactions from teachers and school staff, which is obviously not a good situation for either the student or the adults. Other disorders, such as depressive disorders and anxiety disorders, require so much emotional energy to manage that often little energy is left over to devote to doing homework and paying attention in class. Many mental health disorders are associated with problems with organization and planning, making it very difficult for those afflicted students to set and complete the short-term and long-term goals and tasks required for school success. In sum, students with mental health problems typically find school a daunting and often unsuccessful experience.

While students with mental health disorders often find it hard to deal with school, the reverse is also true: Schools often find it hard to deal with the challenging behaviors that sometimes accompany mental health disorders. Students with disruptive behavior disorders can create havoc in classrooms, particularly if supports are not in place for those students. Teachers can find themselves stressed and dispirited trying to manage the behavior of these students, while at the same time trying to meet the needs of the other students in the room. And it is not just disruptive behaviors that present a challenge for teachers. Just as difficult, though in a very different way, are behaviors that are often associated with mood disorders. Students with mood disorders may seem so lost in their own distress that they lack any kind of motivation in the classroom—or manifest their unhappiness through a prickly irritability. School counselors, administrators, and other school staff can experience the same frustration and helplessness as classroom teachers and are often at a loss for how to assist teachers who are pleading for ideas to help students with mental health disorders.

As difficult as it can be for teachers and school counselors, however, the greatest share of negative consequences falls directly on the students with mental health needs. For students with disruptive behavior disorders, these negative consequences include impaired relationships, a higher incidence of juvenile delinquency, and a greater risk of substance-abuse problems. As adults, they have a greater likelihood of imprisonment, as well as stunted educational and career outcomes (Barkley, Fischer, Smallish, & Fletcher, 2006; Elkins, McGue, & Iacono, 2007; Ferguson, Horwood, & Ridder, 2005). For students with mood disorders, these negative consequences can include difficulties with social relationships, an increased risk of substance abuse, and a higher rate of suicide. Negative adult outcomes include an elevated risk of mental health problems and a diminished sense of basic happiness (Birmaher et al., 1996; Colman, Wadsworth, Croudace, & Jones, 2007; Rao, Weissman, Martin, & Hammond, 1993; Rohde, Lewinsohn, & Seeley, 1994; Weissman et al., 1999). Other mental health disorders also come with their own negative consequences. Finally, for many students with mental health problems, there is an immediate and crippling consequence: a pervasive sense of pain, frustration, and discouragement.

WHAT IF EVERYTHING IS BEING DONE RIGHT?

Even in the best of circumstances, school counselors and other school professionals can benefit from knowledge of intervention guidelines and strategies for working with students with mental health problems. Let's imagine the best possible situation for a child with a mental health disorder, taking the case of a child we will name David. We will assume David's disorder is attention-deficit/hyperactivity disorder (ADHD).

David's ADHD was properly diagnosed by a child psychiatrist following a thorough medical and behavioral assessment. As a part of the medical portion of the assessment, the question of whether to prescribe medication was discussed and a thoughtful decision about medication was made based on the nature of the behaviors and the wishes of David and his parents. David's parents were referred to an ADHD parent-support group, where they are learning how to support David as well as learning behavioral strategies to manage his behavior. David is seeing a community-based licensed professional counselor who is providing emotional support and teaching him organizational and self-management strategies.

The assessment process and the multifaceted support described are excellent. Shouldn't that be enough? Well . . . probably not. Even though David receives ample professional and family support *outside* of school, he still needs additional support for time *inside* of school. He spends six or more hours a day in school and very likely displays behaviors in the classroom that detract from his academic and social success. Because of the pervasive neurobiological impact of ADHD—in other words, the way ADHD has affected the way his brain is wired—David struggles to pay attention in class, tends to blurt out answers that disrupt the class and annoy his classmates, has trouble organizing his material, and becomes easily frustrated and unhappy. And this even with much support from his family and from community health professionals!

Needless to say, many students with mental health problems do not enjoy the kind of support that David receives. In fact, the students with the greatest mental health needs are often the ones most lacking in out-of-school support. This is partly because demands associated with mental health problems exert stress on families—and stress tends to exacerbate symptoms (Hanson et al., 2006). The resulting cycle (stress intensifies symptoms, which leads to increased stress, which intensifies symptoms, and so on) increases the student's need for mental health support.

All of these reasons—the large numbers of students with mental health problems, the way mental health disorders lead to suffering and reduced opportunities, the lack of coordinated out-of-school support for many of these students, and the fact that they spend many hours each week in classrooms—illustrate the importance of finding ways to assist students with mental health needs *in schools and in classrooms*. The ensuing chapters provide many ideas for ways school counselors can work directly with students with mental health problems, both in individual and group settings. Guidelines and strategies for effectively working with students with mental health problems in classrooms are also presented, giving school counselors tools to share with teachers who are struggling to assist students with ADHD, depressive disorders, anxiety problems, or other mental health problems that are so prevalent in today's schools. Dedicated school counselors, teachers, administrators, and other school personnel *can* make a difference in the lives of students with mental health problems.

A CHILDREN'S MENTAL HEALTH MINIPRIMER

To best respond to the mental health needs of youth, school counselors and other educators need some basic knowledge of mental health services and issues. This section will discuss the two systems in this country intended to address children's mental health needs, the diagnostic manual used by virtually all community-based mental health providers, and the best way to think about mental health labels. First, let's begin by examining the current systems in place to address the mental health needs of youth.

DSM Versus IDEA: Two Sides of the Same Coin

There are two main systems in place in the United States to describe and address the mental health needs of children and adolescents (see Table 1.1). The school-based system most often used for addressing the mental health needs of youth is the special education system (some student mental health needs are addressed through plans developed in accordance with Section 504 of the Rehabilitation Act of 1973). The special education system, as governed by the Individuals With Disabilities Education Act (IDEA 2004) is the system mandated in U.S. public schools to provide for the educational needs of students with disabilities. Some of these disabilities are characterized

Table 1.1   DSM Versus IDEA

DSM	IDEA
Main purpose: provide a reliable and valid classification of mental disorders	Main purpose: insure that all children have equal access to public education
Deals with mental disorders	Deals with educational disabilities
Broad scope, addresses all mental health problems	Narrower scope, addresses only problems that affect educational progress
Includes specific criteria for disorders but does not discuss how to assess disorders	Does not include specific criteria for disability areas but does present requirements for assessment (e.g., the assessment must be completed by a multidisciplinary team)
Describes specific disorders (e.g., generalized anxiety disorder)	Describes broad families of problems (e.g., emotional/behavioral disorder)
Classifies patterns of behavior	Classifies patterns of behavior

Source: Adapted from concepts in House, 2002.

by emotional and behavioral problems. In fact, one of the disability categories described in IDEA is specifically intended for students with emotional and behavioral needs. Different states use slightly different labels for this category; some use ED (emotional disturbance), some use BD (behavioral disorder), and my home state of Minnesota uses EBD (emotional/ behavioral disorder).

The community counterpart to the school-based special education system is the community-based mental health system. This is the system with which families interact when they take their child to their doctor with concerns about the child's hyperactive behavior, or depressed mood, or anxiety, or other emotional or behavioral concerns. This is the system families interact with when they take their child to a local counseling clinic or a clinic specializing in child and adolescent emotional and behavioral problems. Professionals in these settings generally conceptualize and diagnose mental health problems using the *DSM* (*Diagnostic and Statistical Manual of Mental Disorders*, American Psychiatric Association [APA], 2000), which is a diagnostic manual that describes scores of mental disorders.

A DSM PRIMER

Terminology

Depending on the level of precision of the speaker, you may hear the terms *DSM, DSM-IV,* or *DSM-IV-TR.* These expressions are often used interchangeably to refer to either the manual or the classification system (based on criteria in the manual):

- *DSM: Diagnostic and Statistical Manual of Mental Disorders.* The original American Psychiatric Association manual was published in 1952. The classification of disorders, based on criteria in this manual, became known simply as the DSM system.
- *DSM-IV: Diagnostic and Statistical Manual of Mental Disorders, Fourth Edition.* The fourth edition, published in 1994, updated criteria for the classification system. Speakers still often refer to the well-known DSM-IV system.
- *DSM-IV-TR: Diagnostic and Statistical Manual of Mental Disorders, Fourth Edition, Text Revision.* This revision, published in 2000, is the most current edition. The criteria remain unchanged from the fourth edition; however, updated supporting research and clinical findings were included.

Why so many acronyms? Partly because *DSM,* by design, is periodically revised to reflect new research findings and clinical advancements. The diagnostic criteria that are the core of *DSM* are currently in their fourth incarnation, hence the label *DSM-IV.* However, in 2000, six years after *DSM-IV* was published, a text revision (the *TR* part) was published that did not change the diagnostic criteria but did include updated research and clinical findings regarding the disorders. Thus, the label *DSM-IV-TR.* Some people, though, may want to refer to the ongoing system of DSM rather than a specific edition, for example, if they were to say, "For the past 50 years, the categorization of mental disorders in the United States was most often done using the DSM." Other people may just want to speak in shorthand. Both groups would use the label *DSM.* For purposes of this book, I will use DSM to refer to the general classification system and simply *DSM* (with italics) to refer to the manual DSM-IV-TR (APA, 2000), which includes the most-current DSM criteria for mental disorders and the most-current supporting literature.

Purpose

DSM is intended to be a universally agreed-upon system of classifying and describing mental disorders. This is an important purpose; if disorders can be reliably and validly identified and classified, then they can be researched and disorder-specific treatments can be developed and delivered. An effective classification system also enhances professionals' ability to communicate with each other regarding clients and patients, as it provides a common language to describe problems.

Multiaxial Format

While the most familiar parts of *DSM* are the diagnostic criteria it includes, it is more than just a collection of disorders and diagnostic criteria. In an effort to provide a more comprehensive portrayal of individuals, *DSM* includes five main components, or *axes*, that can be used to examine and describe a person's problems:

- **Axis I**: This axis includes the majority of clinical disorders that bring people to the attention of mental health professionals, such as mood disorders, anxiety disorders, and disruptive behavior disorders. It also includes "other conditions that may be a focus of clinical attention," which are conditions such as parent-child relational problems and bereavement.
- **Axis II**: This axis is for lifelong conditions that impact multiple aspects of a person's functioning. Included in Axis II is mental retardation and an array of personality disorders, such as borderline personality disorder and antisocial personality disorder. Some mental health clinicians use *Axis II* as a shorthand way of saying that a client has some fundamental personality characteristics that cannot be expected to change (e.g., "I think this client has some Axis II stuff going on").
- **Axis III**: This axis includes medical conditions that are relevant to a person's Axis I or Axis II disorder. Note that there must be a connection between the medical condition and the mental disorder. A person may have ADHD and have been recently diagnosed with breast cancer; however, if there is not a connection between the two, there would be no reason to list the cancer diagnosis on this axis. If a person was diagnosed with breast cancer and subsequently became severely depressed, and the cancer diagnosis contributed to the depression, then it would be included on Axis III.
- **Axis IV**: This axis is for psychosocial and environmental problems that impact a person's Axis I or Axis II disorder. This is DSM's attempt to move beyond a straight medical model and acknowledge the many outside influences that impact people's mental and behavioral functioning. Examples of psychosocial and environmental problems that could be listed on Axis IV for a child or adolescent are parental divorce, extreme poverty, and being the victim of an assault. As with Axis III, problems listed on Axis IV must be related to the person's mental disorder.
- **Axis V**: This axis provides a *Global Assessment of Functioning*, or GAF. GAF consists of a single number that describes a person's overall level of functioning. It is on a scale of 1 to 100; scores below 70 indicate some level of distress or impairment, with scores below 50 indicating very serious problems. The GAF score can be used in a variety of ways, such as giving both a current measure of overall functioning and indicating the highest level of functioning the person has displayed in the past year. Some treatment facilities provide GAF scores at admission and at discharge to portray the amount of progress patients have achieved.

(Continued)

(Continued)

Specifiers and NOS

DSM uses *specifiers* to provide additional information about some Axis I and Axis II diagnoses. Specifiers can be used to reflect the severity of some disorders (mild, moderate, or severe) and describe the course of disorders (e.g., in partial remission or in full remission).

One unique type of specifier is NOS, which stands for *not otherwise specified.* This designation is used when the symptom presentation does not meet full criteria for a disorder, yet significant concerns remain. For example, a person may only display three symptoms of a disorder even though the criteria require at least four specific symptoms. In the hands of a wise and experienced clinician, the NOS label can be a helpful tool to acknowledge real problems that just don't quite fit the formal criteria; in other cases, it can lead to sloppy and imprecise labels. A school counselor who learns that a student has, for example, a depressive disorder NOS label can presume that the student has some depressive symptoms but also should be careful not to place too much weight on the label.

DSM Critique

While DSM is the standard diagnostic system for mental disorders in the United States, it is not without critics. Even with its efforts to create a multiaxial system that accounts for medical, social, and environmental influences on behavior, it is still at its core a system that locates problems within the individual. In addition, it has been criticized for not accounting for cultural variations in behavior and emotional expression and, thereby, identifying a disproportionate number of minority group members with mental disorders (White Kress, Eriksen, Rayle, & Ford, 2005). Finally, some researchers suggest that a categorical system like DSM does not reflect human behavior as well as a dimensional approach that places individuals' behavioral and emotional symptoms on a continuum. In other words, rather than relying on an either-or way of thinking (I am either depressed or not depressed), it is more accurate to describe *how much* of a collection of symptoms a person has (I am more depressed than most people but not as depressed as some).

General knowledge of *DSM,* the disorders it describes, and the way it is used by mental health professionals is very helpful for school personnel for purposes of both communication and credibility (Jones, 1997). Knowledge of *DSM* allows school personnel to speak the language of mental health professionals, thereby facilitating communication. While it is not part of school counselors' role to use *DSM* to diagnose students, knowing enough about *DSM* to be conversant with the language of the mental health system also enhances the credibility of school personnel with both mental health professionals and families, who often learn the jargon of the mental health system through the popular media and through dealings with the mental health system. School counselors who are able to have knowledgeable conversations with parents about children's mental health issues come across as being much more credible and helpful.

THE MEANING OF A MENTAL HEALTH DIAGNOSIS

In addition to developing enough familiarity with mental health diagnoses to be able to talk intelligently with mental health professionals and parents, it is also important that school personnel understand what a mental health diagnosis does and does not mean. It is not unusual for students in K–12 schools to have diagnoses of mental disorders. And yet, these diagnoses are often viewed by teachers, administrators, and even school counselors as being mysterious and unsettling. Particularly in the case of students with more-obscure diagnoses, such as reactive attachment disorder or intermittent explosive disorder, school personnel often know that the diagnoses indicate that something is seriously wrong, but they do not know exactly what the problems are or what can be done about them.

It does not need to be that way. Mental health diagnoses should not elicit fear and anxiety from school personnel. Oftentimes, the negative reaction that school personnel have upon hearing about a diagnosis is not due as much to questions about the specific diagnosis as it is to a general lack of understanding about what mental health diagnoses mean and do not mean. While it is not realistic for school personnel to have a deep and thorough understanding of the detailed criteria and research base for a specific diagnosis, it is possible for them to generally begin thinking about mental health diagnoses in a way that is more useful and realistic. This involves striking a balance. It is a mistake for school personnel to place too much emphasis on a diagnosis, but it is also a mistake to dismiss mental health diagnoses as having no relevance to the schools. First, there are some reasons why school personnel should not overvalue mental health diagnoses:

- *Diagnoses can be influenced by the requirements of insurance companies.* Insurance companies may not reimburse mental health providers unless there is a *DSM* diagnosis and may only provide reimbursement for some *DSM* diagnoses. Accordingly, some mental health providers may shade their diagnostic decisions in a way that provides maximum insurance reimbursement. This is not ethical, but it happens.
- *The diagnostic process is taken more seriously by some clinicians than others.* Some clinicians are more invested in making an accurate diagnostic

decision than others. This may be a function of the agency where the child is seen; the purpose of some agencies is individual and family counseling, and diagnoses may be viewed as necessary evils that are done as expediently as possible. Other clinics or hospital programs have the identification of an accurate diagnosis as their main purpose and specialize in thorough, multidisciplinary assessments.

- *The time devoted to developing a diagnosis differs depending on the agency.* Some agencies or clinics require clinicians to develop at least a working diagnosis after the first session. Others allow more time.

- *Diagnoses often change over time.* It is not unusual for adolescents to have had multiple, and changing, mental health diagnoses over the course of their lives. A file review may show that a 16-year-old with a diagnosis of bipolar disorder had a diagnosis at age 7 of oppositional defiant disorder and a diagnosis at age 12 of dysthymic disorder. This does not necessarily mean that the earlier diagnoses were wrong. They were probably the diagnoses that best fit the array of symptoms displayed at those earlier points in time.

- *The diagnostic criteria and categories are constantly undergoing professional debate, and there is not complete agreement among professionals about the validity of the current criteria.* There is a reason why the DSM system is revised on a regular basis. As researchers learn more about the nature of mental disorders, the criteria should be updated and refined accordingly. But the ongoing revision process illustrates that the current criteria are not perfected.

- *Even if a diagnosis is 100% accurate, it cannot dictate specific school-based interventions.* There is not a one-to-one correspondence between diagnoses and specific school interventions.

Clearly, there are reasons why mental health diagnoses should be viewed with a touch of skepticism. However, it is also true that diagnoses can provide useful information for school personnel. So, given the points made above, let's talk about how diagnoses should be viewed. Mental health diagnoses can be viewed as the best attempt on the part of community-based practitioners, such as psychologists, licensed social workers, licensed counselors, and psychiatrists, to make sense of the unique set of behaviors and emotions displayed by a child or adolescent. Stated differently, diagnoses are practitioners' best attempt to filter the behavioral and emotional symptoms of their young clients through the lens of a set of standard diagnostic criteria (the DSM system) and determine which, if any, diagnoses fit the symptom presentation. A mental health diagnosis is best viewed as a snapshot—a shorthand label that best describes the way a child or adolescent is thinking, feeling, and behaving at one point in time. A diagnosis made at age 7 should not be expected to accurately describe the child at age 16, though it can be a useful marker of the child's mental health history.

There are potent benefits that can come with a mental health diagnosis. Diagnoses can help families, teachers, and school counselors develop a better understanding of why the affected children and adolescents are behaving the way they are. Take the example of a child who seems to ignore directions, spends class time blurting out answers, bothers nearby children, stares out the window, and routinely forgets to complete homework. This child's parents and teachers likely feel considerable frustration and may find themselves taking out their irritation on the child. Imagine now that the student is evaluated and is diagnosed with ADHD. Parents and teachers may look at the child's behavior in a much different light and feel much more apt to respond to challenging behavior with patience and understanding. Perhaps most important, the child may form a more positive self-image, and begin to feel less like a failure and a bad kid and more like a person with a medical condition. The reality is that in the absence of an explicit label such as ADHD, children and adults tend to develop and assign their own unstated labels, which are often pejorative labels such as "willful," "lazy," and "irresponsible." These informal, unconscious labels can be much more stigmatizing than formal mental health labels.

Mental health diagnoses can be used to inform—but not prescribe—school-based interventions. A diagnosis can suggest general intervention approaches and can be viewed as a starting point for the development of more-specific interventions. As noted above, the diagnostic process is not an exact science, so the intervention direction that is suggested by the diagnosis should be viewed as tentative. But that is one of the guiding principles of intervention planning anyway; it is always best to constantly monitor the effectiveness of interventions and modify them if they are not working well.

FINAL THOUGHTS

The two systems designed to help children with mental health problems—the community-based system using *DSM* (APA, 2000) and the school-based special education system—have some similarities and also important differences. Perhaps the most important reason a working knowledge of *DSM* and the mental health system is useful for school counselors and other school personnel is because it helps them serve as better guides for parents and families who are trying to navigate these two similar-but-different systems. It is not unusual for community mental health professionals to have an incomplete or distorted understanding of the programs schools have for assisting youth with mental health needs. It is also not unusual for school counselors and other school personnel to lack a thorough understanding of the community mental health system. So it is very understandable, and even predictable, that parents struggle to make sense of these two systems.

The key point is that there is partial, but not complete, overlap between the way schools and the way physicians and community mental health professionals describe mental health problems. As represented in Figure 1.1, some students with a mental disorder may also receive special education services at school. However, it is also possible for a student with a mental disorder to receive no special education assistance. And it is possible for a student to receive special education services—even in the emotional-behavioral domain—but have no diagnosed mental disorder.

In one sense, the distinctions between educational disabilities, mental health disorders, and subclinical mental health problems are irrelevant for the purposes of intervention. School counselors who want to help students with mental health problems are most in need of practical interventions that they can effectively implement during individual and small-group counseling. Likewise, teachers are most in need of realistic and effective intervention strategies that they can implement in the classroom. The best assessment, one that results in a valid assignment of a special education disability label or a mental health diagnosis, is of little use if it is not followed by effective intervention.

It is critically important that parents, students, and school personnel understand that *the child comes first and the label comes second.* It is crucial that school counselors and other school personnel view labels in the context of the many facets of each individual student. *Labels do not define those*

Figure 1.1   Relationships Among Special Education Disabilities, Diagnosed Mental Disorders, and Mental Health Problems

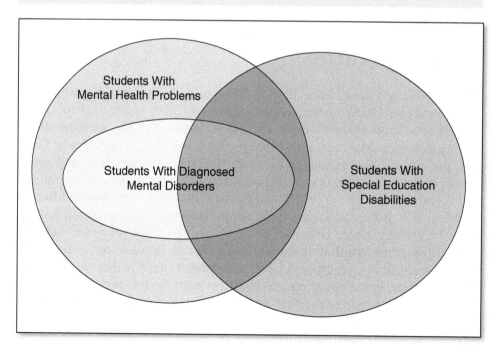

to whom they are applied. Labels can tell us some important things about a student, but the information a label can provide is not nearly as important as knowing what the student likes, how she enjoys spending her free time, what his interests are, what she is good at, and what he worries about. Two students with an identical mental health diagnosis can behave in vastly different ways and respond to school and teachers and interventions very differently. The art and science of mental health diagnoses and interventions is highly individualized.

Finally, it is important to note that even though children's mental health problems are often addressed by distinct and separate school and community-based systems, there are a growing number of programs and initiatives designed to coordinate the efforts of schools and community mental health services in order to better serve children (Weist & Evans, 2005). Good work is being done both in the United States (e.g., Paige, Kitzis, & Wolfe, 2003) and internationally (e.g., Wyn, Cahill, Holdsworth, Rowling, & Carson, 2000) to develop schoolwide systems that promote positive student mental health, including the development of school-based mental health programs. Hopefully, these programs will continue to proliferate, providing students in K–12 schools with better and more-accessible mental health services.

SUMMARY POINTS

- Large numbers of students in K–12 schools have diagnosable mental health disorders, and many more have mental health issues that while not rising to a diagnosable level still create significant problems.
- Mental health disorders come with an array of negative consequences, including social, emotional, and academic problems.
- Mental health disorders among youth are often undiagnosed and untreated. Even when disorders are correctly diagnosed and adequately treated, school-based and classroom-based interventions and supports can still be helpful.
- School counselors are well positioned to provide support to students with mental health disorders or mental health problems, as well as to work with these students' teachers and parents.
- General knowledge about specific mental health disorders is helpful, but learning about the strengths, areas of need, and individual personalities of the student is always more important than knowing the name of the student's mental health disorder.

2

Intervention Basics

The professional literature is replete with good intervention ideas for students with mental health problems. Parents, classroom teachers, administrators, and other school staff can also provide valuable ideas for ways to assist these students. And I hope this book will provide many additional valuable intervention ideas. But it is also helpful to have a broader framework for how best to implement intervention ideas. That is the purpose of this chapter. The following pages describe a number of guidelines for thinking about and implementing interventions, culminating in a simple model of developing specific intervention strategies for individual students.

INTERVENTION GUIDELINES

The following guidelines are intended to provide school counselors with a way to both conceptualize interventions and make interventions more effective. The guidelines tend to be most relevant for classroom interventions, but most also apply to interventions that are delivered directly by the school counselor.

PRINCIPLES OF INTERVENTION

1. Do something different.

2. Take a problem-solving approach.

3. Be faithful—but not rigid—when implementing interventions.

4. Get teacher buy-in.

5. Get student buy-in.

6. Begin with positive interventions.

7. Give new interventions a chance.

8. Have a way of knowing whether the intervention is effective.

9. Don't give up.

Guideline 1: Do Something Different

This guideline may seem painfully obvious, but it is not unheard of for students with mental health problems to continue to struggle in school, while teachers, administrators, and even school counselors continue to behave as they always have. Doing something different does not mean expecting the *student* or the student's family to do something different. It means that the *school* should do something different.

An important aspect of this guideline is the understanding that there are always a variety of things that can be done differently by the adults in school to assist students who are having problems. These do not need to be major changes. In fact, it can often be a mistake to seek major changes, such as moving a student with a disability out of the regular classroom into a self-contained special education classroom, before trying a number of less-severe changes. Relatively minor changes such as changing a student's desk placement, giving advanced warning of upcoming transitions, or scheduling academic-heavy classes in the morning instead of the afternoon can make a big difference in the behavior and adjustment of some students.

Most teachers have a favorite set of interventions that they are used to and that they use frequently. The reason these interventions are favored is because they usually work. When the interventions do not work, though, some teachers have trouble generating additional ideas for things to do differently and may believe they have tried everything. School counselors can play an important role in cases like this by gently suggesting that there are additional things that can be tried and perhaps offering some ideas of things that could be done differently.

Guideline 2: Take a Problem-Solving Approach

The most fruitful way to assist students who are having difficulty in school is to take a problem-solving approach. One advantage of viewing student difficulties through a problem-solving lens is that it helps reduce blame and frustration on the part of teachers and other school personnel. Take, for example, a situation where a student is loud and disruptive in class. Teachers who view that situation as a problem to be solved are less likely to become angry and frustrated with the student and less apt to personalize the behavior.

An important part of a problem-solving approach is to seek to understand both what triggers the problem behavior and what maintains the behavior. *Triggers* are stimuli that elicit the problem behavior. Triggers can be overt behavior, such as a work request from the teacher, or an internal thought or experience, such as a feeling of boredom. What serves as a trigger for one student may not be a trigger for another student. For example, some high school students may feel embarrassed and inadequate when the math teacher calls them to the board to work out a problem and will respond with oppositional behavior. Other students may welcome the attention and revel in the chance to get up in front of the room.

It is also helpful to consider *maintaining variables* in the problem-solving process. Maintaining variables are those factors that reinforce and perpetuate behaviors. For students who enjoy peer attention, having the class laugh at their jokes might serve as a maintaining variable for class-clown behavior. For another student, the feeling of power that comes with defying the teacher may be a maintaining variable for oppositional behavior. (Triggers and maintaining variables are discussed in more detail in Chapter 4.) But the key point is that a problem-solving approach is facilitated by understanding what triggers and maintains the behavior of concern. School counselors can make an important contribution to students with mental health issues by encouraging teachers and administrators to adopt a problem-solving approach.

THE ROLE OF HISTORY IN DEVELOPING INTERVENTIONS

What role should a student's life history play when developing interventions? Should school counselors gather information about a student's developmental history before creating an intervention plan? There is a good argument for doing so. Take the example of a student who is displaying oppositional behavior in class. Now, assume the school counselor discovers that the student has a history of being physically abused. Isn't that helpful information? Wouldn't this suggest that a supportive counseling intervention would be more appropriate than a classroom-based behavioral plan?

(Continued)

(Continued)

Perhaps. But perhaps not. It is easy to assume that there is a causal relationship between the history of abuse and the current school problems. And there may be. But how do we know? Given the thousands of factors that influence minute-by-minute classroom behavior, how do we know that events—even very impactful events—that occurred months or years ago are responsible for classroom behavior today?

Therein lies the rub. A high level of inference is required to connect past history with current behavior. And the level of inference increases with the length of time between the historical events and the current behavior. At best, historical information provides vague and general guidance for intervention development. This is not to say it is worthless information; it just does not provide specific and clear guidance for intervention.

It is possible to look at history in another way, though. Consider what might be called *near history.* Near history is what is known about the student's *recent* behavior and life circumstances, particularly how the student responds to various environmental events. Let's go back to the example of the student who exhibited oppositional behavior in school. Let's assume an exploration of the student's near history revealed that the student became easily distracted and overwhelmed in noisy environments. This suggests several specific interventions, such as allowing the student a quiet, safe place to go when surrounding noise becomes agitating or even letting the student wear ear plugs in class and during passing time.

While old history provides general and vague direction for intervention, near history provides specific and detailed direction for intervention. This is not to say that old history should be completely discounted. If a student has an early history of abuse, or abandonment, or parental divorce, or academic failure, I would want to know that. But as a general rule, *near history is more valuable for intervention than old history.*

Guideline 3: Be Faithful—but Not Rigid—When Implementing Interventions

It makes intuitive sense that an intervention will not be effective if it is not implemented correctly. Indeed, there is much discussion regarding intervention implementation in the professional literature. *Treatment integrity* (sometimes called *treatment fidelity)* is a term used to describe the degree to which treatments are implemented as intended. Higher levels of treatment integrity have been linked to more-effective interventions (Gable, Hendrickson, & Van Acker, 2001). As a general rule, then, school counselors and teachers should do what they can to make sure that interventions are implemented faithfully. Research suggests that there are two factors that impact how faithfully teachers implement interventions.

The first is how acceptable the intervention is to the teacher, and this will be discussed further in the next guideline. The second factor is the complexity of the intervention. In general, the more complicated the intervention, the less likely it will be implemented correctly (Gable et al.). And that makes sense—given everything teachers need to do in a bustling classroom, it is not realistic to expect that they will correctly implement a complex and demanding intervention. This suggests that teachers and school counselors should strive to develop interventions that are practical and simple rather than highly involved.

The rule is that interventions are more effective if they are implemented correctly. But like most rules, there is an exception to that rule. Recent studies have actually found that, in some cases, the best outcomes are associated with *moderate* treatment integrity rather than perfect treatment integrity. For example, in a study of the integrity of treatments for adolescent substance abuse, intermediate levels of treatment adherence led to the best outcomes (Hogue et al., 2008). This also makes some sense. It suggests that, while interventions are less effective if they are not implemented correctly, they are also not maximally effective if they are implemented in a rigid fashion that does not allow for some flexibility. The lesson seems to be to strive to implement interventions faithfully, but allow for some flexibility if warranted by circumstances.

Guideline 4: Get Teacher Buy-In

Perhaps the most important factor in determining the effectiveness of a classroom intervention is whether the teacher believes in the intervention and commits to its success. Teachers who are skeptical of an intervention are unlikely to devote the energy and time that will insure the success of the intervention. On the other hand, my experience with teachers is that they will go to amazing lengths to make an intervention work if they believe it will make a difference in the life of a student. Clearly, then, it behooves school counselors who are consulting with teachers about classroom interventions to get teacher buy-in for any interventions that are developed.

Teachers are more likely to buy in to interventions that they have a role in developing. Accordingly, school counselors are wise to view their role as collaborator rather than mental health expert when it comes to intervention development. Respecting teachers' wishes about the kinds of interventions that they want to implement in their classroom is very important. That said, there may also be times when a school counselor may have a strong hunch that a particular type of intervention will be effective, even if the teacher is not enthusiastic about it. In this case, it will be important for the school counselor to take the time to explain the rationale for the intervention and offer to help as much as possible, with the hope that this will help the teacher become more willing to consider the intervention.

There is one final twist to consider when examining teacher buy-in. It has recently been suggested in the professional literature that teacher buy-in does not necessarily have to precede faithfully executed intervention. Rather, in some cases, teacher buy-in actually occurs *after* they have seen interventions work (Kovaleski, 2007). Apparently, there are no simple rules in this area!

Guideline 5: Get Student Buy-In

Just as it is critical to obtain teacher buy-in, it is also important to get student buy-in. Most students with mental health problems are perfectly capable of participating in discussions about the interventions that will be used to help them. In addition to being respectful of students' right to self-determination, seeking their input and cooperation when developing interventions also greatly enhances the odds that the intervention will work. As an example, reward-based interventions will be more successful if the student is able to have input into what the rewards will be. Adults often have beliefs regarding the rewards children will like—and these beliefs are often wrong. What is rewarding to one student may not be rewarding to another, and what is rewarding to one student may not be rewarding to that same student a month later. It is best to ask students what they are willing to work for.

Student buy-in may take the form of a written commitment. For instance, one possible intervention for behavior problems is a behavior contract that describes expected student behaviors and consequences for both appropriate and inappropriate behavior. Student buy-in can be enhanced by asking the student to sign the contract before it is implemented. Overall, being sure to seek and value the student's perspective is critically important in the success of interventions.

Guideline 6: Begin With Positive Interventions

While schools and teachers are becoming more aware of the value of positive interventions, many educators (and parents) still tend to respond to students' behavior problems with punitive responses. Daily work is not done? Keep the student in at recess! Talking too much during class time? Send the student to the office! Tardy to school? Send the student to in-school suspension! Indeed, for many of us, it is much easier to think of a punitive response to student misbehavior than a positive response.

However, there are a number of reasons to prefer positive responses. One is that, in many instances, they are more effective. I learned this lesson early in my professional career when I was going into elementary school classrooms and conducting developmental guidance lessons. At first, I had much trouble getting second-grade students to listen and to follow my directions. It seemed like I was constantly harping on students to return to their desk, pay attention, listen, and begin working. Then I observed a master teacher and saw her manage these issues by praising the students who were behaving appropriately. I began doing that ("It looks like everyone in this row is ready to listen, great job!") and found that students responded wonderfully. Not only was their behavior better, but I was also much more able to maintain a positive and supportive demeanor—something I valued, given that building relationships with the students was one of my goals.

Part of the reason why the kind of positive responses I used with my second graders worked is that the responses clearly communicated what the students *should* be doing. In contrast, punitive responses tend to focus on what *not* to do, but offer no feedback about what *to* do. A positive approach is more educational.

Finally, punitive responses run the risk of fostering anger and resentment on the part of students. Think about your own job. How would you feel if your boss stood over your shoulder and commented about everything you did wrong? How would that compare with how you would feel if your boss made a point of commenting about your work accomplishments and praising you for your efforts? This is not a perfect analogy to schools, though. You have the opportunity to switch jobs if your boss is overly punitive. Students do not have that power.

All of this should not be taken to mean that teachers should never use negative consequences. As we will see in Chapter 5, students with ADHD often need both positive and negative consequences to manage their behavior. But what I am suggesting is that it makes sense to begin with positive interventions. What is there to lose? If positive interventions prove ineffective, interventions that are more punitive can always be added.

Guideline 7: Give New Interventions a Chance

Sometimes interventions work immediately. Indeed, it is not uncommon to have a honeymoon period with many interventions. Of course, not all interventions work quickly. At the start, interventions can make the problem behavior even worse. And it is hard to tell in the first week or so whether unsuccessful interventions are not working because they are simply ineffective or because they have not been given sufficient time to work. The danger is that teachers and school counselors can abandon perfectly good interventions too early because they are not providing immediate results. If we gave up on all interventions that did not show positive results in the first week, no one would ever complete an exercise program or maintain a diet.

There is no precise rule about how long to maintain an intervention that is not working. I think a good rule of thumb is to give a new classroom intervention one to two weeks before looking to make significant modifications. If some positive changes are not evident after that time, it is probably wise to seek other interventions.

Guideline 8: Have a Way of Knowing Whether the Intervention Is Effective

The design of an intervention is not complete until an evaluation component is included. This should include both a mechanism for evaluation and an evaluation target. The evaluation mechanism is simply the way evaluation data will be gathered. It is best to make this as simple as possible, since more-elaborate systems are hard to maintain in busy classrooms. Ideally, it is objective behavioral data that are gathered. For a student with disruptive hyperactivity, this might be a tally of the number of times he shouts out during a class period or the number of times he is out of his seat without permission. For a socially isolated student, this might be a record of the number of times the student initiated a conversation with classmates during the school day. While this is ideal, there are times where it is unrealistic to obtain objective behavioral data. With students with depression and anxiety, for example, the goal of intervention might be changing internal states of worry and sadness. In these cases, evaluation data might consist of a student's self-ratings of sadness or anxiety on a 1 to 10 scale.

During the development of an intervention, it is also best to set an evaluation target. Gathering baseline data can help inform the decision of what target to set. Going back to the example of a student with disruptive hyperactivity, the teacher might keep a tally of the number of times the student shouted out over a three-day span. If, for example, that student shouted out an average of 10 times per class period, the school counselor and teacher might agree that an evaluation target of reducing that to 3 times per class period would be appropriate.

As with all other phases of intervention development, the evaluation component should be created through collaboration. School counselors can facilitate the process by asking questions such as "How will we know whether this intervention works?" and "What do you think is a reasonable goal for improvement?" School counselors who wish to add to their competencies in constructing evaluation tools and using evaluation data can find valuable information in the book *Evidence-Based School Counseling* (Dimmitt, Carey, & Hatch, 2007).

Guideline 9: Don't Give Up

The problems presented by many students with mental health issues can be difficult, complex, and resistant to change. The teachers who are able to offer the best classroom experiences are those who are persistent and unwilling to give up on the students. In fact, a corollary to this guideline could be *don't expect the first intervention to work*. This may seem to be in direct opposition to the earlier discussion about the desirability of teachers believing in the effectiveness of the interventions they implement. But it is more about teachers (and school counselors) cultivating an attitude that difficult problems are not easily solved, but that with fortitude and perseverance and a willingness to try a number of different interventions, the school life of students with mental health problems can be improved.

AN APPROACH TO INTERVENTION

Many guidelines for intervention for various mental health problems are provided throughout this book. However, these are offered with the understanding that they need to be applied with a liberal dose of professional judgment. The guidelines provide a starting point, but which specific intervention path to follow depends on an understanding of a number of additional factors, including the unique characteristics of the student, the teachers, and the school environment. It is a fundamental mistake to assume that, just because two students share the same mental health diagnosis, they will respond similarly to the same interventions. In light of this reality, it makes sense to follow three basic steps in developing specific intervention plans, which are outlined in the accompanying box.

Let's look at an example of how these intervention steps work. Kevin, an 11-year-old in fifth grade, has a diagnosis of ADHD. Kevin displays considerable hyperactive and impulsive behavior in class, and both his schoolwork and his relationships with his classmates are suffering due to his behavior. His school counselor, in collaboration with the classroom teacher, looks at the general ADHD guideline of *creating systems to provide immediate behavioral feedback* (see Chapter 5 for details) to see whether the guideline makes sense for Kevin. The teacher likes the idea of giving Kevin more immediate feedback and believes that Kevin would respond to a system of feedback where he could earn rewards for appropriate behavior. However, the teacher reports that Kevin has a temper and can be reactive to discipline. The counselor and teacher agree that a response-cost procedure, where reward-earning tokens are taken away from the student for inappropriate

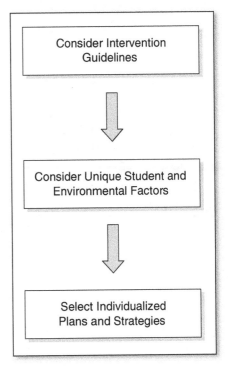

behavior, would likely provoke anger from Kevin and make things worse. But they also agree that a token economy system, where Kevin could earn tokens for positive behavior, has a good chance of being successful. Next, the school counselor talks to Kevin about the intervention. He likes the idea of earning tokens and suggests that tokens can be used to "buy" free time in the gym. The final intervention, then, consists of implementing a system where Kevin's teacher places tokens on his desk when he is sitting calmly and responding appropriately. Each token is worth one minute of free time in the gym at the end of the day.

This example shows how a general guideline can be shaped and individualized based on the unique factors associated with individual students and classrooms. The intervention guidelines should not be used in cookbook fashion. Rather, they should be applied with professional discretion and wisdom.

Finally, it is worth mentioning that the best intervention is often prevention. Many of the intervention guidelines described in these pages are also excellent prevention strategies. For example, teachers who create personal relationships with students, have clear rules and expectations, give specific feedback about student behavior, and accentuate the positive certainly are preventing a number of behavior problems.

SUMMARY POINTS

- Students who are displaying ongoing problems in school need the school to do something different. Doing something is better than doing nothing.
- School counselors and teachers seeking to intervene with a student's problem behavior should take a problem-solving approach that involves identifying factors that trigger problem behavior and factors that reinforce or perpetuate problem behavior.
- It is better to do a good job of implementing simple, practical interventions than to do a poor job of implementing complex interventions.
- Get teacher and student buy-in when developing classroom or individual interventions.
- Strive to use interventions that build and reinforce positive behavior.
- Have a way to evaluate the effectiveness of interventions.
- Interventions should be individualized, not implemented in cookbook fashion.

3

Culture, Race, and Children's Mental Health

Darrell is an African American eighth grader who is new to his school this year. He has had an increasing number of disciplinary problems, mostly stemming from his tendency to get into loud arguments with classmates and with teachers. While some of Darrell's teachers report that he is doing well in their classes (describing him with words like spirited and high energy), others report that he is disrespectful and disruptive. Several of Darrell's teachers have approached the school counselor, wondering if Darrell has a behavior disorder.

Maria, a 16-year-old Latina junior, has been struggling academically ever since she entered high school despite average-range achievement test scores. More recently, some of her teachers expressed concern about her increasing lack of engagement in class and her pervasive sadness. A quick investigation by the school counselor found that Maria generally sits by herself at lunch and does not seem to have close friends at school. She works after school at a local fast-food restaurant, and upon learning of that, one of her teachers was overheard to say, "It is a good thing that she has a head start working in the fast-food business, since she sure won't get into college."

The cases of Darrell and Maria illustrate one of the most complex and critical issues in the field of children's mental health—that of the intersection of race, culture, and mental health. This intricate juncture is infused with issues of racism, stereotyping, definitions of "normal," perceptions, and disturbing realities. While a thorough examination of these issues is beyond the scope of this chapter, the following pages provide an overview and present some key guidelines to assist school counselors in understanding and managing issues of race, culture, and mental health among students.

IMPACT OF CULTURE AND RACE

When discussing a complex issue, it is generally a good idea to start by defining key terms. Defining terms is difficult in this area, however, as *race, culture,* and *ethnicity* have been described as "fuzzy constructs" (Cauce et al., 2002). Race, for example, has historically been considered to be biologically based and clearly identifiable. Yet there is more variability within racial groups than between racial groups, and based on recent research in the biological sciences, the existence of distinct biologically based racial groups has been called a "persistent myth" (Cauce et al., p. 45). Though there is no scientific support for distinct racial groups, race nevertheless is a social construct to which people attach great meaning. Indeed, many people connect stereotypes and prejudices to different racial groups. The perceptions young people have about the racial group or groups they belong to, or see themselves as belonging to, form a central part of their identity. Whether grounded in biological fact or not, race cannot be ignored.

Likewise, culture may have different meanings to different people, but there is no question that cultural influences permeate the way we behave and the way we view the world. In general, culture refers to a set of values, beliefs, and behavioral expectations that are shared by a group of people and are transmitted from one generation to the next. These cultural values, beliefs, and behavioral expectations have a profound impact on the lives of members of the cultural group. Cultural teachings can tell members how to dress, what to eat, and how to express emotions. More relevant for those concerned about children's mental health, cultural teachings can tell members what behaviors are normal and what behaviors are out of the norm, what causes abnormal behavior, and what should be done if a member of a culture displays behavior that deviates from the cultural norm (Schwab-Stone, Ruchkin, Vermeiren, & Leckman, 2001).

It is tempting to link culture with geographical origin, so people with origins in Italy could be said to be steeped in Italian culture, while people with origins in Africa could be described as being part of African American culture. While this may hold true for some individuals, for many it fails to capture the richness of their cultural experience. For one thing, it is increasingly rare for individuals to have origins from just one geographical area. My four grandparents, for example, hailed from four different countries (Sweden, Norway, England, and Wales)—and my ancestry is probably less diverse than that of most people. Furthermore, it defies common sense to assume that an African American teenager growing up in the Bronx experiences the identical cultural influences as an African American teenager growing up in rural Minnesota.

Even though race and culture are constructs that are prone to being viewed in an overly simplistic manner, it is not helpful to underestimate their influence on individual students. There are some inescapable facts that are important when considering the intersection of race, culture, and children's mental health. These facts can be summarized in two broad statements: (1) discrimination and racism permeate our society, and (2) race and culture have demonstrable effects on children's mental health, some of which are overt and clear and others of which are subtle yet pervasive.

Discrimination and Racism in Today's Society

There is no doubt that the United States has made significant progress in reducing racism and racial discrimination in recent decades. Indeed, as this book goes to press our country is being governed by its first African American president. There is also no doubt that racism and racial discrimination remain fundamental problems in this country. In fact, racial- and ethnic-minority membership profoundly affects one's life experiences. A Latino friend of mine, when asked in a job interview whether he had experienced discrimination due to his ethnicity, responded, "You mean today?" There is much concrete evidence to support this statement. As just one example, murder defendants are less likely to be charged with the death penalty when victims are Hispanic than when victims are White (Lee, 2007).

Specific to children and adolescents, statistics in a number of areas clearly reflect significant group differences in the experiences of majority and minority youth. For example, African American children are approximately three times more likely than European American youth to live in poverty and are also more likely to live in neighborhoods plagued by high crime, high unemployment, and inadequate schools (Prelow, Danoff-Burg, Swenson, & Pulgiano, 2004). Minority youth are overrepresented in the juvenile justice system and school programs for students with behavior problems (Cartledge, Kea, & Simmons-Reed, 2002). And of course, there is the well-documented achievement gap between White students and students of color. The most recent report from the National Center for Education Statistics documents substantial gaps between the performance of White and Black students, in Grades 4 and 8, on National

Assessment of Educational Progress (NAEP) tests in math and reading. On the 500-point scale used for the NAEP tests, the average score of fourth-grade White students was 26 points higher in math and 31 points higher in reading than that of Black students. The corresponding numbers in Grade 8 were 27 points in math and 26 points in reading (Vanneman, Hamilton, Baldwin Anderson, & Rahman, 2009). One can make an argument that the achievement gap is more about socioeconomic disadvantage than about race, but that is only partially true. Even controlling for income level, substantial gaps in NAEP scores still exist between White and Black students.

In addition to these disparities, students of color also experience a significant level of discrimination. For example, one study found that 77% of African American adolescents reported experiencing at least one discriminatory incident in the previous three months (Prelow et al., 2004). Not surprisingly, students of color have a heightened awareness of racism and discrimination. As a case in point, a significant percentage of African American students as young as third grade have been found to have expectations that children of their race will be discriminated against (Rowley, Burchinal, Roberts, & Zeisel, 2008). In essence, students of color realize at an early age that the world they live in is a discriminatory place and they are at times the object of that discrimination.

Racial Differences in Mental Health Disorders and Services

Students of color are less likely to receive school-based mental health services than White students. Indeed, while far too many students of all races with mental health problems are unserved or underserved, the percentage of students of color receiving appropriate mental health service is particularly low. One study of over 1,000 youth with mental health needs found that 48% of African American youth and 47% of Latino youth had unmet mental health needs, as compared to 31% of non-Hispanic White youth (Yeh, McCabe, Hough, Dupuis, & Hazen, 2003). A particularly dramatic research finding is that racial differences have been found in the critical area of mental health service usage among youth experiencing suicidal behavior. A study of adolescents who had either attempted suicide or reported suicidal ideation found that African American youth and Latino youth were significantly less likely than White youth to receive mental health services. This finding held true even when differences in the ability to access services was factored in (Freedenthal, 2007). The lack of participation in school-based mental health services among students of color is important not just in its own right but also because school-based services are often gateways to referrals for community-based mental health services (Wood et al., 2005).

Numerous studies have found racial differences in prevalence rates for mental health disorders (e.g., Nguyen, Huang, Arganza, & Liao, 2007).

One study of a large group of children and early adolescents, for example, found that African American and American Indian youth were more likely to experience the disabling impact of psychiatric disorders, particularly as manifested in school problems and disruptive behavior problems (Ezpeleta, Keeler, Erkanli, Costello, & Angold, 2001). Another study of Connecticut middle schoolers found that Hispanic girls had an elevated rate of depressive symptomatology, while Black boys reported both elevated rates of anxiety symptoms and a high rate of disruptive behavior (McLaughlin, Hilt, & Nolen-Hokesema, 2007). While racial differences in reported psychopathology are found in multiple studies, it is not clear what is responsible for these differences. Racial differences in problem behavior appear or disappear depending on whether the behavior is described by parents, teachers, or the students themselves. This confusing state of affairs is illustrated by a study of 600 youth aged 11 to 17 (Lau et al., 2004). The researchers solicited ratings of problem behavior from teachers, parents, and the youths themselves and analyzed the results based on the racial groups represented among the participants (Caucasian, African American, Hispanic, and Asian/Pacific Islander). Among other findings, the researchers found that Caucasian parents reported more internalizing and externalizing problems in their children than the children reported, while the exact opposite pattern existed in the other racial groups, with parents reporting *fewer* problems than the youth. Furthermore, teachers reported fewer internalizing problems among African American youth and fewer externalizing problems among Asian/Pacific Islander youth—this despite the fact that the youth across all racial groups self-reported similar levels of problems. Again, it is unclear what factors contribute to these conflicting findings. Do Caucasian parents overpathologize their children? Or are they just more aware of mental health issues than other groups of parents? And do teachers fail to see internalizing problems among African Americans because their stereotypes of these youth do not include disorders like depression and anxiety? Or do African American youth express (or hide) their internalizing symptoms in a way that does not allow teachers to see them?

The issue of variability in adults' perceptions of children's problem behavior is also relevant for mental health professionals. An early research study involved a presentation of video vignettes of active eight-year-old boys engaged in a variety of tasks (Mann et al., 1992). Mental health professionals from Indonesia, China, Japan, and the United States were asked to rate behavior of the boys in the videos. It turned out that the clinicians from China and Indonesia gave significantly higher ratings of hyperactivity-disruptive behavior than clinicians from the United States and Japan, demonstrating that cultural standards can impact clinicians' ratings of child behavior. In addition to reinforcing the complexity of the issues, all of these findings reinforce the importance of considering race when talking about children's mental health.

A Final Word About the Impact of Race and Culture

While it is instructive to review research that documents measureable differences in children's experiences based on their race and culture, it is just as important to become aware of the more-subtle—and perhaps more-pervasive—ways race and culture impact the human experience. First, it is important to understand that the DSM approach to categorizing mental disorders is fundamentally based on a set of Western cultural assumptions about human behavior and the self, which include the notion that humans are autonomous, independent beings who are able to self-examine and control their own behavior (Schwab-Stone et al., 2001). However, not all cultures promote this particular world view. As an example, one major cultural dimension is individualistic versus collectivistic, with Western culture being individualistic in nature. A component of this individualistic perspective is the Western cultural view of adolescence as a period marked by the process of separation from parents and increased consolidation of an independent, individual identity (Schwab-Stone et al.). For many school counselors socialized in the United States, it may seem like a universal truth that adolescents go through a process of separation and individuation, but this view of adolescence may be at odds with the belief systems of collectivistic cultures. This is just one example of how culture can transmit a fundamental and unique way of viewing the world that appears as a universal truth to members of the culture. No wonder there can be misunderstandings and misjudgments when schools interact with families who are not members of the majority culture.

RECOMMENDATIONS FOR SCHOOL COUNSELORS

It is clear that race and culture are intimately intertwined with mental health issues among children and adolescents, and in order to adequately support students with mental health disorders, school counselors must be cognizant of not only mental health issues but also the way race and culture impact those issues. The following recommendations are a starting point.

RECOMMENDATIONS FOR SUPPORTING DIVERSE STUDENTS WITH MENTAL HEALTH PROBLEMS

1. Assume students of color experience racism.

2. Seek to understand the multiple contextual influences impacting students of color.

3. Explicitly talk with students about racism and prejudice.

4. Strive to impact the broader system.

5. When students of color experience school problems, reach out to their families.

6. Be aware of special issues faced by immigrant students.

7. Do your own work regarding racial and cultural attitudes and beliefs.

Recommendation 1: Assume Students of Color Experience Racism

Despite the progress that has been made in this country in the area of race relations and reducing racial discrimination, racism still permeates our society. Not all youth—particularly younger children—perceive that they have been discriminated against (Szalacha et al., 2003). But a large proportion of students of color do perceive that they have been discriminated against, and there is some research evidence that this perception is linked to negative outcomes (Prelow et al., 2004; Szalacha et al.). Keep in mind, also, that subtle racism can exist and can impact a student of color, even if the existence of the racism is outside the student's awareness. In sum, it is wise for school counselors to operate on the assumption that the students of color in their schools experience racism. It may be hard to translate this assumption into concrete action. But at minimum, if students of color are exhibiting problem behaviors or talking in ways that suggest they have low self-esteem or low aspirations for themselves, it behooves school counselors to consider the possibility that experiences with or reactions to racism may be a part of the issue.

Recommendation 2: Seek to Understand the Multiple Contextual Influences Impacting Students of Color

Family structure, the quality and quantity of friendships, age, academic prowess, the personalities and expectations of one's teachers, school climate, geographical region, local community standards . . . the list of contextual factors that impact students is nearly endless. School counselors tend to be experts at seeing and appreciating the broader contexts that impact students' behaviors and feelings. But when working with students of color, school counselors need to have an even sharper eye for context, as the multiple contextual factors that influence all students may be even more critical.

Let's look at just a few of the many contextual factors that can have a disproportionate impact on students of color:

- *The amount of racial, ethnic, and cultural diversity in the school.* Think about how different school might feel for a Korean American student, for example, if 30% of the student population is Korean American, compared with how it might feel if there are only two

Korean American students in the entire school. Stereotyping a certain race or culture seems particularly rampant when there are few students representing that race or culture (because there are fewer opportunities for majority students' biases to be disconfirmed), and the chance of feeling isolated and different is clearly heightened if there are few racially or culturally similar peers in school. Furthermore, if there are few racially or culturally similar peers, it becomes more likely that students will be expected to be spokespeople for their race or culture.

- *The number of school staff members of color.* White students can generally take it for granted that they will have teachers who—at least racially—are like them. Students of color often do not have this luxury. The opportunity to have same-race mentors and role models is not available to students of color in a school with few staff members of color.

- *The cultural competence of staff members.* While some may disagree with me, my experiences with teachers and other school staff over the years lead me to believe that the large majority of adults in schools want to do right by *all* students, regardless of color or culture. At the same time, it is the rare adult in school who does not unintentionally hold some sort of racial or cultural bias or stereotype. Moreover, the degree to which school staff members are culturally competent varies among schools. Clearly, the global cultural competence of school staff is a contextual factor that impacts students of color.

Recommendation 3: Explicitly Talk With Students About Racism and Prejudice

Racial bias, oppression, cultural intolerance, and prejudice are topics that are rarely discussed in school. There are probably a number of reasons for this, including reticence to bring up controversial topics, the concern that students who are asked about racial bias may begin to see bias even if it is not there, and uncertainty about how to actually initiate the conversation. But I believe that the benefits of talking openly about bias, prejudice, and racial fairness far outweigh any of these concerns.

School counselors who take the risk to talk openly with students about race and racism give the message that they are truly interested in the students' experiences, even if the conversations are hard and can elicit strong emotions. Talking openly about race and racism, particularly with students of color, also allows school counselors to learn firsthand about the practices and policies at the school that may provide disproportionate benefits to majority students and hinder the success of students of color. Institutional racism can be subtle and unquestioned and may not even be noticed until illuminated in the kind of open conversations that I am advocating.

Recommendation 4: Strive to Impact the Broader System

While services such as individual counseling and consulting with teachers about individual students are helpful and necessary for students of color (just as they are for White students), school counselors should not stop there if they wish to be maximally effective. Indeed, efforts to assist students should include a fearless examination of the global school environment, seeking to identify ways in which the school system does not serve students of color and making efforts to make changes where needed.

One way school counselors can start this examination is by disaggregating data to examine how different racial groups are doing in various areas. Often, these data are already being collected and may include standardized test scores, attendance, and suspensions. But it may be necessary to develop informal surveys to gather other data, such as the percentage of students at different grade levels who see themselves as being college bound. Some of the areas school counselors may wish to examine follow:

- Achievement test scores
- Participation in advanced courses
- Grade point averages
- Attendance rates
- Graduation rates
- Rates of suspension and other disciplinary actions
- Rates of aspirations to careers requiring a college education
- Identification and participation in gifted and talented programs

In all of these areas, school counselors could disaggregate data by racial group. Areas of concern could then be highlighted and plans made to address the concerns. For example, if the school counselors in a school with a 40% African American population discovered that only 10% of the students taking Advanced Placement (AP) courses were African American, they could work to convene a task force of teachers, other staff members, and parents to discuss this discrepancy and develop strategies for increasing the number of African American students in AP classes.

Recommendation 5: When Students of Color Experience School Problems, Reach Out to Their Families

Research tells us that minority families are less likely than White families to seek mental health services from formal agencies, preferring instead to explore informal networks of extended families and faith-based institutions (McMiller & Weisz, 1996). There is certainly nothing wrong with drawing upon extended family members and community-support resources to assist youth with mental health problems; in fact, this kind of broad support can be invaluable. But these support people will not likely be able to provide the kind of specialized intervention that can be provided by mental health professionals. Furthermore, the tendency of minority families to look toward informal rather than formal support networks suggests that they may not be as inclined to work closely with teachers and school counselors to assist their children with mental health problems. The end result is that students of color with mental health problems may not receive the full benefit of all the services available to them.

The implication for school counselors is clear; when students of color are experiencing mental health problems, make a special effort to reach out to the students' families. There are benefits of engaging the families in non-judgmental conversation about concerns. Both parties gain a better understanding of the school and home context, and both learn more about the strengths and interests of the student. Perhaps most critically, though, reaching out to families can include informing them about the range of school and community resources that may be helpful to the student. Moreover, the process of reaching out makes school counselors more than just a name on a staff list—families now have a person they know to connect with.

Recommendation 6: Be Aware of
Special Issues Faced by Immigrant Students

Immigrant children face a host of issues in adjusting successfully to American schools, and many of these issues are unknown to both the adults and classmates at school. These issues can include a lack of family support, trauma from war in their home country, refugee-camp experiences, and poverty. Immigrant students' school history in their home country can be inconsistent, and even in the best of circumstances, there would certainly not be a perfect match between the curriculum sequence and level of difficulty in the old school and new school. This is in addition, of course, to more-obvious issues such as differences in language, race, and culture. Immigrant students may respond to these issues by acting out or being silent, by missing school, or by experiencing somatic problems (Goh, Herting Wahl, Koch McDonald, Brissett, & Yoon, 2007). Furthermore, immigrant students may face rejection or harassment from peers who do not understand the language and customs of the immigrant youth. It is not surprising that making friends can be a daunting task for immigrant students.

Part of the necessary task of school counselors who work with immigrant students with mental health problems is to develop an awareness of the myriad issues faced by these students. But gaining awareness is only the first step. It is also critical that school counselors translate that awareness into action. Several strategies have been discussed in the professional literature, such as offering multicultural small groups, connecting immigrant students with a peer buddy or faculty mentor, and delivering developmental guidance lessons designed to enhance the multicultural awareness of all students (Goh et al., 2007). In addition, it is important to provide translators for conversations with immigrant parents, so immigrant students are not put in the position where they need to translate between the school and their parents or guardians. Expecting students to serve as translators places them in a situation where, under the best of circumstances, they are tempted to shade the translation in a way that is to their benefit (e.g., making it sound as though they are doing better in school than they really are) and, under the worst of circumstances, they are forced to usurp the authority of parents and violate cultural rules about who in the family directs the conversation.

In sum, immigrant students face a host of issues over and above those faced by students of color with long-standing roots in this country. When these students exhibit mental health problems, it is imperative that schools and school counselors have an awareness of the complex and challenging context surrounding immigrant youth and take action to provide special support.

Recommendation 7: Do Your Own Work Regarding Racial and Cultural Attitudes and Beliefs

While this chapter barely scratches the surface of the complex intersection of mental health issues, race, and culture, it does make one thing clear: This juncture is permeated by stereotypes, prejudice, racism, and race-based assumptions. It is unrealistic to think that anyone—*anyone*—is unaffected by the cultural and social teachings that lead to stereotypes and racism. While I like to think that school counselors are further along the road to self-awareness than many others, we all have more work we can do. The work is continuous and consists not just of learning about other cultures but, more important, of examining our own race-based and culture-based assumptions and beliefs in an ongoing effort to identify and eliminate our prejudices. The first battleground on which to fight racism and prejudice is within ourselves.

SUMMARY POINTS

- Issues of race, culture, racism, and prejudice are intimately intertwined with mental health problems among youth.
- Students of color are less likely to receive school-based mental health services than White students.
- Talk openly with students about racism and prejudice.
- Seek to address broader systemic issues that may contribute added stressors to diverse students with mental health problems.
- Be aware of special challenges faced by immigrant youth.
- A first step in effectively addressing racial and cultural issues impacting students is to examine one's own beliefs and attitudes regarding race and culture.

4

Disruptive Behavior Disorders

> *Walter's school history has been marked by frequent conflicts with teachers and classmates, and now in eighth grade his behavior has escalated to the point where he is unable to make it through an entire week without either getting kicked out of a class by one of his teachers or suspended for fighting with peers or swearing at teachers or staff. Some of his teachers describe him as being sneaky, while others acknowledge being afraid of him. Walter is also well-known to police in the community for episodes of shoplifting and two recent incidents where he assaulted boys in the neighborhood. The school is at a loss for how to help him.*

> *Jennifer's sixth-grade teachers report that she is becoming increasingly difficult to deal with. She is consistently argumentative, seems irritable most of the time, and frequently refuses to follow teachers' directions. She has alienated most of her classmates, and the friendships she still has seem tenuous. Jennifer's teachers are frustrated; as put by her math teacher, "I don't think Jennifer is a bad kid, but she is constantly questioning the rules and directions. Nothing is easy with her. I try to stay positive with her, but it is hard, and I'm running out of energy."*

Walter and Jennifer are representative of students with disruptive behavior disorders. The conduct of students with these disorders can be trying for both teachers and parents. Disrupted classrooms, intimidation of peers, and violations of hosts of major and minor rules can test the patience and frustration tolerance of even the most placid teachers. Yet students with disruptive behavior disorders are also individuals with unique personal stories that often include victimization and powerlessness—and they may be the very students who are in the greatest need of the support and guidance of teachers, administrators, and school counselors. Indeed, students with behavior disorders are at enormous risk for both short-term difficulties and poor lifetime outcomes. Unaddressed behavior disorders create costs both for affected students and families and for society as a whole. Providing support and intervention assistance to students with disruptive behavior disorders can be one of the most challenging professional and personal tasks undertaken by teachers and school counselors. But it can also be enormously rewarding to see one's efforts literally shifting the life path of a troubled student to a more positive direction.

CORRELATES, ANTECEDENTS, AND OUTCOMES

Disruptive behavior disorders is a broad term that encompasses several DSM (*Diagnostic and Statistical Manual of Mental Disorders,* APA, 2000) categories, as well as an IDEA (Individuals With Disabilities Education Act, 2004) disability area. DSM categories included under the umbrella of disruptive behavior disorders include *conduct disorder* (CD), *oppositional defiant disorder* (ODD), *intermittent explosive disorder,* and *adjustment disorder with disturbance of conduct.* (*Attention-deficit/hyperactivity disorder,* or ADHD, is often considered a type of disruptive behavior disorder as well; though in this book, I will treat it as a separate disorder to better address its unique features.) As mentioned in Chapter 1, the IDEA 2004 disability category that addresses emotional and behavioral disturbances is labeled differently in different states, going by terms such as *emotional disturbance, behavioral disorder,* and *emotional/behavioral disorder.* Thankfully, educators wishing to assist students need not worry about having a mental health evaluation that precisely identifies the particular disorder, because there is little relationship between the type of behavior disorder and the specific intervention strategies that should be used. Rather, a detailed examination of the needs and behavioral characteristics of the individual student is much more important in selecting interventions. Indeed, within the category of disruptive behavior disorders, there are as many unique behavioral presentations as there are students, ranging in severity from mildly annoying and resistant to severely aggressive and antisocial. Furthermore, the nature of the behaviors exhibited by a child or adolescent with a disruptive behavior disorder will change over time and across situations, sometimes substantially. To perhaps reach for a simile, students with disruptive behavior disorders are like storm clouds in the atmosphere of behavior—none are alike, some are mild while others are severe, but all involve disruptions and all are constantly changing.

It is also helpful to have a solid understanding of some of the general characteristics of youth with behavior disorders, as well as an appreciation of what research tells us about the antecedents and consequences of these disorders. While later in this chapter we'll look more closely at the distinctive features of the specific DSM disorders in the disruptive behavior disorders family, let's begin by briefly reviewing what is generally known.

Correlates of Disruptive Behavior Disorders

The tendency of students with disruptive behavior disorders to wreak havoc in schools and classrooms often overshadows the pervasive negative impact of the disorder on their own functioning and well-being. First of all, it is not uncommon for students with disruptive behavior disorders to have one or more additional mental health problems. For example, the comorbidity between CD and anxiety disorders has been estimated to be as high as 55%, ADHD comorbidity estimates are as high as 41%, and comorbidity with depression has been estimated to be as high as 46% (Ollendick, Jarrett, Grills-Taquechel, Hovey, & Wolff, 2008). To be fair, other studies have found significantly lower comorbidity rates, but the main point remains: While dealing with a disruptive behavior disorder, many students are also battling one or more additional difficult and pernicious mental health disorders.

One of the correlates of disruptive behavior disorders—one seen with many mental health disorders—is peer relationship problems. That students with acting-out, volatile, and often-hostile behavior have trouble making friends is not a surprise. Their negative and, in some cases, aggressive behavior tends to intimidate and alienate prosocial peers. These well-behaved peers, in turn, tend to avoid and reject the students with disruptive behavior disorders (Ostrander, 2004). Two consequences follow. First, the students with disruptive behavior disorders feel the sting of rejection, which in addition to being painful in its own right can serve as validation to their distorted view that the world is against them (more about that coming soon). Second, these students tend to gravitate toward other students with behavior problems. This is the worst possible set of social circumstances. Students desperately in need of positive friendships and role models instead end up affiliating with peers who both model bad behavior and often reinforce antisocial behavior. It is as though a person with a gambling addiction moves to Las Vegas and pals around with a bunch of high-stakes gamblers.

In addition to social problems, youth with disruptive behavior disorders typically have patterns of thinking that are negative, being dominated by the pervasive view that the world is a battlefield. These youth tend to feel chronically unloved and abandoned, feeling as though they have been treated harshly by the adults in their world (Bernstein, 1996). Students with disruptive behavior disorders are predisposed to viewing relationships with adults in terms of power, control, and fairness. They often have an exaggerated sense that adults in authority positions—such as teachers and principals—are out to control them and are treating them unfairly. Needless to say, a cognitive set like this fuels argumentative and oppositional behaviors.

Researchers have identified two types of cognitive processes that youth engage in when choosing specific behaviors, both of which impact the decisions they make. The first process, called *response valuation*, involves making a judgment about whether the behavior under consideration is socially and morally acceptable (Fontaine, Burks, & Dodge, 2002). The second process, called *outcome expectancy*, involves making a prediction about whether the behavior under consideration will bring about positive outcomes (Fontaine et al.). Research further suggests that aggressive youth are more likely than nonaggressive youth to view aggression as a socially acceptable and appropriate behavioral choice. In addition, students who believe that aggression will lead to positive outcomes (such as increased power and respect from peers) are more likely to behave aggressively than students who do not hold that belief. Simply put, youth with disruptive behavior disorders are more likely than other students to think that bad behavior is okay and that it pays off.

This discussion might lead one to think that, before deciding to bully, assault, or otherwise aggress upon another person, the student with a disruptive behavior disorder engages in a cool, rational thought process, weighing moral issues and costs versus benefits. In some cases, this may be true, particularly with youth who have a style of behavior called *proactive aggression*. But there are also students with disruptive behavior disorders who have a tendency toward *reactive aggression*. In this type of reaction, the youth responds to perceived provocation or threat with impulsive, unplanned aggression. Students prone to reactive aggression generally have a *hostile attribution bias*, meaning that they consistently perceive the behavior of others to be hostile and provocative even when more-objective observers would rate the offending behavior as being benign. The environment of a high school hallway during passing time is a good laboratory for examining attribution biases. Most students perceive the jostling and bumping to be a simple result of many people crowded into narrow hallways. Youth with hostile attribution biases, on the other hand, are very apt to perceive casual bumps as hostile acts and respond in force. It is the equivalent of someone hearing the phone ring, assuming it is an annoying telemarketer, and answering with an angry rant without knowing for sure who is on the line.

Before we go further, there are two key points that need to be made. The first is that there are important individual differences even among students who display similar patterns of disruptive and aggressive behavior. Take fighting with a classmate, for example. One student might carefully plan when, where, and with whom the fight takes place, all in an effort to maximize power and status among peers. Another student might get into a fight because a peer holds eye contact a fraction of a second too long; perceiving that to be a challenge, the student reactively and impulsively starts fighting. The fights look the same, but the dynamics of how and why they happened are vastly different.

The second key point is that, while teachers, administrators, and parents may see the child or adolescent with a disruptive behavior disorder as behaving in a wildly inappropriate and disrespectful manner, *to the student* the behavior seems justified. If we could peer into the minds of students with disruptive behaviors and see how they think about the world, and about school, and about the adults in their lives, and about the specific situations in which problems arise, their behavior would be very understandable to us (albeit still disturbing and upsetting). Unfortunately, of course, we are not mind readers, and often these students closely guard their thoughts and share only a fraction of their thoughts with the adults in their lives.

Now that we know some of the correlates of disruptive behavior disorders, let's turn our attention to how these disorders develop.

Antecedents to Disruptive Behavior Disorders

Research has identified a number of factors that potentially contribute to the development of disruptive behavior disorders. In fact, disruptive behavior disorders appear to be multiply determined—in other words, there is not one simple cause that we can point to. Among the causal factors are biologically based characteristics such as central nervous system problems, parental characteristics, parent-child relational variables, and life experiences. While a full treatment of this area is beyond the scope of this book (see Bloomquist & Schnell, 2002, for a nice summary of these risk factors), let's briefly look at each of these factors in turn.

It does appear that a subset of children have a genetic predisposition for the types of central nervous system problems that facilitate the development of disruptive behavior disorders (Bloomquist & Schnell, 2002). Children with aggression problems may have deficits in the frontal lobe regulatory systems that inhibit maladaptive behavior (Quay, 1993). And they tend to perform poorly on tests of *executive functioning* (Bloomquist & Schnell), which is the set of cognitive processes that allow people to plan and evaluate their own behavior and regulate their feelings and behaviors. In plain language, this means that some children may have brains that do not allow them to control their aggression as easily as their peers.

In addition to these biologically based factors, there are also a number of characteristics that are often seen in the parents of children who either have or will go on to develop disruptive behavior disorders. Mothers of these students are more likely to be stressed and depressed, are more apt to be disengaged from their children, and are more likely to parent their children in a manner that is characterized by more negative and fewer positive interactions (Lovejoy, Graczyk, O'Hare, & Neuman, 2000). Fathers of children who have or will develop disruptive behavior disorders have higher rates of substance abuse and antisocial personality disorder than fathers in general (Frick, 1994). Furthermore, parents of children with disruptive behavior disorders are prone to negative cognitions regarding children and parenting, such as believing that the children's behavior is due to internal, stable, unchangeable traits or, conversely, that the children could behave well if they just wanted to. Either way, the associated cognition is that they as parents have no control over their children's behavior (Bloomquist & Schnell, 2002). The quality of the parent's relationship also impacts children's behavior. Elevated levels of parental conflict have been linked to aggressive behavior in children, as has parental disagreement about child rearing practices (Bloomquist & Schnell).

The way the parents and children relate to each other has proven to be another antecedent. Parents of children with disruptive behavior disorders tend to inflict harsh and inconsistent discipline, tend not to do a good job of monitoring their children, exhibit minimal warmth toward their children, and say negative things to their children (Bloomquist & Schnell, 2002). Physical punishment in particular has been clearly linked to an increased risk of the development of antisocial and aggressive behavior (Shields & Cicchetti, 2001). On the other side of the coin, the children tend not to comply with parental requests and exhibit aggression. One specific type of parent-child interaction has been repeatedly found in these families. This interaction begins with the child displaying a negative behavior—say whining for a toy in the mall. The parent responds by saying no. The whining not only continues but escalates into a tantrum. The parent, after saying no multiple times, finally relents and buys the child a toy. The end result is that the parent feels bullied and ineffective, and the child's demanding behavior has been reinforced. Essentially, this process trains children to be noncompliant.

Finally, victimization has been identified as being a significant risk factor for the development of conduct problems. For example, one longitudinal study found that children at age 11 who reported one or more experiences of victimization, such as being the victim of theft, vandalism, or assault, were more likely to report significant conduct problems at age 18 (Hilarski, 2004).

Developmental Outcomes of Disruptive Behavior Disorders

In addition to creating a host of co-occurring problems, disruptive behavior disorders significantly increase the risk of later problems in a number of areas. Students with disruptive behavior disorders are at significantly higher risk for ongoing mental health problems, for ongoing problems in school, for later substance-abuse problems, and for being convicted of crimes. The nature of risk varies with the type of disruptive behavior disorder, with more-severe risks being associated with CD and lesser risks being associated with ODD. For example, CD when comorbid with ADHD has been found to be associated with dropping out of school, developing substance-abuse problems, getting fired from a job, and being incarcerated (Biederman et al., 2008). On the other hand, ODD has been found to remit in approximately 70% of students by age 18, indicating that the majority of youth "grow out" of their ODD symptoms (Nock, Kazdin, Hiripi, & Kessler, 2007). Obviously, though, that means that almost a third of students do *not* grow out of their symptoms. In addition, ODD has been found to be a marker for future mental health problems. An astonishing 92% of individuals with ODD were estimated to meet criteria for another mental health problem in a recent study, even if the ODD itself had remitted (Nock et al.). It appears that ODD, even if it recedes, may alter one's life path in ways that leave a vulnerability to other mental health problems.

TYPES OF DISRUPTIVE BEHAVIOR DISORDERS

The school counselor's role in dealing with students with disruptive behavior disorders is much more oriented toward intervention and referral than toward evaluation and diagnosis. Nonetheless, a working knowledge of the various types of behavior disorders can help school counselors better understand the broad nature of a student's behavioral needs, as well as facilitate communication with community-based mental health professionals. The following section will describe the key characteristics of the main DSM disorders in the behavior disorders domain.

Conduct Disorder

According to *DSM* (APA, 2000), the essential feature of CD is a repetitive pattern of behavior in which the basic rights of others or major age-appropriate societal norms or rules are violated. Clinically significant symptoms such as intimidating others, stealing, setting fires, and physical cruelty to people or animals must be present for at least a year. CD is the most severe of the disruptive behavior disorders and is associated with a very high risk for significant negative long-term outcomes. Clinical correlates that often accompany CD include lack of empathy for others, lack of remorse after antisocial acts, and a tough façade hiding low self-esteem. Clearly, this is the heavyweight division of behavior disorders.

While the estimated prevalence rates for CD of 1.5% to 3.4% may seem rather low, CD accounts for 30% to 50% of the referrals for psychiatric evaluations. CD is more common among males (APA, 2000). In addition,

CD tends to present itself differently in boys and girls. Boys are more apt to manifest their CD through confrontational aggression, stealing, vandalism, and school behavior problems. Girls are more likely to display nonconfrontational behaviors such as lying, truancy, running away, substance abuse, and prostitution (APA).

DSM (APA, 2000) lists two subtypes of CD: (1) early onset versus late onset and (2) degree of severity. Early onset is assigned if the CD is diagnosed prior to age 10. The categories of severity are mild, moderate, and severe. Early onset CD is associated with higher levels of aggression and poorer long-term outcomes as compared to late onset CD; youth with late onset CD often have a significant ecological component to their behavior, such as gang involvement or substance abuse.

Oppositional Defiant Disorder

This is a disorder whose name captures its essence—oppositional and defiant behavior. DSM (APA, 2000) describes the essential feature of ODD as being a recurrent pattern of negativistic, defiant, disobedient, and hostile behavior toward authority figures that persists for at least six months. To be diagnosed with ODD, students must display symptoms such as frequently losing their temper, arguing with adults, defying adults' rules and requests, appearing touchy or easily annoyed by others, and blaming others for their misbehavior. As with all DSM diagnoses involving children and adolescents, these behaviors must be beyond what is appropriate for their developmental level. Recent data from the National Comorbidity Study Replication estimated the lifetime prevalence of ODD to be 10.2% (Nock et al., 2007).

Youth with ODD are experts at testing the limits—and testing the patience of teachers and administrators. In fact, the emotional reaction that students with ODD tend to elicit from the adults in their world is one way they can be differentiated from youth with CD. The behavior of students with ODD typically elicits irritation, frustration, and anger from teachers and parents and other authority figures. The behavior of students with CD, on the other hand, is more likely to elicit concern and even fear from adults. Students with ODD tend to be irritating; students with CD can be scary.

While oppositional behaviors are not unusual in young children, and tend to gradually diminish as children age (Bongers, Koot, van der Ende, & Verhulst, 2004), ODD tends to develop in reverse fashion, with the pattern of oppositional behavior gradually becoming more prevalent over time. ODD generally appears by age 8, with a gradual onset in which symptoms develop over a period of months or years (APA, 2000). Behaviors associated with ODD often first manifest themselves at home and then expand to the school setting. Youth with ODD tend to display their most intense oppositional behaviors with familiar adults (particularly adult authority figures) and may behave beautifully with unfamiliar adults. There is a lesson here for school counselors: If you meet individually with a student who has been referred for ODD behaviors, and the student appears pleasant and polite, don't dismiss the parents' or teachers' concerns as being overblown. As you have more contact with the student, or if you are placed in the role of an authority figure, you may see more of the oppositional behaviors.

There are several developmental routes that ODD can take once it is established. The behaviors can continue to become more intense, leading to a diagnosis of CD. At this point, the diagnosis of ODD is overridden by the CD diagnosis; by definition, youth with CD cannot also have an ODD diagnosis. ODD can be viewed as a gateway to CD, as CD is preceded by ODD in virtually all cases. The reverse is not true, however; ODD may or may not lead to CD. It is similar to the relationship between college football players and professional football players; virtually all NFL players were first college football players, but only a portion of college football players go on to play in the NFL. In some cases, the pattern of oppositional behavior gets neither better nor worse, leading to the maintenance of an ODD diagnosis. There is also a developmental route where oppositional behaviors diminish over time, leading to a removal of the ODD diagnosis. ODD is more prevalent among boys in childhood, but this gender difference disappears in adolescence, with as many girls as boys having the diagnosis.

Intermittent Explosive Disorder

Most teachers who have been in the field for awhile can think of students who behaved well most of the time, who did not seem intent on defying rules, and who seemed to care about the feelings of others but periodically displayed episodes of intense and often frightening rage. This pattern characterizes *intermittent explosive disorder*. DSM (APA, 2000) categorizes intermittent explosive disorder as an impulse control disorder and describes its essential feature as the "occurrence of discrete episodes of failure to resist aggressive impulses that result in serious assaultive acts or destruction of property" (p. 663). *Discrete* is an important element of the definition; it means that the individual's typical behavior pattern is appropriate and prosocial and that the behavioral explosions represent a clear departure from the individual's normal behavior. Some students with intermittent explosive disorder may feel a sense of rising tension preceding the explosions and, afterward, feel a sense of relief and even exhaustion. Along with the relief, though, may also be a sense of intense guilt and remorse. There may be precipitating events that seem to set off the behavior, but the behavioral reaction is well out of proportion to the triggering events. Far from being intentional or proactive, the behavioral thunderstorms associated with intermittent explosive disorder really do seem out of the individual's control and often feel as frightening to the individual as to the audience.

Minimal research has been done on intermittent explosive disorder, and no reliable prevalence figures are available. There is some preliminary evidence, though, that it may be important to examine the unique manner in which the explosive episodes develop and resolve in each individual. For example, one study of explosive rages in a group of youth with Tourette syndrome found four different subtypes of rage, differentiated by factors such as whether the rage was displayed just with close family members or if it was displayed in multiple settings (Budman, Rockmore, Stokes, & Sossin, 2003). It seems that school counselors working with students who display episodic rage should carefully examine the manner in which the rages present themselves to see whether there are any clues that might suggest intervention routes. One case study has been described in the literature in which child-centered play therapy was quite effective in reducing rages in an elementary-aged boy with intermittent explosive disorder (Paone & Douma, 2009).

Adjustment Disorder With Disturbance of Conduct

All of us are familiar with the experience of being exposed to a difficult life event—the death of a loved one or the loss of a job, for example—and responding with uncharacteristic behaviors and emotions. When these behaviors or emotions become more serious than is typical, or when they begin to interfere with one's ability to function well at school, work, or socially, they may indicate the presence of an *adjustment disorder*. According to *DSM* (APA, 2000), adjustment disorders are significant sets of emotional or behavioral problems (or both) that occur within three months of exposure to an identifiable stressor. There are subtypes of adjustment disorders to reflect whether the adjustment problems are manifested as problems of mood, of anxiety, or of conduct. If the adjustment problems primarily consist of conduct problems, the disorder is labeled *adjustment disorder with disturbance of conduct*. The key requirement for diagnosing a child or adolescent with an adjustment disorder is that there must be a clear link between the youth's behavior and a stressor of some kind, such as parental divorce or being exposed to violence.

Of all the diagnostic categories available for disruptive behavior disorders, adjustment disorder with disturbance of conduct is generally the most benign, because by definition, it describes a situation where the individual's behavior is a reaction to an outside stressor rather than a continuation of a lengthy and often intractable pattern of disruptive behavior. As a group, youth with behavior-related adjustment disorders can be viewed as needing support and a listening ear rather than extensive behavioral intervention. If the stressor is particularly severe, there may be a need for intense counseling interventions, but the behaviors can be viewed as symptoms of psychological distress. The core issue is the stressor and how the youth is responding to that, not the behavior.

INTERVENTION GUIDELINES

The high level of disruptiveness students with behavior disorders bring to schools and classrooms, along with the host of negative outcomes for the students themselves, makes effective school-based interventions a priority. The following guidelines provide directions for intervention for school counselors, teachers, and other school personnel. As noted in Chapter 2, these guidelines should be combined with knowledge about the unique issues and personality of the specific student and the context in which the problems occur in order to devise a specific, tailored intervention plan.

INTERVENTION GUIDELINES FOR STUDENTS WITH BEHAVIOR DISORDERS

1. First, do no harm.
2. Begin by seeking to understand the behavior.
3. Select comprehensive and lengthy interventions where possible.
4. Make a personal connection.
5. Focus on antecedents.
6. Set and monitor goals.
7. Communicate in a way that encourages good behavior.
8. Make it pay to behave.
9. Address dysfunctional thinking.
10. Build positive behavior.

Guideline 1: First, Do No Harm

This initial guideline serves as an important reminder that some attempts at intervention can actually exacerbate the problems of students with disruptive behavior disorders. A body of research indicates that gathering antisocial, high-risk youth together and providing group-based interventions can increase rather than decrease problem behavior. Researchers observed the minute-by-minute interactions in these groups and identified a process they coined *deviancy training* (Dishion, McCord, & Poulin, 1999). In this process, the group responds with laughter or other reinforcing behavior to a youth who makes a comment about breaking rules. Dishion and his colleagues, for example, followed boys in the Oregon Youth Study over time and found that youth whose early friendships were characterized by deviancy training displayed significantly greater increases in substance use, delinquency, and violent behavior two years later as compared to boys who did not have deviancy training.

The phenomenon of deviancy training is not pervasive. Research indicates that many peer-oriented interventions at the elementary level have proven effective in group settings. Even at the middle school level, where youth seem particularly at risk for deviancy training, the effects are moderated by including prosocial peers in intervention groups. But the overall research sends a clear message to school counselors: Be cautious of forming a group consisting exclusively of antisocial and aggressive students, particularly at the middle school level. Furthermore, be vigilant when running groups with any types of students to make sure that deviant or rule-breaking comments from some group members are not reinforced by other group members.

Guideline 2: Begin by Seeking to Understand the Behavior

Imagine you go to a doctor for chest pains, and after a minute of asking about your symptoms, the doctor advises you to schedule bypass surgery. Or imagine you take your car into the shop for a rattle in the engine, and after hearing your description of the problem, the mechanic tells you that you need a new $3,000 transmission. Think you might be skeptical? Yet when it comes to students' behavior problems, we often use a similar approach, selecting cookie-cutter, one-size-fits-all interventions based on the behaviors we see, without first trying to figure out what is motivating or maintaining the behavior.

It makes more sense to begin by looking underneath the behavior to try to determine what is causing or supporting it. As discussed in Chapter 2, exploring triggers and maintaining variables is a wise first step. In the case of disruptive behavior disorders, there are numerous possible factors that can be triggering and maintaining the problem behavior. Some of these factors are listed in the accompanying text box (see "A Sample of Triggers and Maintaining Variables"). Let's look at an example to emphasize the value of identifying triggers and maintaining variables. Let's say that two 7th-grade students, Maria and Kevin, both display the same behavior pattern: making increasingly loud, disruptive comments in math class until the teacher must send them out of class. In Maria's case, the triggering stimuli are under-the-breath comments from several classmates, who know that they can get Maria going by egging her on. Once Maria starts making loud comments, her behavior is reinforced by the laughter and approval of the classmates. The triggering stimuli for Kevin, on the other hand, is his intense level of discomfort in math class, rooted in his poor math skills and his fear that he will be exposed to his peers as being dumb. His disruptive and loud comments are maintained by his removal from the unpleasant situation and the accompanying reduction in his feelings of anxiety and fear. This is a classic case of negative reinforcement, where an aversive stimulus is removed contingent upon a response.

A SAMPLE OF TRIGGERS AND MAINTAINING VARIABLES FOR DISRUPTIVE BEHAVIORS AT SCHOOL

Triggers

- Feeling sick, tired, or hungry
- Feeling distressed over events occurring before school
- Being asked to work on an academic task that seems difficult
- Being verbally corrected in front of peers
- Having a request denied by a person in authority
- Being verbally challenged by a peer
- Being in the vicinity of (and trying to impress) high-status peers
- Being in an area of the school without adult supervision

- Feeling bored
- Being under the influence of substances
- Being asked to participate in an activity that feels emotionally threatening
- Being told to do something in an authoritative manner
- Being laughed at by a peer
- Being rejected by a peer
- Being in the vicinity of (and trying to dominate) low-status peers

Maintaining Variables

- Feeling of power and control
- Feeling of freedom and escape
- Satisfaction of adhering to a personal code (e.g., "No one is going to disrespect me.")
- Avoidance of classroom situations that seem threatening
- Peer attention
- Tangible rewards (e.g., obtaining a CD by means of theft)

- Feeling of arousal—the "rush"
- Feeling of emotional- and physical-tension reduction
- Removal from classroom situations that seem threatening
- Teacher attention
- Peer approval

Author's note: lists are not exhaustive.

Even though the behavior displayed by Maria and Kevin looks the same, the meaning of the behavior is very different. Interventions that will work with Maria will not work with Kevin, and vice versa. Maria would benefit from interventions such as changing her desk placement, switching her to a different section of the same math class, or using a group contingency so that the entire class benefits from improvements in Maria's behavior. None of those interventions would significantly impact Kevin, who needs additional academic support in the math area, as well as assurances from his math teacher that he will not be called on in class in a manner that will embarrass him.

In addition to remembering the mantra that students' behavior problems must be individually analyzed for unique sets of triggers and maintaining variables, it is helpful to keep in mind some common distinctions that characterize either the behavior or the personality of students prone to problem behavior. Being aware of these distinctions can help school counselors better understand and better prevent behavioral issues among students. The first distinction, which we talked about before, is *proactive* versus *reactive* aggression. You'll recall that proactive aggression is intentional, goal-directed aggression motivated by the youth's desire to gain something, such as power or material goods. Proactive aggression can be considered learned behavior that has been rewarded in some way in the past (Brown & Parsons, 1998). Reactive aggression, in contrast, is an impulsive behavioral reaction to perceived threats or provocation. Different intervention strategies are recommended for each of these types of aggression. Proactive aggression, given that it is designed to achieve some sort of goal, is best dealt with by making sure the behavior is not rewarded and, rather, is followed by negative consequences of some sort. So an elementary-aged student who pushed around a smaller classmate and took a video game from the classmate would have to give the video game back, write a letter of apology to the student, and spend time inside at recess for a week. Reactive aggression, in contrast, is best dealt with by a two-pronged approach of minimizing the triggers that set off the behavior and helping the student replace hostile attributions with more-realistic attributions. As an example, a high school student who has been in several reactive fights in the hallway during passing time would be given permission to pass between classes five minutes early and would also work with the school counselor to develop an awareness that minor jostling in the hallways at school are almost always the result of unintentional contact that happens when many students are in a small space.

A second helpful distinction is that of *understimulated* versus *overstimulated* students. Another way of putting this is that some students tend to become easily aroused (overstimulated) and others tend to require a great deal of environmental stimulation to become aroused (understimulated).

Students who tend to get easily overstimulated may find the environment of an active, noisy classroom very distracting and even aversive. In addition to being unable to attend well or do their best work in such a classroom, they may also become edgy and irritable. Interventions in such a case might include finding a desk placement in a corner of the room that is a bit less chaotic, moving the student to a classroom that is more sedate, or even allowing the student to wear headphones to play soft music. Students with disruptive behavior disorders, however, are more likely to be understimulated. These students become easily bored and often engage in thrill-seeking, sometimes risky behavior in order to feel alive. A student who is chronically understimulated may shoplift, for example, not for material gain but for the adrenaline rush that comes with taking and walking out with the item. Interventions for these students might consist of finding prosocial outlets for thrill-seeking behavior, such as competitive sports or other kinds of challenges.

A final distinction that can help school counselors better understand and assist students with disruptive behavior disorders is that of *chronic* versus *acute* problems. Chronic, of course, means of long duration or frequently recurring, while acute means of short duration or sudden onset. How long does a problem have to exist to be considered chronic? The general guideline used in *DSM* (APA, 2000) is one year. For example, a tic disorder must exist for a year to be called chronic, and dysthymic disorder, which is a type of chronic depressive disorder you'll hear more about in Chapter 6, involves depressive symptoms that have been experienced for at least a year among children and adolescents. While duration is only one variable among many that go into intervention planning, the presence or absence of chronicity does provide some information that can be helpful. Chronic problems are more likely to be linked to long-term internal deficits or family and other environmental concerns. Furthermore, chronic problems almost always have been subject to various formal and informal interventions (which obviously have not worked, at least not completely). It is helpful to examine these past interventions and their impact, to avoid repeating unsuccessful interventions and perhaps employ a strengthened version of previous interventions that proved partially successful.

Acute behavior problems, on the other hand, are more likely to be born of environmental changes or even trauma. For example, when dealing with a student whose problem behavior in the past four months has been a clear departure from previous appropriate behavior, the wise school counselor will investigate what happened four months ago, looking for broad triggering events. Students with acute problems typically have a satisfactory history of managing their emotions and behaviors and coping with problems, so at times it can be helpful to focus on ways they can reestablish previously successful coping strategies.

Guideline 3: Select Comprehensive and Lengthy Interventions Where Possible

Research has repeatedly demonstrated that interventions are most effective with youth with disruptive behavior disorders if the interventions are comprehensive and long lasting. That of course jibes with common sense. Interventions that target multiple risk factors; that positively impact the individual, the school environment, and the family; and that persist over a length of time are clearly more likely to make a difference than those not having these qualities. Not only does it make intuitive sense that more-lengthy strategies should have more impact, but also this has been demonstrated empirically. For example, one study examined the impact of a prevention program delivered to two groups of elementary-aged students at risk for emotional disturbance, one of which received the program for one year and one of which received the program for two years. The children receiving the program for two years had substantially better outcomes (McConaughy, Kay, & Fitzgerald, 2000). Clearly, rather than seek a single, brief magic bullet, school counselors and other school personnel should think of extended, multifaceted interventions.

While we can all agree that the best interventions for students with disruptive behavior disorders are comprehensive and long-term, many schools may lack the resources to implement these types of expensive and time-consuming programs. Even if that is the case, though, it is still possible to honor the spirit of this guideline. For example, a school counselor who is working on behavioral goal setting with a student could make a point of contacting the student's parents and enlisting their help in working on the goals in both the school and home settings. As another example, a school counselor who is working with a teacher to devise a behavior-management plan for a student could contact the student's other teachers and work to coordinate the efforts of all the teachers so they are using similar rules and strategies. These are, admittedly, minor efforts and do not approach the level of comprehensiveness of ideal programs, but actions like these give students with disruptive behaviors the impression that the key people in their lives are on the same page and are providing similar and consistent rewards and consequences.

Guideline 4: Make a Personal Connection

School-based interventions for students with disruptive behavior disorders consist mostly of trying to manage the school environment in a way that minimizes the triggers to problem behaviors and insures that positive behavior is rewarded. But it is also important not to lose track of the personal relationship between the student and the school counselor. It may be tempting to believe that highly resistant and oppositional students are incapable of having a meaningful connection with a school-based adult. Indeed, often these students are unappreciative at best and stone-cold resistant at worst when school counselors and others try to help them. In fact, consistent with their perception that adults don't understand them and treat them unfairly, these students often feel compelled to work under protest (Bernstein, 1996). Rather than viewing students with disruptive behavior disorders as being in some sort of special category that makes them unable to profit from counseling and relate well to adults, though, it is more fruitful to think in terms of a continuum of amenability to adult intervention. Students on the unamenable end of the continuum are no doubt highly challenging, but they should not be viewed as being unable to establish relationships with helping adults. It is best to view relationship building with students at this end of the continuum as being more difficult and more time consuming but possible. In fact, these students are *most* in need of positive adult role models and mentors. Bernstein (1996) offered several sensible ideas for building therapeutic relationships with youth with disruptive behavior disorders:

- If a student presents as being resistant and uncooperative, simply reflect that feeling rather than try to break down the resistant wall with a frontal assault. Statements like "You look like you would rather be anyplace than here right now" or "I know it's no fun to be forced to see a counselor" can serve as the first small steps to a working counseling relationship.
- Display interest and curiosity about the unique life of each student. In addition, become informed about adolescent culture as a whole. Having an awareness of the types of music, performers, movies, and video games that are currently popular with youth will help school counselors be better able to ask conversational questions that do not seem hopelessly anachronistic to teens.
- During early sessions, avoid both excessive numbers of questions (which can feel interrogatory and can elicit annoyance) and lengthy silences (which can feel uncomfortable).
- It can be helpful to engage students with disruptive behavior disorders in conversations about others rather than about themselves, given that they are very unlikely to offer detailed descriptions of their own problem behaviors or inner feelings, particularly in early sessions. This might include inquiring about whom they hang out with, what they think of their classmates, and who they believe treats them unfairly.
- Avoid passing judgment. These youth may revel in the chance to talk to a listening adult about their views on current events and issues. While these views may be shockingly antisocial, it is important to listen nonjudgmentally, particularly in early sessions. Later, when a therapeutic relationship has been built, counselors can feel freer to use versions of "I care about you and want the best for you, which is why I am worried about _____."

Finally, once a counselor develops a personal connection with a student, that foundation of trust can smooth the way to deliver one of the most powerful messages possible: *I believe in you.* In my experience, even the most hardened students at some level crave to know that important adults accept them and believe in them. This sentiment cannot be delivered falsely, and it is important to include in the message that this does not mean that you expect the student to be perfect. If you genuinely believe in a student, share that. If you believe in his potential, tell him so. If you believe that you see a better side of her than other adults do, or than even she sees, tell her so. Most of us have had the privilege of having someone we respect tell us that they believe in us. If you have had that experience, you know how powerful it can be. And you can imagine what it would be like not to ever hear that message.

Guideline 5: Focus on Antecedents

In Guideline 2, I talked about the importance of understanding both the triggers and the maintaining variables associated with problem behaviors. The focus of this guideline is the former: the triggers, or antecedents to problem behaviors. In the language of behavior therapy, this means examining the stimulus cues associated with problem behaviors. School counselors and other school personnel who are able to identify what is triggering the episodes of problem behavior for a student are in a position to alter the environment of the classroom or other areas of the school to minimize the occurrence of the triggers, thereby ameliorating the problem behaviors.

The impact of antecedents on our own behavior is readily apparent. How often are you working on a task at your computer only to find yourself automatically checking your e-mail whenever you get the signal that you have a new message? A variety of internal and environmental triggering stimuli can be powerful influences over problem behavior. As discussed in Chapter 2, it is best to look for *immediate* antecedents to problem behavior, because the further back in time we go to look for antecedents, the greater the degree of inference we are making and the more likely we will be wrong. Moreover, we have greater control over the immediate antecedents to school behavior problems. For example, if we determine that a student we are working with responds with aggressive noncompliance when called on in class (an immediate antecedent), we can work with the student and teacher to figure out how to change the dynamic. But if we suspect that the year-old divorce of the student's parents contributes to the problem behavior, we (a) can't be sure that is true and (b) are unable to alter that antecedent. The rule of thumb is to start by seeking the most-proximal antecedents; then move on to look for more-distal antecedents.

In many cases, a combination of proximal and distal events serves as antecedents to problem behavior. Let's look at one illustrative example. Marta is a fourth-grade girl who has been displaying flurries

Figure 4.1   Problem-Analysis Interview

1. What are the problem behaviors you are concerned about? (Select one behavior to begin working on.)

2. When does it happen?

3. What do you do when it happens?

4. What do other students do?

5. When doesn't it happen?

6. What do you do then?

7. What do the other students do when it doesn't happen?

8. What is important to the student, and how does she or he get it now?

9. Based on what we've talked about so far, have you thought of any changes you can make in your classroom to improve the situation?

Note: With slight modifications, this interview format can be used with parents, with other adults involved with the student, or directly with the student.

of argumentative and oppositional behavior throughout the school year, and her teacher has asked the school counselor for help. The school counselor is aware that Marta's parents separated last year and that Marta spends weekends with her father. While this may be a distal antecedent to the problem behavior, the counselor decides to look for more-immediate antecedents. Using the problem-analysis interview (Figure 4.1) with Marta's main teacher, the school counselor is able to discern that the behaviors are most severe early in the week. In addition, Marta seems to be most oppositional during reading and language arts. A classroom observation further reveals that Marta's level of disruptive behavior escalated immediately before the oral reading portion of class. During a follow-up conversation with Marta, the school counselor asked her how she felt about reading, and Marta acknowledged that she hated reading and didn't like reading in front of the class. Based on this information, the school counselor and teacher developed a list of factors that seemed to be serving as antecedents to the problem behavior. They also implemented interventions to address each antecedent, as shown in the following table.

Antecedent	Intervention
Fear of looking foolish during oral reading due to low reading skills	Provide afterschool academic support in reading; work with her teacher to avoid calling on Marta for oral reading of difficult passages.
Adjustment to Mom's home and school routine after spending the weekend with Dad	Check in on Monday morning with the school counselor to see how the weekend was and preview the upcoming day.
Parental separation	Invite Marta to join a family change group run by the school counselor.

It is clear that identifying antecedents to problem behaviors can help generate effective interventions. A final point is not to forget one of the most important sources of information when it comes to identifying antecedents: the student. While students have varying levels of insight about their own behavior, it can be fruitful with most students to ask questions such as "What do you think sets you off when you lose your temper" and "When are you most likely to get in trouble with your teachers?"

Guideline 6: Set and Monitor Goals

Goal setting is an integral part of many counseling approaches. Benefits of therapeutic goal setting include helping clients focus their attention and efforts in a defined direction, as well as mobilize their energy (Egan, 2010). Furthermore, developing goals can engender a sense of hope by creating a clear pathway to change. Think about your own life. There are probably multiple examples of times you formally or informally set goals and used those goals to move in a new life direction. Perhaps you set a goal of becoming a school counselor, beginning an exercise program, or creating a better relationship with someone you worked with. People who are effective in managing their lives tend to naturally set goals for themselves.

Goal setting is particularly important for students with disruptive behavior disorders. They often have lives that are disorganized and aimless, lacking in positive long-term aspirations or short-term goals. Working on specific and achievable goals can provide motivation and help them focus their energies. Moreover, achieving those goals can be one of the most rewarding and esteem-building experiences students can have.

The rub here, of course, is that students who have a pattern of oppositional behavior with adults are likely to oppose the efforts of school counselors to help them set goals. Youth with disruptive behavior disorders are prone to view goal setting as attempts to control them and exert authority over them. That makes it critical for counselors to present goal setting as a collaborative activity. Getting buy-in from the student is necessary, even if that means that the goals that are finally selected are not the exact ones the counselor would prefer. Take the case of Jack, who has been on a downward spiral of loud oppositional and defiant behavior in math class. The school counselor would love for Jack to embrace a goal of responding to the teacher's request with compliance rather than contempt. Jack, however, views compliance as letting the teacher win, which he is unwilling to do. So perhaps the best goal that Jack can agree to is to talk to the teacher in a normal tone, with no profanity. Once this goal is achieved (and the counselor has time to work with Jack on seeing himself in a more positive light), Jack may be better able to commit to goals that are even more prosocial.

Guideline 7: Communicate in a Way That Encourages Good Behavior

The words we choose when we talk to students with disruptive behavior disorders are important. Clearly, there are some ineffective and shame-producing verbal approaches to avoid, such as yelling, browbeating, lecturing, and judging. In addition to avoiding these approaches, though, teachers and counselors can also choose ways of communicating with youth that maximize the chance that they will respond with compliance and positive behavior.

One communication strategy is to begin with high-probability requests (Frey & George-Nichols, 2003). What this means in a classroom is that a teacher would begin by asking a student with disruptive behavior disorders to do something the teacher is virtually certain the student will do, possibly something the student enjoys doing. Once the student has done that—and the teacher can praise or reward the response—the teacher then asks the student to do something that requires more effort. The underlying concept is to build behavioral momentum and help the student get in the habit of complying. The following dialogue illustrates this concept:

Teacher: Stacey, please go over and check the gerbil cage to see if he has enough water in his water bottle.

Student complies.

Teacher: Great, thanks. Now take out a piece of paper and write your name on the top.

Student complies.

Teacher: Alright, good. Now, write a paragraph with at least three sentences talking about the animal you liked best at our field trip to the zoo yesterday.

Another way to communicate that encourages good behavior is to *offer choices within parameters*. This gives students a sense of freedom, while also giving the teacher a measure of control. So rather than saying, "Jessica, take out your math book and get to work on the assignment for today," a teacher could say, "Jessica, you need to get started on today's math assignment within the next five minutes. Would you like to start now, so you can get done earlier, or would you like to spend five more minutes on your writing project?" Offering choices takes a bit more effort and may require some creativity, but it is typically appreciated by students and can help avoid the knee-jerk resistance students with disruptive behavior disorders often have to teachers' directives.

A final communication strategy is to always seek to tell students what *to* do rather than telling them what *not* to do. Some examples follow.

Telling Students What *Not* to Do	Telling Students What *to* Do
Stop talking.	Listen.
Stop pushing.	Keep your hands to yourself.
Stop goofing around.	I'd like your attention on me.

None of these communication strategies is magic, and none is foolproof. When used intentionally, however, they can increase the likelihood that students will comply. And it is always easier to act in a way that facilitates compliance from the start than to deal with the consequences of noncompliant behavior.

Guideline 8: Make It Pay to Behave

The more technical term for this guideline is to *manage contingencies*, but contingency management is really just arranging students' environment so that it pays for them to behave. Let's look at a classroom example to illustrate this concept. Assume there are two English teachers in your school who teach in adjacent classrooms. Both know their content inside and out, there is no difference in the subject matter they present, and students are randomly assigned to each teacher. Yet one teacher consistently has students who are more engaged and display fewer behavior problems than students in the other class. When you observe both classrooms, you notice one distinct difference: The teacher with the engaged, compliant students routinely recognizes students who are working hard and writes encouraging comments on written assignments. The teacher with less-compliant students corrects problem behavior but does not recognize appropriate behavior, and her feedback on written assignments consists strictly of pointing out their errors. From the students' perspective, it pays to behave for the first teacher but not the second.

There are several considerations when trying to arrange classroom and school environments so that it pays for students to behave. Perhaps the most important consideration is to recognize that what is reinforcing—in other words, what will serve as effective "pay"—can be very different for different students. Some high school students find teacher praise very rewarding, while others would rather give up their driver's license than be singled out for public praise from a teacher. Some elementary school students are very motivated if they are given independent reading time contingent upon finishing their assignment, while others couldn't care less about reading but would work like a demon to earn points toward an early recess. The key point is that rewards for students with disruptive behavior disorders must be individualized. It is a mistake to assume that rewards that most students like will be reinforcing for the specific student you are working with.

A related point is that the best person to decide what reinforcers to use for a particular student is the student. While adults tend to have a general understanding of what children and adolescents like, the true experts in this area are the students. One tool that can be effective is a *reinforcement menu*. Research indicates that students work harder for reinforcers they have selected than they do for ones that are selected for them. So it behooves counselors and teachers to develop menus that can be provided in the classroom or in the school; then ask the student which item from the menu the individual would like to work for.

A final consideration is that to be effective, reinforcers must be contingent upon the display of desirable behavior. This seems obvious, but in practice it can be challenging. For example, if a student with ODD has significant oppositional behavior in the morning but has a very good afternoon, should the afternoon behavior be rewarded? Or conversely, if the student has a stellar day up until a difficult last hour, should the youth be rewarded for a good day? To make these types of judgments, it is best to consider the unique circumstances of the individual student, particularly the baseline level of inappropriate behavior. In the case of a student who is displaying disruptive behavior multiple times during the day, it may make sense to reward the student for a half day or even an hour of positive behavior. On the other hand, rewards should be withheld from a student who has any substantial behavior issue at any point during the school day if that student has demonstrated the ability to behave appropriately for days at a time.

Taking into account all the previous considerations, let's now examine two classroom systems that help make it pay for students to behave. The first, the *token economy*, is an effective classwide intervention system for rewarding good behavior. Part of the appeal of a token economy is its simplicity. After collaborating with students to construct a set of classroom rules, the teacher then obtains a supply of poker chips or tickets (the "tokens" in token economy). The teacher periodically gives a token to individual students who are following the rules and displaying prosocial behavior. The students can save the tokens and, at a designated time, redeem them for a reward of some sort. At the elementary level, the reward might consist of being able to buy an item in a school store. At the secondary level, the reward might be selecting an item from a menu of rewards such as 15 minutes of computer time or a no-homework-for-one-day coupon.

The second classroom system aimed at the elementary level is called the Good Behavior Game. This intervention is particularly well suited for classrooms where peer laughter or encouragement is serving as either a trigger or a maintaining variable for problem behavior. Similar to the token economy, the Good Behavior Game begins with the teacher and students discussing what they would like the classroom to look like, including both the specific behaviors that lead to the class being a good and pleasant place to learn and the behaviors that interfere with a good classroom environment (called "fouls"). The teacher then divides the class into teams and creates a competition to decide who "wins" the game. There is a scoreboard, similar to a sporting event, listing wins for each team, as well as fouls. The Good Behavior Game has strong empirical support at the elementary level and has even been promoted as a "behavioral vaccine" for problem behaviors (Embry, 2002). A more detailed description of the Good Behavior Game can be found in a manual by Embry and Straatemeier (2001).

Guideline 9: Address Dysfunctional Thinking

Not surprisingly, interventions for youth with disruptive behavior disorders generally have a behavioral focus. But it is important not to ignore the role of cognition in behavior. Attitudes, beliefs, world views, perceptions, thoughts . . . all are integrally connected with behavior. As discussed earlier in this chapter, students with disruptive behavior disorders are prone to hold beliefs that fuel negative behavior. In addition, they are susceptible to beliefs and thoughts that damage their self-esteem. School counselors and teachers should do what they can to challenge these cognitions.

Students with disruptive behavior disorders typically hold sets of self-serving patterns of thinking that inhibit their ability to make good moral judgments about their own behavior and to empathize with others (Bernstein, 1996). These patterns of thinking include a sense of entitlement and an ability to rationalize antisocial behavior ("Sure, I took her iPod. Why not? She has lots of money to buy another one, and I wanted it"), in addition to a tendency to minimize their own behavior ("I didn't hurt him bad—I didn't even hit him that hard"). School counselors can challenge these statements by shifting the focus to the long-term consequences of these thinking patterns (Bernstein). Posing thoughtful questions is one way to do this, being sure not to come across as an authority figure giving a lecture. Questions like "What kind of reputation do you think you'll have if you continue to steal things from other people? Is that what you want?" and "What do you think your employer will do if you threaten coworkers at your job site?" can be helpful. Bernstein suggests engaging youth with oppositional behavior in lengthy conversations about moral and social norms to help them move beyond the "me first" level of moral reasoning. Ask questions such as "Why does our society have laws? What would happen if everyone did whatever they wanted? Are there rules of behavior among your friends? Why is that?"

Exercises in perspective taking can also be instrumental in helping students with disruptive behavior disorders begin to develop a sense of empathy (Bernstein, 1996). Bernstein suggests sharing stories from peers who have been victimized in which the individual talks about the shame, guilt, fear, and anger that resulted from the victimization. These can be written accounts or, even better, audio recordings of the victims talking about their experiences. Another approach to help foster empathy among students with disruptive behavior disorders is to explore episodes from their past when they have been the victim rather than the aggressor. Indeed, most aggressive and violent youth have histories full of abuse, neglect, and emotional pain. Finding ways to help them talk about those painful experiences can be a way to help them connect better with the pain of others.

Guideline 10: Build Positive Behavior

Teachers, administrators, parents, and school counselors who are faced with a child or adolescent displaying significant problem behaviors typically have one fundamental question: What can I do to stop these behaviors? The situation is generally framed as an issue of helping the student reduce or eliminate whatever behaviors are causing problems. However, rather than having this single focus, concerned adults can view their role as being twofold: (1) to reduce problem behavior and (2) to increase positive, prosocial behavior. Take the example of an eighth grader who has been in a pattern of oppositional behavior in school and has had two recent incidents of responding to a teacher's direction with a string of angry profanities. The inclination of most teachers and administrators is to figure out what consequence should apply, be it in-school or out-of-school suspension, being removed from classes, or forced apologies. The focus would be on the negative behavior, and understandably so. The behavior is clearly inappropriate and disruptive.

But there is another way to view the situation. It is also possible to view this as being a case of a student who has not learned how to effectively manage emotions, and who has poorly developed ability to control impulses, and who has not learned the social skills required to appropriately express frustration or inadequacy. Rather than focus exclusively on punishments and consequences, school personnel and school counselors could focus on helping the student recognize and express feelings better, control impulses better, and talk to adults in a prosocial manner. This is not a matter of choosing one approach over the other or of abdicating the use of consequences. Rather, it is taking a two-pronged approach to intervention, where students with disruptive behavior disorders both experience appropriate consequences for their behavior *and* learn better ways of managing their feelings and actions.

One important advantage of taking this two-pronged approach to behavior is that it helps teachers and counselors draw attention to the things the student does right. Harping on negative behavior tends to just reinforce the self-image of behavior disordered students that they are unsuccessful students and flawed people. In addition to the advantage of recognizing and acknowledging positive behavior, the two-pronged approach also provides a route to intervention—that being teaching and shaping prosocial behavior—that may both come more naturally to teachers (it is a type of education, after all) and be more effective. The negative behaviors of students with disruptive behavior disorders may be strongly habitual, and an approach focusing on building skills instead may be met with less resistance.

One purpose of focusing on positive behavior is to assist students in developing a belief in a positive and rewarding future and helping them commit to pursue that future. A specific way to do this is by using an intervention based on the notion of *possible selves*. Possible selves are people's ideas of what they might become, including both what they wish to become and what they are afraid they may become (Markus & Nurius, 1986). The school counselor can implement a possible selves intervention by having thorough conversations with a student about the kind of person the student hopes to become and the kind of person the student does *not* want to become. It is helpful to set specific points in time to ground these conversations, talking about possible selves when the student is 16, and 20, and 30, and so on. The desired possible selves can serve as an embodiment of the student's long-term goals, while the unwanted possible selves can serve as a motivator to change current behavior that is pointing in that direction.

Once the possible selves are well developed, the conversation can shift to connecting current behavior, so it aligns with the desired future selves. For example, if seventh grader Antonio states that his desired self at age 20 is to be in college playing basketball, then the school counselor can center the conversation around the choices Antonio needs to make now in order to make that possible self come true (e.g., "So for sure you'll need to pass math class to get you on track for college eligibility. And getting your homework done is the key part of that. Okay?"). It is also possible to use a more short-term possible selves approach, projecting out just one year. Figure 4.2 provides an example of a Possible Me Tree that looks out one year.

Let's look at one final positive intervention approach, one that is the purest example of focusing on positive behavior. *Self-modeling* is an ingeniously simple intervention that requires a bit of technological sleight of hand. In preparation for the self-modeling intervention, recordings are made of the classroom behavior of a student whose behavior is negative or disruptive. The recordings are then modified so that the negative behaviors are edited out. What remains is a recording of the student behaving appropriately in the classroom—complying with teacher requests, working on assignments, paying attention, and interacting positively with classmates. The edited recording is then repeatedly shown to the student. Multiple studies have indicated that this process leads to significant improvements in a range of student problems, including selective mutism (Kehle, Owen, & Cressy, 1990), academic on-task behavior (Clare, Jenson, Kehle, & Bray, 2000), and disruptive behaviors (Kehle, Clark, Jenson, & Wampold, 1986). While self-modeling does require some technological expertise, and should

Figure 4.2   Sample Possible Me Tree

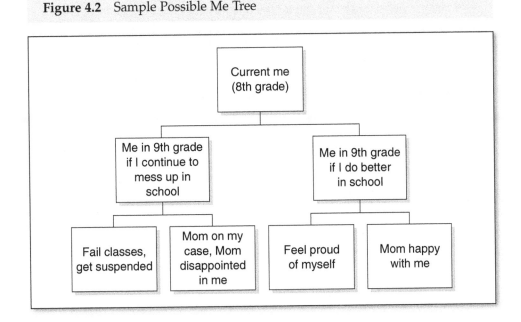

be preceded by parental permission due to the use of video recordings, it is an intriguing and potentially powerful intervention.

A final thought. As you read through the guidelines in this chapter, the thought may have crossed your mind that many guidelines contained ideas that apply to *all* students, not just those with disruptive behavior disorders. And you would have been absolutely right. Many of the ideas in this chapter *do* apply to all students. That in itself is a powerful statement. It means that students with disruptive behavior disorders are not alien creatures whose thoughts and feelings are qualitatively different from "normal" students. Rather than viewing these students as being beyond hope, it is more helpful to view them as students who have varying combinations of biological vulnerabilities, personal histories, and patterns of thinking that make them more likely to behave inappropriately and less likely to respond to standard levels of intervention. Think of them as needing more-intense and more-creative intervention strategies to succeed in school. And think of them as needing caring adults—including you—to believe in them.

SUMMARY POINTS

- Students with behavior disorders are at high risk for a host of short-term and lifetime negative consequences.
- Students with behavior disorders can appear tough and resistant but often have personal histories replete with victimization and powerlessness.
- Effective intervention for problem behavior begins by seeking to understand and address the triggers and functions of the behavior. Avoid one-size-fits-all intervention approaches.
- Making a personal connection with students with behavior disorders is critical. Making a connection can be hard work but can be done.
- Work around resistance by avoiding excessive questioning, displaying genuine curiosity about students' lives, and refraining from passing judgment about their behavior.
- Make it pay to behave by finding out what is reinforcing for the student and then providing that contingent on positive behavior.
- Work to decrease problem behavior *and* increase prosocial behavior.
- The message "I believe in you" can be a powerful positive force for students with behavior disorders.

5

Attention-Deficit/ Hyperactivity Disorder

Anthony, a fourth-grade boy, has been making life miserable for his teacher. While he is viewed by the adults in school as being a nice boy who wants to do well in school, he seems to be in constant motion in class, jumping out of his seat, looking out the window, and blurting out answers. Anthony displays solid academic ability, but his grades are poor due to his messy work and his penchant for completing assignments but then either losing them or forgetting to turn them in. His desk, locker, and backpack are all disorganized messes. The most concerning aspect of Anthony's fourth-grade year is that he appears to be getting increasingly discouraged and down on himself because of his school problems.

High school has been a very difficult experience for Erika. After muddling through middle school—despite her teachers' belief that she is bright and talented and was capable of much better grades—her grades have plummeted in ninth grade. Several of her teachers have contacted her school counselor with concerns, saying things like "Erika's head is in the clouds" and "I like her, but she is constantly zoned out in class." Erika's parents report that she spends at least two hours a night at the kitchen table doing homework but that at the end of that time she typically has accomplished very little. Promises of rewards and restrictions of privileges have had no impact, except to add frustration to both Erika and her parents. All the adults in Erika's life are worried about her dropping out of school, though they feel helpless about how to prevent that.

Anthony and Erika have *attention-deficit/hyperactivity disorder,* or ADHD. ADHD is a neurologically based developmental disorder that affects students' ability to organize and regulate their behavior, which ultimately impairs their ability to be successful academically and to build good relationships with peers and adults. As illustrated in the cases of Anthony and Erika, students with ADHD are not only challenging and often frustrating to have in class but also prone to low self-esteem, alienation from school, and pervasive unhappiness. Yet there are a number of things school counselors, teachers, and other school personnel can do to make school a better place for students with ADHD. In this chapter, we will examine a number of those ideas and strategies. First, though, let's look at the characteristics, consequences, and developmental course of ADHD.

IMPACT, DEVELOPMENTAL COURSE, AND RACE AND GENDER DISPARITIES

Traditionally, the core characteristics of ADHD have been viewed as high levels of activity, impulsivity, and inattention. *DSM* (American Psychiatric Association [APA], 2000) outlines three subtypes of ADHD that encompass these characteristics. The first, *attention-deficit/hyperactivity disorder, predominately hyperactive-impulsive type,* is characterized by behaviors such as fidgeting, excessive running or climbing, blurting out answers in class, and having difficulty waiting for a turn (APA). These are students who can pass for human tornados. These behaviors must be maladaptive and beyond developmental expectations, as is the case with the DSM behavioral symptoms listed for all of the ADHD subtypes. In other words, contrary to what my seventh-grade math teacher used to claim, it is not possible for every student in a junior high to be ADHD. Only students who display behaviors well beyond the norm for their age can be considered ADHD.

The second ADHD subtype listed in *DSM* (APA, 2000) is *attention-deficit/hyperactivity disorder, predominately inattentive type.* This subtype is characterized by behaviors such as having difficulty sustaining attention to work or play tasks, frequently being forgetful, being easily distracted, and being poorly organized (APA). Students falling in this subtype seem like they have their head in the clouds most of the time. The third subtype, *attention-deficit/hyperactivity disorder, combined type,* is present in cases where diagnostic criteria for both the hyperactive-impulsive subtype and the inattentive subtype have been met.

While there is some professional dispute about the prevalence rate for ADHD, *DSM* (APA, 2000) reports a rate of 3% to 7%, with boys being over-represented in this group. A quick bit of math tells us that this means that the odds are that a typical classroom includes at least one student with ADHD.

It is not just the relatively high prevalence rate that makes ADHD so problematic in today's schools; it is also the multiple aspects of children's functioning that are impacted by ADHD. Classroom behavior, learning, social relationships, decision making, and long-term planning—all are put at risk by ADHD. Let's look more closely at how ADHD impacts the lives of students who have this disorder.

The Impact of Attention-Deficit/Hyperactivity Disorder

While the behavioral presentation of ADHD centers on hyperactivity, impulsivity, and inattention, the overall impact of ADHD is much more pervasive. Students with ADHD often struggle academically, have difficulty making and maintaining friendships, tend to make poor decisions, and are often beset with feelings of discouragement and low self-esteem. In the academic realm, even when controlling for IQ, students with ADHD tend to underperform compared to students without ADHD, receiving lower grades, lower ratings of academic progress by teachers, and lower scores on achievement tests (Molina et al., 2009). It is not surprising that school is hard for students with ADHD. Research indicates that the speed of mental computation is diminished in individuals with ADHD and that verbal working memory skills are poor in comparison to those without ADHD (Barkley, 1998). In the language realm, students with ADHD have been found to talk more than other children, but their speech tends to be disorganized and less fluent than that of peers (Barkley). This seems to not be a language issue per se but, rather, a difficulty with an underlying disorganization of thinking.

THE VIDEO GAME CONUNDRUM

One of the puzzling aspects of ADHD is that most children and adolescents with the disorder seem perfectly capable of attending and focusing on certain tasks or activities, such as activities that involve novelty, frequent reinforcement, and high-magnitude rewards. One such activity is video games. Video games can transform impulsive, hyperactive, inattentive youth into focused and effective gamers. It is as though the ADHD melts away—at least as long as the youth is playing the game.

This transformation can be confusing for parents and teachers. Questions arise. "My son can't possibly have ADHD—he can focus on video games for hours." "He is just fine when he is in the computer lab. If he can behave there, why can't he behave in my class?" The attentive and focused behavior youth with ADHD display when they are playing video games tends to magnify the blame they receive when they are inattentive and unfocused in other settings.

(Continued)

(Continued)

While this now-I'm-ADHD-now-I'm-not phenomenon may be most striking with video games, there are other activities and tasks that also seem to banish ADHD symptoms, all of which involve high levels of stimulation, novelty, and reinforcement. High levels of reinforcement do the trick. Wealthy teachers can try an experiment. Begin a class period by telling the class that every student who is perfectly attentive and well behaved for the next hour will receive $1,000. Suddenly, the number of ADHD behaviors will drop to zero. Of course, there are limits to the transformative power of even high levels of reward. The promise of $1,000 for an hour's worth of perfect behavior will be effective, but if the time frame is extended to a week of perfect behavior, students with ADHD will certainly have some slipups.

The impact of video games and other high-reinforcement activities results in a marked inconsistency in the display of ADHD symptoms for many students. Confusing as this can be, it is really a blessing in disguise, because the inconsistency holds the key to intervention. The reason for this is that the behavior is really *not* inconsistent—it is just highly reactive to the characteristics of the task. Students with ADHD will predictably do very well when they play video games. And they will predictably do poorly when they are faced with a monotonous, low-reinforcement, unexciting task—like homework. So school counselors can work with teachers to examine the activities and tasks that students with ADHD are presented and then work to add additional reinforcement and novelty to those activities.

It is not just the academic demands that are problematic for students with ADHD; they also have trouble with the social aspects of school. Social relationships in general are challenging for children with ADHD. Compared to the general population, children with ADHD tend to have fewer friends and are more apt to be socially rejected (Barkley, 1998). Both boys and girls with ADHD are prone to impaired social relationships with peers, siblings, and parents (Greene et al., 2001). It is easy to see why social relationships are difficult for youth with ADHD, particularly those with the type of ADHD where hyperactivity and impulsivity are problem areas. Similar to their behavioral presentation in other areas, the social behaviors of these youth tend to be erratic and poorly controlled. They tend to want friends but act in the kind of overly loud and intrusive manner that peers find off-putting. In fact, the disruptive behavior and unpredictability of students with ADHD leads peers to react with criticism and rejection (Barkley, 1998). Children with ADHD often don't understand why they struggle with friendships, simply feeling disliked and unlikeable.

In addition to academic problems and social difficulties, ADHD is connected with a myriad of specific impairments related to decision making, organization, and planning. Students with ADHD tend to have diminished ability to think ahead, anticipate consequences, and develop and follow through on long-range plans (Barkley, 1998). Furthermore, students with ADHD have difficulty effectively regulating their emotions, tending to have greater emotional reactivity and lower tolerance for frustration than other students (Barkley). On top of all this, youth with ADHD are prone to sleep difficulties, with problems falling asleep and staying asleep being common.

Developmental Course

Before beginning to describe the developmental course of ADHD, it is worth offering the reminder that there is no single, unitary developmental course for *any* disorder, including ADHD. Each individual with ADHD will have a unique life path, impacted by hundreds of variables that impact everyone (compulsory schooling, going through puberty, etc.) and hundreds of variables that are unique to that one individual. That being said, though, there is strong research evidence that illuminates the developmental routes often taken by individuals with ADHD.

The developmental story for children with ADHD often begins before they are born, with the ADHD status of their parents. ADHD runs in families; the risk of a parent with ADHD having a child who also has ADHD has been found to be as high as 54% (Barkley, 1998). As infants, children who go on to receive a diagnosis of ADHD often display precursors to the disorder, being more likely to have a high activity level, low persistence in pursuing play objects, strong intensity of response, and a tendency to be overly demanding. As preschoolers, children who are on a developmental path to ADHD are likely to display persistent problems with social interactions with parents and peers, excessive activity, inattention, and emotional difficulties ranging from anger to fearfulness. Also often present are difficult temperamental characteristics such as moodiness, sleep problems, and difficulty adjusting to change. It is not just the child's temperament that serves as a risk factor, though. Parental variables such as maternal smoking and drinking during pregnancy, marital discord, psychiatric illness, and a negative, commanding parenting style also tend to be present in children with ADHD. It seems to be a matter of the child's vulnerability combined with an environment that places strong demands on the child—demands the child is not able to meet.

The mean age of onset of diagnosable ADHD symptoms is between ages 3 and 4, but some elaboration about ADHD symptoms at this age is necessary to avoid misconceptions. It is common for preschool children to be the subject of parental and teacher concern about inattention (up to 40%), though most of these problems resolve within six months. Even among four-year-olds with sufficient symptomatology to receive a diagnosis of ADHD, only about half still have an ADHD diagnosis by later childhood and early adolescence. While the presence of periods of inattention and hyperactivity during the preschool years is not a reliable predictor of ADHD, there is a subset of children at that age who have more *durable* symptoms, such as being difficult to manage at age 3 and still difficult to manage at age 4. These children are much more likely to display ongoing conduct and ADHD problems.

Preschool children with persistent ADHD symptoms are described by parents as being restless and always on the go, frequently climbing and getting into things. They are demanding and often defiant. They elicit many more commands, criticisms, and punishments than other children and create high stress among parents. Parenting young children with ADHD is challenging work, and the magnitude of the challenge often leads parents to question the adequacy of their parenting skills. Preschool children with ADHD tend to do poorly in daycare and are often described as being demanding, overly noisy, and intrusive.

THE AGE-OF-ONSET CONTROVERSY

DSM (APA, 2000) explicitly states that some symptoms of hyperactivity-impulsivity or inattention must be present before age 7 in order for a person to be diagnosed with ADHD. The reasoning for this diagnostic requirement is clear: If ADHD is a neurological disorder, then evidence of the neurological issues should be apparent early in a child's life. Just as a 14-year-old, for example, would not suddenly acquire cerebral palsy, neither would she suddenly acquire ADHD. Children who do not meet full diagnostic criteria by the age 7 marker are not precluded from being diagnosed with ADHD when they are older. In fact, it is common for children and adolescents to receive a diagnosis of ADHD well past age 7. In these cases, a developmental history would reveal the presence of some level of impairment caused by ADHD: This is based on the assumption that the neurological issues were already there but did not lead to significant problems until the child or adolescent was in an environment that included demands for controlled behavior and sustained attention. Students with inattention as their primary ADHD symptom are particularly likely to be able to survive elementary school and even middle school, only to fall apart when they are in a high school setting that requires exactly what they do not have: the ability to focus and attend for lengths of time.

The age 7 requirement does provide a safeguard of sorts for ADHD misdiagnosis among older children and adolescents. There are multiple reasons why older students might begin displaying symptoms of inattention or hyperactivity, such as drug abuse, exposure to trauma, and sleep deprivation. If there was no sign of these symptoms at an earlier age, then ADHD is not the culprit, and by definition, ADHD cannot be diagnosed. So the age 7 rule helps clinicians rule out ADHD in these cases and turn their attention to other more likely causes.

This all makes good sense. But a recent study raises concern about the use of the age 7 cutoff to either confirm or disconfirm an ADHD diagnosis. The researchers conducted a five-year follow-up of a large group of twins who had originally been selected because of the presence of inattentive symptoms in at least one of the pair of twins (Todd, Huang, & Henderson, 2008). The strength of this study is that the researchers had good data from both the parents and the children at both initial testing and five-year follow-up, including the estimated age of onset of ADHD symptoms. The researchers found that both parents and children estimated significantly later age of onset at the five-year follow-up compared with the initial testing, averaging over six months later among parents and a year later among children. The important consequence of this is that a significant proportion of the youth who met all other criteria for ADHD did not meet the age-of-onset criterion.

The overall lesson is that memories of both parents and children are fallible when it comes to retrospective reporting of ADHD age of onset, and there seems to be a systematic tendency to err on the side of later age of onset. While having a specific age of onset seems objective, in practice it may result in an underidentification of older youth with ADHD.

Children with ADHD enter kindergarten at high risk for academic failure. Not only do they have behaviors that make it hard for them to learn, but their basic academic readiness skills are often delayed. Yet once children with ADHD enter school, their life and the lives of their family can become even more difficult. Indeed, the demands of the school setting represent the single greatest source of distress for children and their parents, and this continues through high school. Often, school is the setting where the problems and symptoms of ADHD are most noticeable and problematic. The things children are expected to do in school (sit still, listen, follow directions, inhibit impulsive behavior, organize, interact socially, and follow through on instructions and activities) are exactly the demands that are exceedingly difficult for most children with ADHD.

The vast majority of children with ADHD are identified by first grade as having problem behavior (Barkley, 1998). High numbers also have learning difficulties, which compounds the problem. Homework becomes a source of stress and conflict. At home, there is often conflict over household chores, and children with ADHD often need more direction and supervision to complete self-help skills such as dressing oneself. Patterns of social rejection also can develop in the elementary years. Social skills are often delayed, and even those youth with good social skills are apt to use them too much or too intensely. They are often seen by peers as intrusive, loud, and overwhelming. Not surprisingly, by the late elementary years, youth with ADHD are often struggling with feelings of depression and social inadequacy but don't have enough insight to link their own behavior to the way others respond to them. A subgroup of students has developed conduct problems; studies on the overlap between ADHD and behavior disorders have found comorbidity of 20% to 67% with oppositional defiant disorder (ODD) and 20% to 56% with conduct disorder (CD; Barkley).

As youth with ADHD move into early adolescence and later adolescence, there typically is an improvement in symptoms of hyperactivity, inattention, and impulsivity. However, that improvement is often offset by the increasing demands for independent and responsible conduct. These students are also faced with the additional issues all adolescents face, such as dating, identity development, physical development, and peer-group development, all of which add stress.

Contrary to the old notion that ADHD is "outgrown" in adolescence, current research indicates that up to 80% of children with hyperactivity display significant continuing symptoms into adolescence and young adulthood (Barkley, 1998). School outcomes are consistently poorer for students with ADHD; students with ADHD have been found to be over three times more likely than non-ADHD students to be retained, suspended, and drop out. These negative school outcomes are particular magnified if the ADHD is accompanied by conduct problems.

The increase in risk associated with conduct problems is part of a larger issue of comorbidity. A large body of literature documents the strong likelihood that ADHD will be accompanied by one or more other disorders, including ODD, CD, mood disorders, and learning disorders. The exact comorbidity figures vary depending on the study, but the research suggests that up to a third of children with ADHD also have a diagnosable mood disorder, a quarter have a diagnosable anxiety disorder, over half have ODD, and up to half have CD (Barkley, 1998). These are stunning figures and point to both the level of distress experienced by many students with ADHD and the high level of challenge in figuring out how to intervene effectively with these students.

Race and Gender Considerations

Race and gender have complex and significant relationships with the manifestation, diagnosis, and treatment of ADHD. Most of the studies on racial differences in ADHD have compared African American with White children. Studies have consistently found that African American children display higher levels of ADHD behavior than White children, whether the behavior was assessed by teacher report, parent report, or classroom observation (Miller, Nigg, & Miller, 2009). However, despite this disparity, African American children receive an actual diagnosis of ADHD only two-thirds as often as White youth. Part of the explanation for this curious state of affairs is that parents of White children are more likely than parents of African American children to accept and endorse the label of ADHD for their children, even given similar levels of hyperactivity, impulsivity, and inattention (Hillenmeier, Foster, Heinrichs, & Heier, 2007). It is hard to know what to think about this phenomenon. On the one hand, African American students may be less likely to experience any stigmatizing effects of an ADHD label due to their parents' reluctance to endorse that label. On the other hand, African American students may also be at higher risk for having undiagnosed and untreated ADHD.

Research findings also paint an interesting picture about gender differences in ADHD. Research indicates that ADHD is more common among males. For example, data from the National Health Interview Surveys over the past decade indicate that boys are more than twice as likely as girls (ranges of 10% to 12% vs. 3% to 5%) to have a diagnosis of ADHD (Pastor & Reuben, 2008). However, ADHD is far more likely to be overrepresented among boys in studies that examine children seen by clinics as opposed to studies that examine general community samples of youth (9:1 vs. 3:1–2:1, respectively), which suggests that girls may be underreferred for ADHD (Sciutto, Nolfi, & Bluhm, 2004). In one interesting study, 199 elementary school teachers were presented with fictional case studies in which the gender and type of symptoms of the child was systematically varied. It turned out that teachers were more likely to refer boys than girls even given identical symptoms, particularly in cases where hyperactivity was the main symptom. In fact, teachers were 50% more likely to refer hyperactive boys than hyperactive girls (Sciutto et al.). Clearly, these teachers—and probably adults in general—are more likely to view ADHD as a disorder that afflicts boys rather than girls.

Further research on gender and ADHD found gender differences not just in prevalence of ADHD but also in the severity and nature of ADHD symptoms. One meta-analysis discovered that across many studies girls with ADHD displayed symptoms of hyperactivity, inattention, and impulsivity that were less severe than boys. Moreover, girls displayed more internalizing problems and fewer externalizing problems than boys did (Gershon, 2002). A more-recent study of elementary-aged students with ADHD, however, found that boys and girls showed similar (and substantial) levels of impairment in the academic, social, emotional, and behavioral domains (DuPaul et al., 2006). While these research findings cannot be neatly integrated into a consistent set of conclusions (which is not unusual; research tends to be messy, much like the real world), they do suggest that in individual cases girls can be as severely affected by ADHD as boys, even though boys have a higher incidence of ADHD than girls do.

INTERVENTION GUIDELINES

The pervasiveness and severity of the negative outcomes of children with ADHD make it essential that schools and school counselors strive to develop interventions to assist these students in their journey through school. The following guidelines can provide some ideas for intervention.

> ## INTERVENTION GUIDELINES FOR STUDENTS WITH ADHD
>
> 1. Take a disability perspective.
> 2. Create systems to provide immediate behavioral feedback.
> 3. More action, less lecturing.
> 4. Make rewards and consequences more powerful.
> 5. Increase structure.
> 6. Plan the environment.
> 7. Provide outlets for high activity levels.
> 8. Provide organizational assistance.
> 9. Develop ADHD-friendly instructional practices.

Guideline 1: Take a Disability Perspective

It can be easy for the adults in the lives of students with ADHD to become frustrated and to wonder why the students can't just settle down and pay attention like other students. After all, students with ADHD have no visible disabilities, and they can have periods of time when they seem very focused and very productive. But a small thought experiment can provide a fleeting sense of what it is like to be a child with ADHD. Think of a time when you were stressed and sleep deprived—for example, when you were cramming for final exams when you were in college or when you were on deadline for an important project at work. Remember what it was like to go days without sleep, keeping yourself going with lots of caffeine? You probably felt shaky, and unfocused, and had trouble tracking. You wanted to concentrate, but found your mind wandering despite your best efforts. You found yourself making careless mistakes, and forgetting things, and losing track of what you were trying to accomplish. What you are remembering is the kind of experiences that students with ADHD have every day. And of course, they cannot change that by getting a few good nights' sleep. How well do you think you would have done in school, and in your career, had you always functioned the way you did during those stressful and sleep-deprived days?

What I hope this exercise illustrates is that ADHD is not simply a label that is applied to children who choose not to concentrate or who lack motivation. In fact, ADHD among children and adolescents should be viewed by teachers, parents, and other involved adults with a *disability perspective* (Barkley, 1995). This means that children with ADHD should be viewed as having a disability just as real as children with physical disabilities or other types of disabilities. Not only is this stance appropriate given the neurological roots of ADHD, but also it helps foster a sense of empathy and ward off frustration and judgment on the part of the adults involved with the child. Let's look at a specific example. Assume Jackie, a junior in high school, has the inattentive subtype of ADHD. In class, Jackie rarely attends to the teacher and typically spends her time either talking with friends or doodling. How might most teachers respond to Jackie? Well, it depends on how they view the situation. If they do not understand the nature of ADHD and fail to take a disability perspective, they might become impatient and frustrated with Jackie and even feel personally offended that Jackie seems to have minimal interest in their class. On the other hand, if they are well educated about ADHD and take a disability perspective, they are much more able to avoid taking Jackie's behavior personally and to focus on what they can do to help make her experience in class a good one.

Guideline 2: Create Systems to Provide Immediate Behavioral Feedback

One of the hallmarks of students with ADHD is their lack of ability to consistently regulate their behavior at a developmentally appropriate level. Compared to their classmates, students with ADHD have much more trouble with tasks such as controlling their behavior, organizing their material, staying on task, and using foresight and planning skills. This difficulty with self-regulation has an important implication for schools, teachers, and parents: Students with ADHD need more of our help in regulating their behavior. In the classroom, this translates into a need for immediate and overt behavioral feedback (Pfiffner & Barkley, 1998). Immediate, regular behavioral feedback also helps provide the structure and predictability that students with ADHD need. Indeed, research consistently supports the value of using behavioral methods to improve outcomes for students with ADHD (Fabiano et al., 2009).

The guiding question, then, for a student with ADHD is, "How can we figure out a way to provide immediate behavioral feedback that makes sense for the age, circumstances, and unique personality of this student?" This is a question that school counselors can ask teachers who are struggling to manage the behavior of students with ADHD, in addition to being one that counselors can pose to parents who are trying to manage the behavior of their child with ADHD. The feedback system should be individually tailored for the student to the extent possible. What works for one seventh-grade student with hyperactivity and inattention may not work for other seventh-grade students with hyperactivity and inattention. Some possible ways of providing immediate behavioral feedback follow:

Subtle Strategies

There are a number of subtle, under-the-radar strategies teachers can implement in classrooms to provide feedback to students with ADHD. One strategy is *proximity control,* which is simply having the teacher walk toward the student who is off task or behaving inappropriately and using the teacher's presence to calm and redirect the student. The power of proximity control can be enhanced by having the teacher gently tap on the student's desk, to provide a more-immediate redirection cue. Another subtle strategy that can be implemented by teachers is to develop a *secret signal* with the student. The secret signal provides a way for the teacher to give immediate and clear feedback to the student without anyone else in the class knowing about it. The following box provides more detail about how to develop and implement a secret signal. While subtle strategies are appealing because of their ease of use, many students with ADHD need more-overt strategies to provide immediate behavioral feedback. But if nothing else, subtle strategies can be paired with more-potent strategies to create a more-powerful intervention's package.

THE SECRET-SIGNAL STRATEGY

The secret signal is a tactic that allows a teacher and a student to communicate privately about the student's behavior in the midst of a busy classroom. To implement this strategy, the teacher and student begin by meeting and agreeing upon the signal to be used by the teacher, which is known only by the teacher and the student. The signal should be something simple, such as a tug on the ear, or a wink, or a brief nod of the head. The student and teacher also agree upon what the secret signal is intended to mean—in other words, what message the signal communicates. The signal might mean that the student is getting off task and should redirect attention to the classroom activity. Or the signal might mean that the student is sitting calmly and attending well. So the secret signal can be used either to redirect inappropriate behavior or to reinforce positive behavior.

Let's look at two examples:

Shawn is a 13-year-old boy with ADHD who struggles with inattention and distractibility. Shawn and his math teacher, Mrs. Roberts, meet and agree to try the secret-signal strategy. In fact, Shawn enjoys the idea of having secret communications with Mrs. Roberts that no one else knows about. After talking about several types of secret signals, Shawn and Mrs. Roberts agree that the signal will be Mrs. Roberts pulling twice on her left ear. They also agree that Mrs. Roberts will give the signal when Shawn's attention is starting to wander. So when Mrs. Roberts pulls on her ear, it is a signal to Shawn that he should bring his attention back to the task at hand.

Jennifer is a 10-year-old girl with ADHD who is overly active in class and who is also prone to inattention. In a meeting with Jennifer, her parents, and her teacher Mr. Jeffrey, the group decides to try the secret-signal approach. Given that Jennifer is often not looking at Mr. Jeffrey in class, they agree that the secret signal will be verbal, specifically having Mr. Jeffrey clear his throat. In an effort to focus on the positive, it is agreed that the signal will indicate that Jennifer is doing what she should do at that moment—paying attention or working quietly on seat work. To add to the power of the secret signal, Mr. Jeffrey devises a simple behavior chart for Jennifer, and each time he gives her the secret signal, she has permission to add a sticker to the chart. After earning 10 stickers, Jennifer is given 15 minutes of extra computer time.

The secret signal is a simple but powerful strategy that can be used in a number of ways. While it can be implemented with students with a variety of problem behaviors, it is well suited to use with students with ADHD.

Strategies for Elementary-Aged Students

As with all types of interventions, ADHD interventions should be developmentally appropriate. Intervention strategies for elementary-aged students with ADHD should be more visible and concrete than interventions for older students. An example of a visible and concrete intervention strategy that works well with students with ADHD is a behavior chart. This is a chart students can keep taped to their desk that lists key behaviors along one axis and time periods along the other axis (see the sample classroom-behavior chart that follows). For example, Royce might be having trouble blurting out answers in his math class. A chart for Royce could include a column for raising his hand before speaking. The math class could be divided into two time periods, to provide more feedback to Royce. At the end of each time period, Royce's teacher could walk over to his desk and, if Royce had been raising his hand appropriately, place a smiley face or a sticker on the chart. Many variations can be made with the chart; some of which are listed in the following box. The key point is to individualize the chart as much as possible rather than use a one-size-fits-all approach.

BEHAVIOR CHARTS 101

When used correctly, behavior charts can be a simple, flexible, and effective way to provide students with additional feedback about their classroom behavior and, if desired, can also be used to determine whether any tangible consequences have been earned. Guidelines for the effective use of behavior charts, as well as some examples of the varied ways behavior charts can be used, are included here.

(Continued)

(Continued)

Guidelines for the Use of Behavior Charts

- *Individualize the charts.* Rather than making hundreds of copies of your favorite behavior chart and using it for every student you work with, create individualized charts for each student. This small investment of time will pay benefits by creating charts that are tailored to the specific needs of each student.
- *Be prudent in choosing behaviors.* It generally works best to select a limited number of behaviors (2 to 3) that are directly related to the problems the student is having. In addition, strive to select behaviors that do not overlap. For example, having both "Refrain from shouting out in class" and "Wait to be called on before speaking" is redundant.
- *Create the chart in cooperation with the student.* Students are much more likely to buy in to the chart if they have a hand in its development. Issues such as which behaviors to target, what reinforcers to use, and what time frame to use should all be discussed with the student.
- *Respect students' need for privacy.* Many students, particularly older students, find behavior charts embarrassing and don't want their peers to know about the charts. Respect this by making sure the chart is not conspicuous and the chart is not marked in view of other students. One way to do this is to have the teacher hold on to the chart during class and discreetly mark the chart at the end of the class.
- *Modify freely.* Behavior charts should always be viewed as a work in progress. If they are not working, make changes. Try changing the time frame, the reinforcers, or the specific behaviors. Often the person who has the best ideas of what to change is the student who is using the chart.

Variations in the Use of Behavior Charts

- *Alter the time frame.* Some students may need very frequent feedback and a chart divided into hour-long segments. Others may respond to daily or even weekly charts.
- *Comprehensive versus targeted.* In some cases it may be preferred to select as wide a range of behaviors as possible, such as when students' ADHD behaviors are generally well controlled and they just need an overall "boost" from the chart. Two examples of comprehensive sets of behaviors follow.

Example 1	Example 2
Verbally appropriate	Work
Physically appropriate	Respect
Work completion	Belong

The advantage of comprehensive charts is that they cover all the bases and provide feedback over an array of behaviors. The disadvantage is that they are less effective in providing specific feedback in pockets of concern. For example, a student with ADHD may sit nicely in her seat and never blurt out, but she may have significant trouble with inattention, organization, and work completion. For her, a chart that targets these latter behaviors is a better choice. In this case, the chart might include the behavior categories of "Comes prepared," "Begins working promptly," and "Maintains focus on work." Another advantage of targeted charts is that they do not seem as overwhelming for students who are struggling. Just as novice golfers do much better if they focus only on one or two tips instead of the hundreds of actions that make a good golf swing, students with ADHD often do better when they focus on just a small handful of behavior goals.

- *Points versus stickers versus checks.* There are several different ways the cells of the chart can be marked by the teacher. Each cell can be marked with points—which also can be varied. Generally, a 1 to 3 scale works well, though some students may benefit from a 1 to 5 scale to provide more fine-tuned feedback. Elementary students may respond to stickers that are placed on the chart if they behave well. A simple check mark can also be used.
- *Self-reinforcing versus tied to external reinforcement.* For some students, getting a sticker or a rating of *3* on a 3-point scale is highly reinforcing in itself. Other students may need the extra power of having the ratings tied to additional reinforcements or consequences. For example, a student on a point-based scale might earn 30 minutes of extra time in the gym after accumulating 50 points. For even greater power, the results of a chart can be tied into home-based reinforcements or consequences.

As discussed in Chapter 4, another intervention strategy that can be used with elementary-aged students is a *token economy*. This well-known behavioral approach allows students to earn tokens for appropriate behavior, which can then be used to buy rewards of various kinds. Provision of the tokens can be linked to classroom rules or to specific behaviors that a student is working on. For example, a student with ADHD might earn tokens for raising a hand before speaking. The rewards can be selected from a reward menu (perhaps including rewards such as extra computer time, being line leader, or having a classroom popcorn party) or can be "bought" from a school store, stocked with items such as pencils and stickers. The teacher can determine the number of tokens it takes to purchase a certain reward. When implementing a token economy with a student with ADHD, it is most effective to deliver tokens frequently at the beginning and then taper off to the point where tokens are

	Class Period			
Sample Classroom-Behavior Chart				
Student's name _____ Date _____				
Behavior	Math (First Half)	Math (Second Half)	Reading (First Half)	Reading (Second Half)
Raise hand before speaking				
Talk nicely to other students				
Pay attention to teacher				
Complete assigned work				

given intermittently for appropriate behavior. In this way, students do not become dependent on the tokens.

Note that the token economy is a reward-based, positive intervention. A variation of the token economy that builds in a negative consequence is called a *response-cost procedure.* In this procedure, the student is given some sort of reinforcing proxy at the beginning of the day or class period. If the student misbehaves, the reinforcers are taken away. It is as though you received your daily salary in a stack of $10 bills first thing in the morning, and then your boss took bills away from you if you did not perform. An example of what this might look like would be giving a third-grade student with ADHD 10 tokens at the beginning of the day. Each time the student blurted out, the teacher would take back a token. The tokens the student had remaining at the end of the day could be used to shop at the school store. The specific behaviors that would warrant the repossession of a token would be agreed upon by the student and the teacher before the procedure was implemented.

The response-cost procedure is often particularly effective with students with ADHD. There is something about taking back a token that has a more-profound effect on behavior than just rewarding positive behavior. Students with ADHD, in general, need more than just positive reinforcement. The pervasive impact of the disorder often requires the greater incentive of both rewards and negative consequences to alter behavior. However, a response-cost procedure should be implemented with care and in cooperation with the student. As can be imagined, taking away tokens or other reinforcer proxies can be frustrating and upsetting to some students and, if not done thoughtfully, can escalate negative behaviors.

Strategies for Secondary-Level Students

The highly visual, concrete strategies for providing immediate behavioral feedback that work well with elementary students are typically not received well by high school students. The challenge with high school students is to still find ways to provide immediate feedback, while doing so in a more-private manner. Many of the subtle strategies discussed earlier, such as proximity control and a secret signal, can work effectively with high school students. Another intervention approach for secondary students is to employ *strategic teacher attention.* Essentially what this approach involves is having the classroom teacher provide positive attention when the student is behaving appropriately and withdrawing attention when the student is not behaving appropriately. Sounds easy, right? In reality, this can be a very difficult intervention, as many teachers understandably either focus their attention on the students in class who are creating problems or offer praise that is so general that it gives students little information about what they did to earn the praise. But praise that is immediate, warm, and genuine and that specifies the behavior ("Thanks for getting started right away, Jason; I really like the way you got out all your materials and got right to work!") has been proven effective with students with ADHD (Pfiffner & Barkley, 1998). The key to the effectiveness of teacher attention—the part that makes it *strategic*—is to be very deliberate; offer positive attention immediately and contingent upon the display of appropriate behaviors. Strategic teacher attention can be particularly helpful if the behaviors that are praised are incompatible with other behaviors that have been problematic for the student. For example, a teacher could intervene with a student who gets up and wanders around the room during independent work time by intentionally and quickly offering praise when the student stays seated and attends to work.

While strategic use of praise and positive attention can be powerful, praise alone is generally insufficient with students with ADHD. Students also need to receive immediate feedback about their inappropriate behavior. Reprimands and corrective statements are a necessary part of an intervention plan for most students with ADHD. Just as with strategic teacher attention, the effectiveness of reprimands depends on how and when they are delivered (Pfiffner & Barkley, 1998). Reprimands should be provided immediately after the inappropriate behavior and should be brief and to the point. Reprimands are more effective when they are delivered in close proximity to the student. Furthermore, reprimands should be offered without emotion. It is not just what *is* included in the reprimand, it is what is *not* included that is important—specifically *not* including sarcasm, demeaning statements, or a sense of disapproval.

I have been referring to high school students in this section. But what about middle school students? Should the elementary-aged strategies be applied to them? Or the secondary strategies? The answer depends on the needs and the developmental level of the middle school student in question. Middle school students are in that wonderful grey area between childhood and adolescence, and the principle of individualizing interventions is even more important for these students than for students at other levels.

Guideline 3: More Action, Less Lecturing

Lecturing is rarely an effective intervention for any student, but it is particularly ineffective for students with ADHD. As a rule, students with ADHD are more responsive to adults' *behaviors* than they are to adults' *words*, especially if those words come in the form of a lecture. One troubleshooting guideline that can be used when a student with ADHD is struggling in school is to look at whether there are sufficient tangible consequences (both positive and negative) built into the student's intervention plan. School counselors can help teachers make a shift from lecturing to taking decisive action in response to problem behavior. It is generally not helpful to spend time giving lengthy explanations to a child with ADHD about why behavior is inappropriate and all the negative outcomes that will accrue if the actions continue. Rather, give a token when the student is behaving well. Or use a response-cost procedure to remove a token when the student is not behaving well. Or walk over and stand by the youth's desk when attention wanders. Or take some other type of appropriate action . . . but don't lecture.

Guideline 4: Make Rewards and Consequences More Powerful

In addition to making consequences more immediate, teachers are wise to make consequences and rewards more powerful for students with ADHD. This is simply a matter of doing what works, as students with ADHD tend to be less sensitive to normally occurring rewards and consequences than other students. Accordingly, what works best with students with ADHD is to arrange for them to receive rewards and consequences that are a step above what the general student population receives. Some examples follow.

Student Behavior	Response to Typical Student	Response to Student With ADHD
Student raises hand to be called on.	Teacher calls on student.	Teacher specifically thanks the student for raising her hand and then calls on her.
Student gets out materials and begins work promptly.	Teacher thanks the student for good work habits.	Teacher thanks the student for his good work habits and gives him a token.
Student blurts out an answer, interrupting another student.	Teacher asks the student to raise his hand and then goes back to the other student.	Teacher asks the student to raise her hand, removes a token from the student's desk, and then goes back to the other student.

Guideline 5: Increase Structure

Increasing the level of structure in the school setting can be helpful for students with many mental health problems, but it is particularly helpful for students with externalizing disorders such as CD, ODD, and ADHD. Increasing structure means making the school environment more predictable and consistent, so students know exactly what is expected of them and also know what will happen both if they do what is expected and if they do not do what is expected. For many students with ADHD, added structure not only leads to better behavior but also creates a feeling of comfort and security. As structure increases, the likelihood of having misunderstandings about class expectations decreases.

There are a number of ways that teachers can add structure to their classrooms. Some ideas are listed here:

- *Be predictable.* Adding structure begins with focusing on the attitude of the teacher. Simply pointing out the benefits to students with ADHD of having a predictable teacher and a predictable classroom can help teachers adopt the goal of being more consistent and predictable in their enforcement of classroom rules and their general behavior in the classroom.
- *Make rules clear and explicit.* Structure is increased when classroom rules are clearly worded and prominently posted in the classroom. Classroom rules are most effective when they are developed through dialogue with students at the beginning of the year—rather

than thinking of rules as something teachers impose on students, think of them as a written record of the shared agreement between students and the teacher regarding the way the classroom should operate and the way people in the classroom should behave. Regularly reviewing and discussing the rules can further strengthen the structure of the classroom.

- *Provide an advanced organizer.* Teachers can add structure by regular use of advanced organizers, which are brief statements highlighting what is going to happen in the classroom (Pierangelo & Giuliani, 2008). These can be previews of a larger part of the day ("This morning we will start out with reading and then move to social studies, where we will have a special guest to talk about Native American culture") or a class period ("We will start out math class today by reviewing yesterday's homework assignment and then move into a lesson on fractions. You'll be working with your partner for that part"). Liberal use of advanced organizers can add predictability to the school lives of students with ADHD.

- *Set learning expectations.* It is helpful to begin lessons by explicitly stating what students are expected to learn by lesson's end. In addition to being a good teaching technique, it has the added benefit of adding predictability and structure to the lesson.

- *Set behavioral expectations.* In addition to setting learning expectations, it is beneficial to set behavioral expectations on a regular basis. This is best done in a confident, matter-of-fact manner (e.g., "Rather than making comments or asking questions while the video is playing, keep them in your head or write them down. When the video is done, we'll have a discussion where you can ask questions or make comments").

- *Signal impending transitions.* Students with ADHD often have difficulty with transitions, as shifting gears is often hard for them. A helpful strategy that adds predictability is to provide advanced warning of impending transitions. Giving a five-minute warning of the end of a class period, for example, provides students with a cue that they will be shifting their focus in a few minutes.

While it can be helpful to suggest some of these structure-enhancing ideas to teachers, it is often most effective to develop ideas in collaboration with teachers. Asking questions such as "What are ways that you can make your classroom more predictable and expectations for students more clear?" can often generate many good ideas. Of course, it is important not to imply that the way the classroom is currently run is too loose or poorly organized. A helpful way to approach the conversation is to stress that students with ADHD need more structure due to their neurologically based hyperactivity, inattention, and impulsivity. Make it clear that it is not a matter of the classroom being poorly run, but a matter of making sensible modifications for the special needs of ADHD students.

Guideline 6: Plan the Environment

The physical environment of the school can have an impact on the behavioral adjustment of students with ADHD, and school counselors who are consulting with teachers about how to best educate students with ADHD are wise to assess the physical environment of the classroom. Here are some things to look for when trying to design a classroom environment conducive to learning and appropriate behavior for students with ADHD:

- *Consider desk placement.* Something as simple as the location of the desk of a student with ADHD in the classroom can make a significant difference in how the youth behaves. Some experts have suggested that the desks of students with ADHD be placed either in close proximity to the teacher or near a student who is a positive role model (Pierangelo & Giuliani, 2008). The reasoning for having the desk placement near the teacher is clear: It allows the teacher to more easily monitor and provide feedback to the student. Essentially, it provides built-in proximity control. Bear in mind, however, that students' responses to the class environment can be idiosyncratic. Some students with ADHD may do very well seated next to the teacher, but others may perform better seated in a corner of the classroom away from distractions. When deciding on desk placement, also consider factors such as where the windows are (if any) in the classroom, where the door is, and how the individual student responds to being in the front or back of the class. The bottom line is figure out what works best for each student.
- *Provide low-distraction work areas.* It may be possible to create low-distraction work areas in the classroom itself if space permits, such as developing reading nooks or having some study carrels along a back wall. It can also be helpful to have one or more rooms in the school that are available for use as quiet, low-distraction work areas that students can go to for test taking, quiet reading, or other work tasks (Pierangelo & Giuliani, 2008).
- *Consider the level of light and sound in the room.* Some students with ADHD are sensitive to classrooms that are overly noisy or very bright. It is worth thinking about whether light and sound are impacting students, and trying to problem solve some ways of reducing the level of light and noise. In addition, given that teachers naturally differ in the amount of noise and activity they have in their classrooms, it can be helpful when choosing teachers for a new

school year to try to match students with classrooms that have the level of bustle that best suits them.

It need not be all guesswork when trying to plan the environment for students with ADHD. The simple act of asking these students what kind of environment is best for them can produce many good ideas. Many students with ADHD have at least some idea of the kind of desk placement and noise level that is best for them. Adding the student voice to the observations of the teacher and your own observations can be a powerful source of good data.

Guideline 7: Provide Outlets for High Activity Levels

Consider the last time you attended a full-day workshop. If you are like most people, by the end of the day you were restless and antsy to get up and move. Now multiply that feeling tenfold and you have an appreciation of what it feels like to be a hyperactive student with ADHD who is expected to sit quietly in a desk for substantial periods of time. It can be very helpful if these students can be afforded regular opportunities to move, walk, run, or engage in other kinds of physical activity. Some ideas for how to do this are listed here:

- *Allow students to stand during seat work.* While it seems oxymoronic to complete seat work standing up, just the act of standing can help students with ADHD manage their energy better. It may even be helpful to experiment with a stand-up desk. If either of these options is considered, it would be important to place the student's desk in an area of the room that will not serve as a distraction to the other students.
- *Allow students to use calming manipulatives.* Elementary school teachers are very familiar with the battle to keep students from bringing and playing with small toys at school, and these teachers may blanche at the suggestion that students be *encouraged* to play with small manipulatives. But these objects can give students with ADHD something to do with their hands and can actually help them focus better. Calming manipulatives serve as the kinesthetic equivalent of white noise. The key, of course, is to select manipulatives that provide an outlet for high energy rather than serving as a distraction. Silly putty or Koosh balls can be good calming manipulatives for many students.
- *Let students with ADHD be errand runners.* It can be a helpful energy release to give students with ADHD the chance to run class errands. There is also the added benefit of the mini self-esteem boost that comes with being given the responsibility of running an errand.

- *Consider active counseling sessions.* It is no surprise to school counselors that stereotypical 50-minute, talk-oriented counseling sessions do not translate well to schools or youth. Most school counselors already favor sessions that are briefer and include activities such as drawing, watching videos, and written exercises. This type of non-talk therapy can be extended for students with ADHD to provide an energy release as well as to present counseling in a delivery vehicle that is conducive to children and adolescents. Counselors can have therapeutic discussions with students while shooting baskets, while taking a walk, or while engaging in other physical activities.

Guideline 8: Provide Organizational Assistance

The organizational skills of students with ADHD are almost universally poor. The neurological impact of ADHD tends to impair executive functions such as planning, foresight, and decision making. These impairments, in turn, tend to translate into lost homework assignments, overdue assignments, chaotic and messy desks and lockers, and ineffective or nonexistent organizational systems. A recent study, though, found that a concentrated intervention focused on organizational assistance helped students improve not only their organizational skills but also their class grades (Langberg, Epstein, Urbanowicz, Simon, & Graham, 2008). It seems clear that one way that teachers and school counselors can assist students with ADHD is to provide them with organizational assistance.

There are a number of ways that organizational assistance can be rendered (U.S. Department of Education, 2004). For some students, having an assignment notebook or a binder with sections for each class works well. A system of color-coded folders may work. For other students, having a homework partner may be effective. What can be most critical with many students with ADHD is to have a designated adult who is in charge of helping the student stay organized. This may involve regularly checking with the students about upcoming assignments and periodically working together to clean and organize desks and lockers.

Guideline 9: Develop ADHD-Friendly Instructional Practices

Rather than being prescriptive or concrete, this guideline is more inspirational. It serves to encourage teachers and school counselors to brainstorm how they might modify the way the curriculum is presented to give students with ADHD every opportunity to succeed. Knowing the struggles many students with ADHD have in school, it behooves educators and counselors to do whatever they can to give these students the best possible chance to succeed. This is not to say that teachers are not already making strong efforts to deliver the curriculum in a way that helps all of their students succeed. But most teachers, if given the chance to sit down and focus solely on the needs of a single student, can generate at least a few ideas for things that they can do to provide more opportunities for success. A question like "Are there any other ways that the curriculum might be presented that would provide _____ with more opportunities to succeed in your class?" can often stimulate several good ideas. Some additional ideas are provided here:

- *Divide work assignments into smaller units.* Successful students (and adults) have the skill of being able to take large assignments and break them into smaller, more-manageable tasks. Students with ADHD tend to lack that skill. Medium-sized assignments seem daunting; large assignments seem impossible. Rather than being able to figure out a manageable task that will get the big project started, they just see a huge assignment and can't imagine where to start. Accordingly, teachers and school counselors can help students with ADHD by splitting large assignments into smaller chunks. For example, rather than assigning a full book report, a teacher could choose to have a student with ADHD hand in minireports on each chapter of the book.
- *Minimize repetition.* It is worth considering whether it makes sense to expect a student with ADHD to complete every single problem and assignment that the class is assigned. Some students with ADHD are very capable of handling all classroom assignments; for them, expectations should remain high. But others struggle under the weight of the assignments and fall easily into the cycle of not completing work, then having to take unfinished work home to complete, then not finishing the homework, and so on. For these students, it is often more sensible to pare down the number of assignments or problems they are expected to do, to stay out of the negative cycle. It is better to have a student complete 5 of 5 problems than to be given 20 problems and not complete any.
- *Attend to the visual presentation of worksheets.* Students with ADHD can become overwhelmed with too much visual information on a page. This is illustrated in Figures 5.1 through 5.3. It is not just students with ADHD that can get lost in large numbers of words or numbers on a page. Look at Figure 5.1. Does it seem just a *little* overwhelming? In contrast, since the problems in Figure 5.2 are in a larger font and are surrounded by plenty of white space, students with ADHD are less likely to become overwhelmed or lose their place. And Figure 5.3 provides even more visual assistance in separating the problems, making it even less likely that students will lose their place. These figures also serve as examples of how to break a larger assignment into smaller segments. Finally, teachers can make worksheets even more ADHD-friendly by quickly using a highlighter to highlight key points, directions, or phrases.

Figure 5.1 Sample Worksheet

Name _____

Multiplication Reinforcement

Chapter 3

1. 123 ×1	2. 135 ×2	3. 176 ×3	4. 113 ×4
5. 213 ×5	6. 257 ×6	7. 284 ×7	8. 295 ×8
9. 377 ×9	10. 326 ×8	11. 399 ×7	12. 335 ×6
13. 123 ×11	14. 135 ×22	15. 176 ×33	16. 113 ×44
17. 274 ×55	18. 249 ×66	19. 238 ×77	20. 220 ×88

Figure 5.2   Sample Worksheet

Name _____

Multiplication Reinforcement

Chapter 3

1. 123
   $\times\,1$

2. 135
   $\times\,2$

3. 176
   $\times\,3$

4. 113
   $\times\,4$

Figure 5.3   Sample Worksheet

Name _____

Multiplication Reinforcement

Chapter 3

1. 123 $\times\,1$	2. 135 $\times\,2$
3. 176 $\times\,3$	4. 113 $\times\,4$

SUMMARY POINTS

- The impact of ADHD is pervasive, affecting academic performance, peer relationships, decision making, organizational ability, emotional regulation, and self-esteem.
- Students with ADHD need frequent immediate and overt behavioral feedback in classrooms in order to be successful. Feedback systems such as token economies, the secret-signal procedure, or behavior charts can be helpful.
- Effective interventions for students with ADHD involve action, not lecturing.
- Students with ADHD benefit from added structure in the classroom. Strategies to increase structure include making rules and expectations clear and explicit, providing advanced organizers, and being as predictable as possible.
- Make the physical environment of the classroom "ADHD friendly" by attending to things like desk placement and level of light and sound.
- Provide organizational assistance to students with ADHD by aids such as assignment notebooks, color-coded folders, and homework partners.

6

Mood Disorders

> *Emily, a high school junior, has recently been looking morose and disengaged at school and seems to be withdrawing from interaction with her friends and classmates. She has failed to complete homework in the past several weeks, and when asked about homework by her teachers, she has responded with uncharacteristic irritability and sarcasm. She appears tired and just not herself.*
>
> *Jason's fourth-grade teachers have expressed concerns about his lack of energy and motivation. In a pattern that teachers report has been going on all year, Jason seems lethargic most days and rarely laughs or smiles. He frequently misses school because of stomachaches and headaches. While he seems to be academically capable, his performance at school has been marginal at best. When teachers shared their concerns with Jason's mother, she replied, "That's just the way he is. I wish he was happier, but that's just not the kind of kid he is."*

Even though both of the students featured display a different set of issues and problems, they have one thing in common—both may be suffering from a mood disorder. *Mood disorders* are a family of disorders with core symptoms of disruptions of normal mood and affect. Like all other disorders, these core symptoms of abnormal mood are woven into a complex and highly individualized package of additional symptoms, strengths, and vulnerabilities. In addition, mood disorders can present themselves very differently in children and adolescents as compared to adults. For example, children and adolescents can be diagnosed with a mood disorder even though they do *not* display a depressed mood, as diagnostic criteria for several types of mood disorders include depressed mood as a required symptom for adults but not for youth (APA, 2000). For children and adolescents, the disruption of mood can be in the form of elevated irritability rather than depressed mood. While it may seem counterintuitive to think that a student could have a mood disorder and not have a depressed mood, this diagnostic quirk actually makes sense when one considers the differences between children and adults. Youth are typically much less aware of their internal experience than adults, and they may lack the ability to recognize their core moods and then accurately express those moods in words. Indeed, the closest some adolescents can come to describing what their depression feels like is to say that they always feel "bored." What this means is that, in real life, children and adolescents with mood disorders may not fit the stereotype of a sad, tearful waif but may instead come across as touchy, irritable, and disengaged.

PATTERNS ASSOCIATED WITH MOOD DISORDERS

Mood disorders impact multiple areas of functioning, including thoughts, feelings, and behavior. Moreover, an individual's patterns of thinking and behaving can have a significant effect on the development, course, and unique expression of a mood disorder. Let's explore this further.

Mood Disorders and Negative Patterns of Thinking

A substantial body of research points to a link between negative thought patterns and depressive symptoms (Garber, Weiss, & Shanley, 1993; Gladstone & Kaslow, 1995; Ostrander, Weinfurt, & Nay, 1998). From Aaron Beck's notion that depressed individuals tend to have a negative view of themselves, the world, and the future (Beck, Rush, Shaw, & Emery, 1979) to the assertion of Martin Seligman and his colleagues (Burns & Seligman, 1991) that depressed persons often have a negative explanatory style (i.e., view their failures as being due to personal failings on their part, while refusing to take credit for their successes), a number of theorists and researchers have pointed to the crucial role cognitions play in depression.

Youth with mood disorders are predisposed to see the world through a lens of pessimism and low self-worth. Similar to youth with disruptive behavior disorders, children and adolescents with mood disorders typically have attributional styles (i.e., characteristic ways of assigning reasons for why people think and behave the way they do) that do not serve them well. The nature of these attributional styles, however, is different for students with mood disorders versus disruptive behavior disorders. While students with oppositional and aggressive behaviors generally overemphasize the aggressiveness and violence in the thoughts and actions of others, students with mood disorders are inclined to believe that others view them as being worthless, unlovable, and incompetent. Furthermore, youth with mood disorders are prone to experiencing pervasive feelings of guilt, worthlessness, and self-loathing. When provided with feedback about their performance—such as a grade on a test, a comment from a teacher about their classroom behavior, or an offhand joke from a friend about the way their hair looks in the morning—students with mood disorders interpret that feedback in the most negative manner possible. Let's assume, for example, that Holly receives a D grade on a math test. Holly feels devastated by the grade. A close examination of her underlying thoughts shows that her negative thinking started with her belief that she had done a terrible job on the test, which then mushroomed to the beliefs that the test grade was more evidence that she is not just stupid in math but is a stupid person and that she will always be dumb. In other words, Holly's attributed her low grade to negative qualities that were *personal, pervasive,* and *permanent* (Seligman, 1995). On top of all this is the fact that negative thoughts and cognitions can snowball, making students with mood disorders at risk for experiencing the type of negative thought spiral depicted in Figure 6.1.

The negative attributions and beliefs associated with mood disorders are often not easily recognized, as they generally exist at a level that is outside of one's conscious awareness. Furthermore, individuals with mood disorders often have negative schemas that are out of their awareness and which filter their experiences. *Schemas* are deep-seated and pervasive lenses through which we view the world. An example may help illustrate the impact of a negative schema. Fourteen-year-old Andy, because of growing up in a family saturated with criticism, has developed a schema that could be titled "The world is a harsh place, and I need to be on guard at all times." This schema will filter Andy's experiences, making him particularly sensitive to criticism and prone to perceive more criticism in messages given to him by others than may be intended. Let's listen in on the internal dialogue of Andy and two of his friends when they hear identical messages from a teacher:

Teacher:	You did well on this test, but I think you can do better.
Internal dialogue of Friend 1:	Great! I didn't even study, and I still did well!
Internal dialogue of Friend 2:	My teacher thinks I can do even better! She must think I have good potential!
Andy's internal dialogue:	Does she think I didn't try hard enough? She's never liked me. *None* of my teachers like me!

Figure 6.1   A Self-Talk Downward Spiral

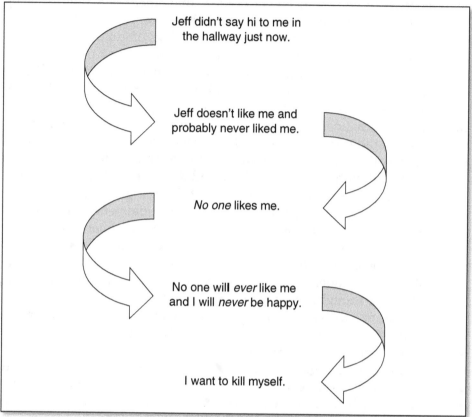

Jeff didn't say hi to me in the hallway just now.

Jeff doesn't like me and probably never liked me.

No one likes me.

No one will *ever* like me and I will *never* be happy.

I want to kill myself.

Mood Disorders and Negative Patterns of Behaving

Mood disorders exert a powerful influence on one's behavior, and as can be seen in Figure 6.2, the relationship between the mood disorder and behavior is reciprocal and can lead to negative behavior spirals. The behavior-influencing effect of mood disorders is partly physiological. Mood disorders can sap energy, disrupt healthy sleep patterns, and lead to a feeling of wearing a weighted jacket. Getting out of bed in the morning can seem insurmountable; simple acts such as getting out of one's desk to sharpen a pencil or making an appointment with the school counselor can seem overwhelming.

Mood Disorders and Social Functioning

Students with mood disorders almost always have social problems of one kind or another. Indeed, social isolation, low levels of social support, and social difficulties are common correlates of depression (Mesman &

Figure 6.2   A Behavioral Downward Spiral

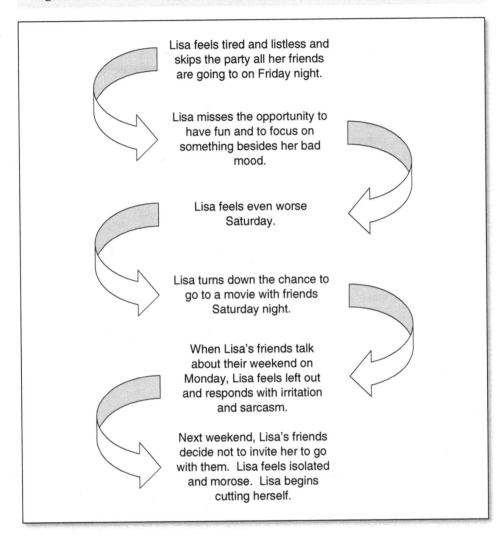

Lisa feels tired and listless and skips the party all her friends are going to on Friday night.

Lisa misses the opportunity to have fun and to focus on something besides her bad mood.

Lisa feels even worse Saturday.

Lisa turns down the chance to go to a movie with friends Saturday night.

When Lisa's friends talk about their weekend on Monday, Lisa feels left out and responds with irritation and sarcasm.

Next weekend, Lisa's friends decide not to invite her to go with them. Lisa feels isolated and morose. Lisa begins cutting herself.

Koot, 2000; Schraedley, Gotlib, & Hayward, 1999; Vitaro, Pelletier, Gagnon, & Baron, 1995). One recent study, for example, found that as compared to peers with few depressive symptoms, elementary-aged children with high levels of depressive symptoms were more likely to attempt to solve social problems by asking others to help them (thereby abdicating the chance to solve problems themselves) and by using hostile strategies (Rinaldi & Heath, 2006). It should not be assumed that social problems are a consequence of depression—in other words, that the depression comes first and leads to later social difficulties. Some research suggests an opposite relationship exists, with low social competence contributing to the development of later depressive symptoms (Cole, Martin, Powers, & Truglio, 1996).

TYPES OF MOOD DISORDERS

Becoming familiar with the specific types of mood disorders will not only enhance school counselors' confidence in dealing with students but can also boost their credibility and help them communicate better when interacting with parents and health professionals. In addition, knowledge of the type of mood disorder can inform intervention efforts, serving as one factor to consider when developing intervention strategies.

Diagnostic and Statistical Manual of Mental Disorders (*DSM*, APA, 2000) outlines three major types of mood disorders: major depressive disorder, dysthymic disorder, and bipolar disorder. Each of these is complex, and bipolar disorder in particular includes several subtypes, but for the purposes of school-based intervention, having a general understanding of the similarities and differences between the major mood types is usually sufficient. All three, by the way, could be considered *clinical depression*—a popular term used to describe depression diagnosed and treated by mental health professionals. In addition to these varieties of mood disorders, there is a type of adjustment disorder that features depressed mood as its primary symptom. Given its link to depression, it will be discussed in this chapter along with the various mood disorders. Bipolar disorder, due to its unique and challenging combination of symptoms, will be dealt with in a separate subsection at the end of the chapter.

Major Depressive Disorder

Major depressive disorder (MDD) most closely fits the general public's picture of what depression looks like, often including symptoms such as being crushed by sadness, not being able to get out of bed in the morning, and being overwhelmed by dark thoughts. MDD is an intense, hard-hitting mood disorder that has major impacts on a person's mood, thinking, and behavior. According to *DSM* (APA, 2000) criteria, for individuals to receive a diagnosis of MDD, they must display at least five of nine specified symptoms for at least two weeks. These symptoms include a loss of interest or pleasure, feelings of worthlessness or guilt, difficulty concentrating, changes in sleeping habits, and depressed mood. All of these symptoms must be judged by the mental health professional to be clinically significant, which is a way of saying that the symptoms must have a serious impact on the person's life. MDD is an episodic disorder, meaning that it generally impacts people for a limited period of time. The typical course of MDD begins with a lead period, during which milder symptoms of anxiety or depression are experienced, followed by the development of full-blown MDD (Lewinsohn, Clarke, Seeley, & Rohde, 1994). When untreated, MDD generally lasts longer than four months (APA, 2000). There is good news regarding the natural course of MDD: In most cases, individuals recover fully from an episode of MDD and return to their original level of functioning (APA). The bad news is that an episode of MDD increases the risk for subsequent episodes. In fact, approximately 20% to 40% of children and adolescents who have an initial episode of MDD will have a subsequent episode within two years, and 70% will have one or more subsequent episodes by adulthood (U.S. Department of Health and Human Services, 1999). Furthermore, the suicide risk for people with MDD is a great concern. One study that examined outcomes for individuals 10 to 15 years after being diagnosed with MDD during adolescence found that 7% had committed suicide and a disproportionate number had attempted suicide (Weissman et al., 1999).

Prevalence

Estimates indicate that approximately 5% of children and adolescents will experience an episode of MDD (Shaffer et al., 1996). Some quick figuring tells us that these percentages translate to about one student in a small-sized class or 40 to 60 students in a school of 1,000 students experiencing MDD during their youth. If we look at a single point in time (as opposed to rates of students who will experience MDD over the span of their youth), the numbers are not quite so dire, indicating that 1% to 6% (depending on the study) will be in the midst of an episode of MDD (Kessler, Avenevoli, & Merikangas, 2001). Even these lower single-point estimates, though, translate to at least 10 students in a school of 1,000 who are currently experiencing the full impact of MDD.

Gender Considerations

Studies of overall rates of depression (as opposed to studies of the specific subtypes of depression) consistently find that adolescent girls are more likely to experience depression than adolescent boys (Costello, Erkanli, & Angold, 2006). While prepubertal boys and girls are equally likely to experience depression, gender differences emerge around age 14 (Wade, Cairney, & Pevalin, 2002). Both biological and psychosocial explanations have been suggested for adolescent girls' higher depression risk. It may be that the stronger social orientation of adolescent girls may leave them more emotionally vulnerable when they experience social difficulties, adding to the risk of depression (U.S. Department of Health and Human Services, 1999).

There is also some emerging evidence that depression may manifest itself differently in boys and girls. One study of depressed youth aged 11 to 20 found that girls had higher levels of body dissatisfaction, guilt, low self-worth, self-blame, feelings of failure, sad mood, concentration difficulties, sleep problems, and health concerns. Boys, on the other hand, were found to have higher levels of anhedonia (lack of feeling), morning depressed mood, and morning fatigue (Bennett, Ambrosini, Kudes, Metz, & Rabinovich, 2005).

Dysthymic Disorder

Dysthymic disorder (also called *dysthymia*) is a mood disorder characterized by chronic depressive symptoms that are less intense than those of MDD but much longer lasting. Dysthymic disorder is to MDD what a weeks-long, low-level headache is to an intense but short-lived migraine. In order to be diagnosed as having dysthymic disorder, a child or adolescent must have depressed or irritated mood most of the day, for more days than not, for at least one year (two years for adults; APA, 2000). In addition, at least two of the following symptoms must be present: poor appetite or overeating, sleep problems, low energy or fatigue, low self-esteem, poor concentration or decision-making problems, and feelings of hopelessness (APA). Other symptoms that, while not required for a diagnosis, have been linked to dysthymic disorder include feelings of inadequacy, loss of the ability to experience pleasure, feelings of irritability, social withdrawal, and excessive ruminations and feelings of guilt. While dysthymic disorder features a symptom pattern that is less intense than MDD, the long-term impairment may be greater (U.S. Department of Health and Human Services, 1999), presumably because of the stress of dealing with an unpleasant array of symptoms for a period of years. Indeed, while dysthymic disorder can be considered an episodic disorder, the average episode for a child or adolescent lasts for a dispiriting four years (Kovacs, Obrosky, Gastonis, & Richards, 1997). Because of the extended duration of episodes, many children and adolescents with dysthymic disorder come to see their depressed state as normal, forgetting what it is like not to be beset by depressive symptoms. It is possible to have both dysthymic disorder and MDD, a condition sometimes referred to as *double depression.* Individuals with double depression are at particular risk for negative outcomes.

Prevalence

The prevalence of dysthymic disorder among adolescents has been estimated to be approximately 3% (Garrison et al., 1997). The lifetime prevalence estimate for dysthymic disorder is 6% (APA, 2000), meaning that about 1 out of every 17 individuals can be expected to experience dysthymic disorder in the course of their lifetime.

Gender Considerations

While research has not specifically examined gender differences in dysthymic disorder among youth, it is reasonable to assume a similar gender pattern as exists for MDD, with equal numbers of young boys and girls affected and more adolescent girls than boys being affected. There is tentative evidence that boys with dysthymic disorder manifest more irritability, while girls are more prone to fatigue and concentration problems (Bennett et al., 2005).

Adjustment Disorder With Depressed Mood

As noted in Chapter 4, adjustment disorders are significant sets of emotional or behavioral problems that occur within three months of exposure to an identifiable stressor (APA, 2000). If the adjustment problem primarily consists of depressed mood, the disorder is labeled *adjustment disorder with depressed mood*. Adjustment disorder with depressed mood is the most common type of mood problem among youth (U.S. Department of Health and Human Services, 1999). Thankfully, it is also the most benign, and the mood problems are generally short lived and fully resolve over time. While the level of subjective distress that accompanies this disorder should not be minimized, it can be helpful for school counselors to think in terms of providing extra short-term support to students with adjustment disorder with depressed mood rather than implementing major interventions. Rearranging deck chairs will usually suffice, since the *Titanic* is not sinking.

INTERVENTION GUIDELINES

When faced with challenging problems such as how teachers and schools can best serve students with mood disorders, savvy school counselors turn to the professional literature for guidance. Unfortunately, little research has been conducted on effective school-based interventions for mood disorders, particularly interventions that can be implemented by classroom teachers to assist individual students. The broader literature on childhood depression and clinic-based treatment of mood disorders, however, provides some guidance in shaping interventions. In the remainder of this chapter, a set of intervention guidelines will be presented. These guidelines are extrapolated from current research findings so as to anchor them on the firmest possible empirical ground. Where possible, the guidelines are supplemented with examples of how they can be used to generate specific strategies for individual and group settings as well as classroom settings.

INTERVENTION GUIDELINES FOR MOOD DISORDERS

1. Construct a relationship.

2. Expand awareness of feelings.

3. Emphasize the connections between events, thoughts, and feelings.

4. Challenge pessimistic and constricted thinking.

5. Create a network of support.

6. Maximize opportunities for success.

7. Build social skills.

8. Provide concrete evidence of work performance and improving skills.

9. Increase engagement in pleasant events.

10. Increase the level of physical activity.

11. Provide education about mood disorders.

12. Be flexible about work expectations.

Guideline 1: Construct a Relationship

The counseling literature is replete with examples of the benefits of a good, trusting relationship between counselor and client. A solid working relationship has been linked consistently to successful counseling outcomes for both adults (Horvath & Symonds, 1991) and children and adolescents (Shirk & Karver, 2003). Indeed, among factors common to all therapies (i.e., not uniquely associated with a specific therapy), the working alliance between the client and the therapist is the most frequently mentioned in the psychotherapy literature and is estimated to account for the greatest amount of variance in psychotherapy outcomes (Wampold, 2001). There is research evidence to support the value of therapist empathy for adult clients with mood disorders; a study of adults seeking therapy for mood disorders found that clients of therapists who were rated as being the warmest and most empathetic improved significantly more than clients of therapists with lower empathy ratings (Burns & Nolen-Hoeksema, 1992).

In addition to the research evidence, there are commonsense reasons why school counselors and other school personnel should work to build relationships with students with mood disorders. While all children and adolescents can benefit from positive adult relationships, youth with mood disorders may have the most to gain, given that the social difficulties that often accompany mood disorders may leave them with few social connections (Field, Diego, & Sanders, 2001a; Vitaro et al., 1995). More generally, students are more apt to listen to and accept adults' challenging and even supportive statements if these statements are offered in the context of a caring relationship. In fact, the development of a caring relationship between a counselor and a student may be a prerequisite to the student's acceptance of cognitive or behavioral treatment techniques (Stark, 1990). As applied to school counselors working with students with mood disorders, constructing a good relationship means developing rapport; being viewed by the student as a caring, interested person; and coming to a mutual agreement on the goals and techniques of the counseling sessions.

Individual Applications

While effective school counselors seem to naturally and effortlessly build trusting relationships with students, there are two specific strategies counselors can use to enhance their relationships with students with mood disorders:

- *Communicate understanding.* People of all ages, but particularly youth with mood disorders, are drawn to those who seem to understand them at a deep level. School counselors can, first, strive to fully understand both the verbal and nonverbal messages from students with mood disorders and, second, communicate this understanding back to the student. It is this two-stage process that is the key to truly communicating understanding. Communication may sound like the following:

  Even though the realistic side of you knows that you have some friends, the feeling that keeps washing over you is that no one likes you.

  Your teachers and parents don't understand how tired you feel all the time and how hard it is to concentrate on school work.

  All you want to do is stay in your room, even though you know in your heart that you are an outgoing person.

- *Get on the same page.* Students will generally feel better about counseling and work harder if they have a role in developing counseling goals and approve of the techniques to achieve those goals. Accordingly, wise school counselors will have clear and open discussions with students at the beginning of counseling regarding the goals and techniques to be pursued. For example, if negative thinking patterns seem to be contributing to a student's depressed mood, before beginning to dispute those cognitions, it would behoove the counselor to discuss the connection between negative thoughts and depression and make sure this makes sense to the student. Doing so will increase the likelihood that the student will genuinely participate in the intervention efforts and feel good about the counseling relationship.

Classroom Applications

It is also helpful for teachers to do what they can to construct a relationship with students with mood disorders. While it can be challenging for teachers at the secondary level to develop a close relationship with every one of their students given the high number of students they see, it is possible for teachers to take some actions to strengthen their relationships with students with mood disorders. Two helpful strategies follow:

- *Use names.* Teachers can make a point to address students by name and make some type of personal comment to the students during every class period. Even trivial comments can communicate personal interest and caring, which is just what students with mood disorders need.
- *See symptoms rather than bad behavior.* It is helpful for school counselors to educate teachers about some of the behaviors associated with mood disorder. In particular, it is helpful for teachers to know that irritability is a common and predictable component of depression in youth (APA, 2000). School counselors can help teachers view irritability as a symptom of a mood disorder rather than as a defiant and oppositional personality style. Just as parents of toddlers feel more successful and view their children more positively if they know that oppositional behavior among toddlers is normal and healthy, teachers can feel much more positively about students with mood disorders if they understand that irritability is a symptom that is simply a part of the disorder. This will increase the likelihood that they can look past the irritability and work to forge a caring relationship with the student.

Guideline 2: Expand Awareness of Feelings

Students with mood disorders tend to experience their feelings a bit like sailors experience the ocean. Just as sailors can be battered by ocean waves while being unaware of the vast expanse of water under the surface, children and adolescents with mood disorders experience the ups and downs of their feelings without a clear awareness of the rest of their inner emotional life. Indeed, youths with mood disorders may not only be unaware of *why* they feel the way they do (Stark, Rouse, & Kurowski, 1994), but also unable to correctly identify the feelings they experience. For example, an angry, irritable adolescent may be unaware that sadness is what fuels his anger. Another angry student may be unaware that unacknowledged grief is at the core of her anger. Clearly, the first step in assisting students with difficult or distressing feelings is to help them gain an awareness of what those feelings actually are.

Individual and Group Applications

A number of strategies can be used to expand students' awareness of their feelings. For example, let's look at three simple activities that can be used in either individual or group counseling:

- *Emotional Vocabulary.* To begin the activity Emotional Vocabulary (Stark et al., 1994), a set of index cards is created, each with the name of an emotion listed on it. If used in a group setting, the cards are first placed facedown in front of the students, who take turns picking a card. Upon picking a card, each student in turn reads the emotion, talks about what the emotion feels like, and provides an example of a time the individual experienced the emotion. Group leaders can follow up with a variety of processing questions, such as asking how many group members have experienced that feeling, how often they experience the feeling, and what actions they take to manage the feeling.
- *Emotional Pie.* This activity (Stark et al., 1994) simply consists of having students draw a large circle on a piece of paper and then divide the resulting pie into segments based on how often they experienced particular feelings in the past day or week (see Figure 6.3). School counselors working with younger students can ask them to divide their pie based on how often they had experienced the basic emotions of happy, sad, mad, and afraid. Older students can be provided with a more-extensive list of feelings or be allowed to select their own feeling words. This activity can also be used as a part of classroom lessons on feelings.
- *Emotional Thermometer.* This is another simple technique in which the school counselor draws a large thermometer on a board or a large piece of paper and then asks the students to rate the emotional intensity of various situations they have experienced (Merrell, 2008). The intent of this technique is to teach children that the strength of emotions varies depending on the situation.

In addition to formal techniques, school counselors can expand students' awareness of feelings by modeling

Figure 6.3 Emotional Pie

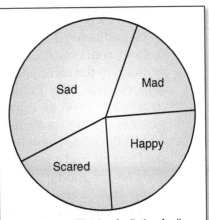

Directions: "Think of all the feelings you have had in the past week (or day). Divide your pie into as many pieces as feelings you recognized, with the size of the pieces showing how often you experienced each feeling." For younger children, demonstrate by drawing your own feeling pie.

appropriate disclosure of feelings and focusing on the emotional component of students' conversations. Questions such as "I hear your anger coming through loud and clear, but is there also some sadness that's a part of it?" and "Do you think there is a connection between the lack of energy you've been feeling and the death of your grandma?" can be helpful in increasing students' understanding of their emotional lives.

Guideline 3: Emphasize the Connections Between Events, Thoughts, and Feelings

Attribution theory (Weiner, 1985) suggests that people differ in the degree to which they believe they have personal control over the positive and negative events in their lives. There is some evidence that individuals with depressed mood are predisposed to attribute their negative life experiences to internal, stable factors (Abramson, Metalsky, & Alloy, 1989; Wall & Hayes, 2000). They believe, in essence, that they are the cause of their own misery and that they will always be miserable. One way students with mood disorders can begin to change this mindset and feel as though they are more in control of their moods is by learning that there is a connection between what they think and what they feel. And changing the way they think about a situation can affect how they feel about the situation. There are a number of simple strategies that can be used to teach students the connection between thoughts and feelings.

Individual and Group Applications

- *Share contrasting examples.* An easy way to introduce the thoughts-feelings connection is to provide examples of two students who are exposed to the same situation but feel very differently because of the different way they think about the situation. For example, one student gets a D on an exam and feels terrible because he believes the grade is further confirmation that he is dumb. Another student gets a D on the same exam but feels great because she knows she did not study at all and views the grade as confirmation that she is smart and can get good grades if she applies herself.
- *Employ a thought diary.* The connection between situations, thoughts, and feelings can be further explored by having students keep a diary in which they record the situations they are in, how they felt in each situation, and what was going through their minds while they were in the situation (see Figure 6.4). Younger students, as well as adolescents new to the notion of the thoughts-feelings connection, will require assistance completing the thought diary. The school counselor can talk through difficult situations with students and help them identify the feelings and thoughts that were generated in the situations. In addition to looking for *negative*

thoughts that are fueling sadness or low self-worth, counselors should look for situations in which the student has *positive* thoughts and is able to view a potentially difficult situation in a way that avoids an emotional meltdown. These situations can be used as indications of progress: "Last week when you were in a similar situation, you blamed yourself, but today you were able to tell yourself that it was not your fault. That's great—you are really making good progress in taking control of your thinking!" They can also be thought of as life-lines to help pull students out of negative thought spirals: "Remember last month when you were teased by your best friend? You were able to tell yourself that she was having a bad day and was just taking it out on you. And you were right, since she apologized later. Could you tell yourself something like that in this situation?"

Guideline 4: Challenge Pessimistic and Constricted Thinking

As we discussed, research tells us that the thoughts and schemas of children and adolescents with mood disorders are frequently negative, pessimistic, and self-blaming. Finding ways to challenge the pessimistic and constricted thinking of students with mood disorders, therefore, is an important part of school counselors' intervention efforts.

Figure 6.4   Thought Diary

Situation	What I Felt	What I Was Thinking
Example: 16-year-old girl		
Hearing a group of girls laughing in the hallway just as I walk by	Embarrassed, left out, self-conscious, ugly, and inadequate	They are talking about me and laughing at how fat and underdeveloped I am.
Example: 9-year-old boy		
Missing an open goal in the soccer game and having a teammate yell at me	Bad and sad	I'm terrible at soccer. I'll never be good. My teammates hate me.

Individual and Group Applications

There are a number of concrete strategies and activities that school counselors can use in individual or group settings to challenge the pessimistic thinking of students with mood disorders:

- *Identify thinking errors.* Assist students in identifying pessimistic or distorted thinking by having them evaluate their thoughts using a list of possible thinking errors (Merrell, 2008). Items on this list include thinking in black-and-white fashion, using binocular vision (i.e., seeing problems as being bigger than they really are or seeing personal strengths as being smaller than they really are), and accepting criticism but not compliments.

- *Encourage alternate interpretations.* School counselors can simply ask students, "What's the evidence?" or "Is there another way to look at it?" when they describe their distorted thoughts (Stark et al., 1994). The underlying message—which can be stated repeatedly to the students—is that there are always multiple ways of interpreting an event, and we may as well choose the interpretation that serves us best.

- *Review and rehearse thoughts.* This strategy involves three steps, beginning with a review of events the students recently experienced where they felt down or depressed and probing for underlying pessimistic or negative thoughts. The thought diary is helpful in this review process. Once these thoughts are identified, the second step is for the school counselor and the students to jointly develop realistic and productive replacement thoughts that can be employed in future situations. The final step is to discuss situations that are likely to occur in the future that historically have elicited negative feelings. Students can rehearse how they will choose to think about them, so they do not experience a negative emotional reaction. These situations can be very specific (e.g., what to say to yourself when your best friend makes fun of your hair again) or more general (e.g., what to say to yourself when you get lower than an A on a test).

- *Develop positive self-statements.* Work with students to develop positive statements they can say to themselves in situations that typically elicit depressive or difficult feelings. The key is to develop statements that are individualized and feel realistic to the student. As an example, rather than the generic "I am smart," a student faced with a difficult math test might use the statement, "I have never failed a math test before, and even if I do, I am still an A student in my other subjects."

Classroom Applications

The way in which teachers challenge the negative thinking of depressed students is largely dependent on the personality of the teacher, the personality of the depressed student, and the relationship they have. In some cases, the teacher can simply reflect back to the student a pessimistic statement and ask the student to consider whether it is really true: "I heard you say that you're sure you will fail this test. Do you think that's really true? Is there another way to think about it that might be more helpful to you?" In other cases, the teacher could make a more-challenging statement: "I heard you say that you'll fail this test for sure. You've gotten at least a C on every exam so far this semester, so it's just not realistic to expect that you'll do so much worse on this one." In both cases, though, the teacher listened for evidence of pessimistic thinking on the part of the student and challenged that thinking in some way. The role of the school counselor becomes one of educating teachers about the damaging role of negative thoughts in students with mood disorders and encouraging teachers to challenge these negative thoughts in some way.

Guideline 5: Create a Network of Support

School-based supportive networks can be very helpful for students with mood disorders. Given the connection between mood disorders and social problems (e.g., Mesman & Koot, 2000), the establishment of positive social relationships is a particularly important intervention goal for students with mood disorders. Fostering supportive relationships between students with mood disorders and teachers, coaches, police-liaison officers, school nurses, and other involved adults can provide students with the sense that they are not alone in their struggles and they have a team of adults in their corner. Ideally, peers are also members of this supportive network.

Group Applications

If properly used, counseling groups can serve as ready-made networks of support. The group itself can serve as a supportive environment where students can receive affirming messages from multiple persons (Brigman & Earley, 1991). Furthermore, many find it easier to talk with peers in a counseling group than with adults in school (Greenberg, 2003). Group leaders can use several strategies to maximize the amount of support available in groups:

- *Organize single-issue groups.* Students who share a similar issue or life circumstance may be more likely to understand and support each other (Greenberg, 2003). It can be helpful, therefore, to construct groups when possible around a shared issue, such as a grief group or a group for students who have experienced a separation or divorce. School counselors can even consider constructing a group specifically for students with mood disorders, though labeling it as a "Mood Disorders Group" or a similar label that implies a diagnosis is not advised (Ritchie & Huss, 2000).

- *Foster support with intentional leader behavior.* Group leaders can encourage support within the group by modeling supportive responses following members' disclosures. It is also helpful for leaders to listen carefully for any supportive statements offered by group members and explicitly thank members for giving such statements. Group leaders can also conduct activities that encourage support between members. One example is a compliment-book activity. For this activity the group leader gives each member precut sheets of four-by-four-inch paper, as well as a single four-by-four-inch sheet of heavy paper. The members are told that the papers will be used to make a compliment booklet and are asked to place their name and any decorations they wish on the heavy sheet for use as a cover. The covers are collected and then, one after another, each cover is pulled out and the name read. When a name is read, all members write a compliment to that student on one of the sheets of paper. The sheets are collected and stapled to the cover, completing the compliment booklet. Group leaders who are concerned that some of the members may include uncomplimentary comments may wish to quickly scan the comments as they are being collected and discard those that are not positive.

Staff Applications

School counselors can enhance the network of support for students with mood disorders through informal consultation with a variety of school staff members. Teachers, teaching assistants, coaches, administrators, support staff, and other staff members can be enlisted to provide support. Staff members need not be informed about the presence of the mood disorder, just that the student is having a tough time and could use some extra support. For example, the network of support for one depressed seventh-grade boy was enhanced by asking the school's police-liaison officer to make a special effort to talk to the boy in the halls and during lunch. This was an easy two-minute consultation, yet it provided the student with a significantly greater sense that there were supportive adults in the building who cared about him.

Guideline 6: Maximize Opportunities for Success

A behavioral explanation for depression is that individuals with depression are not able to obtain sufficient positive reinforcement from their environment (Lewinsohn, 1974). This suggests that a useful intervention for students with depressed mood is to increase the amount of positive reinforcement they receive. One way to do this is to increase the amount of success they are experiencing in school—certainly a laudable goal for all students but one with even greater benefits for students with mood disorders.

Classroom Applications

- *Enlist teachers' help.* The people with the greatest expertise in figuring out how to help students succeed in the classroom are classroom teachers. The vast majority of teachers I know are very willing to make special efforts to assist students with special needs and circumstances, if they are aware of which students need extra help. School counselors can appeal to teachers to make special efforts to help students with mood disorders succeed (without necessarily sharing the students' diagnosis). Possible strategies can range from substantial efforts such as providing extra afterschool tutoring to easy interventions such as changing desk placement so the student is seated closer to the teacher.
- *Provide assistance with memory.* Research suggests that depression has specific effects on memory. Children with high levels of depression have been found to struggle with tasks requiring immediate recall of learned material (Lauer et al., 1994). Paradoxically, depressed children also are prone to overestimate their memory skills, which can lead them to neglect using learning and memory strategies that might facilitate recall (Lauer et al.). The good news is that depressed children perform as well as nondepressed children on memory and learning tasks when they have the opportunity to learn the material over repeated trials (Lauer et al.). This research implies that teachers can improve the learning performance of children with depression by providing repetitive reviews of important material and encouraging the students to use learning strategies rather than rely on raw memorization. For example, in a class session on the Great Lakes, students could be taught the mnemonic HOMES to remember the Great Lakes rather than being asked to simply memorize them.
- *Prize effort, not intellect.* Research also consistently indicates that students with mood disorders often have negative academic self-concepts (Masi et al., 2001; McGee, Anderson, Williams, & Silva, 1986). This, in turn, suggests that it would be helpful for teachers to give students the message that success in class comes from putting in the effort to learn skills rather than from just being "smart." If students with mood disorders perceive that only smart students are capable of being successful in a class, they may become discouraged and give up, given that skewed academic self-concepts may lead them to believe they are unintelligent. Teachers can help students avoid this trap by giving an overt message that the purpose of the class is for students to learn new skills and that success in the class comes with effort, not just being smart.

Guideline 7: Build Social Skills

Students with mood disorders often have poor social relationships (Vitaro et al., 1995), so improving their social competence by teaching them social skills makes good sense. This is particularly important because a lack of social competence and poor social relationships can create a situation where students are not able to obtain positive social reinforcement, which is a condition that has been theorized to contribute to depression (Lewinsohn & Gotlib, 1995). Social-skill building can be done in a number of ways.

Individual and Group Applications

- *Role-play.* School counselors can foster the social-skill development of students with mood disorders by role-playing social situations with the students, using either contrived scenarios or social situations that the students have actually experienced. During or following the role play, counselors can model and discuss appropriate social skills. Role play can be particularly helpful in preparing students for specific upcoming social situations, such as how to initiate and maintain a conversation with peers during lunch.
- *Build students' social vocabulary.* It is often helpful to provide students with a social vocabulary of individualized phrases that can be used to initiate conversations, maintain conversations, and deal with interpersonal conflict. While it is true that social skills encompass a large and complex array of skills and behaviors, it is also true that sometimes what keeps a student from striking up a conversation with a classmate is not being able to think of anything to say. Just providing that student with one or two specific conversation starters (e.g., "Hey, did you see the game last night?" or "How'd you do on that math test? I thought it was really hard") can be enormously helpful. Of course, school counselors can also help build the social vocabularies and social skills of all students by presenting developmental guidance lessons, focusing on basic social skills such as building and maintaining friendships and resolving conflict.

Classroom Applications

Teachers can assist in the process of building the social skills of students with mood disorders by paying special attention to the students' social behavior and sharing these observations with the school counselor. This can assist the school counselor in specifically targeting skills areas that are most deficient.

Guideline 8: Provide Concrete Evidence of Work Performance and Improving Skills

Students with mood disorders are inclined to view the world through the lens of negative expectations and low self-esteem (Masi et al., 2001; Stark, Ostrander, Kurowski, Swearer, & Bowen, 1995). Nonspecific positive comments (e.g., "You have been doing very well in my class this semester") can be discounted or distorted and the positive intent of the comment lost. It is helpful for teachers, therefore, to present positive feedback to students with mood disorders in a manner that minimizes the chances that the feedback will be misinterpreted or discarded.

Classroom Applications

- *Stay factual.* A way to contest depressive distortions is to provide factual, objective, concrete evidence of success. Statements such as "I notice you have learned 25 new spelling words in the past three weeks" and "Your score on the MCA reading test was among the five highest scores in this grade" are much more difficult for students to discount because they are factual and specific.
- *Use visual aids.* In addition to providing specific and factual verbal feedback, it can be helpful for teachers to keep a visual record of students' increasing skills. One option for providing this type of visual feedback is to create a simple bar graph, where progress (e.g., number of books read, number of math skills mastered, or number of projects completed) can be charted and represented with an increasing bar. At the secondary level it is generally best to do this privately, since adolescents may be uncomfortable with public displays of their progress. One possible way to insure privacy would be to use a graph kept in the teacher's desk.

Guideline 9: Increase Engagement in Pleasant Events

Research suggests that among adolescents a lack of pleasurable social engagement is linked to the development of mood disorders (Joiner, Lewinsohn, & Seeley, 2002). Furthermore, research has suggested a link between pleasurable events and depression—specifically that individuals who engage in fewer pleasant events are more likely to feel depressed (Wierzbicki & Rexford, 1989). There are multiple reasons for this, including the diminished energy frequently felt by students with mood disorders and the tendency to underestimate the amount of enjoyment they will experience during the event. Regardless of the reasons, increasing the number of pleasant events students with mood disorders participate in is an important part of an intervention package and can help pull students out of negative behavior and thought spirals.

Individual and Group Applications

- *Schedule pleasant events.* School counselors can ask students with mood disorders to list 10 events or activities they enjoy and then to set a goal of engaging in at least one of those activities every day. These can range from listening to favorite music to going to a movie to having a hot fudge sundae. This intervention can be done either in an individual session or in a counseling group.
- *Incorporate a review of pleasant events into group check-in.* In group counseling, part of the check-in process at the start of each group session can be a review of the types of pleasant events each member engaged in since the previous group session. The group leader and other group members can celebrate instances when a group member successfully engaged in a number of pleasant events; if a student has not engaged in pleasant events, the group can help discuss any barriers experienced by the student and problem solve ways the student can be more successful during the ensuing week.

Guideline 10: Increase the Level of Physical Activity

Research points to a clear link between increased physical exercise and improvements in depressive symptoms (Craft & Landers, 1998; Field, Diego, & Sanders, 2001b). School counselors can use this finding to assist students with mood disorders.

Individual and Group Applications

- *Create an exercise program.* During individual counseling, school counselors can help students with mood disorders develop a regular exercise program and encourage the students to stick with the program. Counselors may find it beneficial to collaborate with physical education teachers in figuring out appropriate and fun ways to add more physical activity into the lives of students with mood disorders.
- *Find a workout buddy.* Pairing students with an exercise partner can provide a double benefit, both increasing compliance with the exercise plan and building social relationships. A visual record of progress (e.g., number of miles walked) can provide extra reinforcement.

Guideline 11: Provide Education About Mood Disorders

Mood disorders can feel mysterious, unpredictable, and frightening to students living with them. Learning more about typical signs, symptoms, causes, and treatments can help students make sense of what they are experiencing and provide them with hope that they can overcome or at least manage the disorder. Helpful information can be found on a number of professional websites (e.g., www.aacap.org/cs/root/facts_for_families/ the_depressed_child; www.nimh.nih.gov/health/topics/depression/ depression-in-children-and-adolescents.shtml) and in books such as *Recovering from Depression: A Workbook for Teens* (Copeland & Copans, 2002), and *Depression Is the Pits, But I'm Getting Better: A Guide for Adolescents* (Garland, 1997). School counselors can provide students with pertinent information during individual or group sessions. Furthermore, it can be very helpful for school counselors to provide information about mood disorders to all students via special programs or developmental guidance lessons (Evans, Van Velsor, & Schumacher, 2002).

Teachers can also benefit from information about depression. Educating teachers about the risk factors contributing to depression, signs of depression, and developmental issues impacting depression can better equip teachers to recognize early signs of mood disorders and increase the likelihood they will appropriately refer to the school counselor students exhibiting signs of a possible mood disorder (Evans et al., 2002). Parents, as well, can benefit from information about mood disorders.

Guideline 12: Be Flexible About Work Expectations

Mood disorders often impede academic performance. There are multiple reasons for this, including the impact of depressed mood on energy level and concentration (Christensen & Duncan, 1995; Livingston, Stark, Haak, & Jennings, 1996), the tendency of depression to lead to a perception that even small tasks require large expenditures of effort (APA, 2000), and the role of depression in leading to low academic self-esteem and beliefs that one is unable to be successful (Masi et al., 2001). There may be times when students with mood disorders are simply unable to keep up with a normal workload. Providing these students with flexibility and understanding regarding work expectations can prevent them from entering a downward spiral and becoming further and further behind at school.

Classroom Applications

- *Enlist teachers' help.* School counselors can be instrumental in helping teachers see the need for flexibility with students with mood disorders. Counselors can assist teachers and students in negotiating an understanding that considers the student's diminished energy level and concentration and, at the same time, appreciates the teacher's need to have the student learn the required material. A useful analogy to help teachers appreciate the need for flexibility is chemotherapy treatments for cancer. It is the rare teacher who would refuse to allow some flexibility in work expectations for a student with cancer who is undergoing chemotherapy. Yet severe depression, like chemotherapy, can also create somatic difficulties and diminished energy.

If there is a clear link between a student's mood disorder and impaired school performance, school counselors can advocate for either an evaluation for special education services or development of an accommodation plan under the auspices of Section 504 of the Rehabilitation Act of 1973 (i.e., a 504 plan). Students with mood disorders deemed eligible should be provided with a written 504 plan that includes simple, concrete accommodations (see Smith, 2002, for an example). The guidelines presented in this chapter can be used to generate ideas for appropriate accommodations.

BIPOLAR DISORDER

Shana, a 14-year-old eighth grader, has been in a downward cycle since the first week of school. She has a reputation as being moody, volatile, and unpredictable. Some days she is quiet and withdrawn, while on other days she is aggressive, loud, and argumentative. Even though her teachers like her and want her to succeed, they are frustrated by her behavior. Shana has also alienated many of her old friends with her volatile behavior, and rumors are going around school about her alcohol use and sexual activity. She is failing three of her four academic classes.

Felix has had a very difficult time in fourth grade. His teachers use words such as troubled, unpredictable, *and* tightly wound *to describe Felix's behavior and mood. While Felix has had some good days and is viewed by school staff as having a good heart, on more days than not, he is highly irritable and prone to angry outbursts. His teachers report that he seems to want to have friends but acts in a manner that pushes his classmates away. Consequently, he seems lonely and isolated. Felix is bright, but his work production is erratic. His teachers are at their wits end trying to figure out how to help him, and his parents are equally frustrated.*

Shana and Felix have *bipolar disorder,* one of the most challenging mood disorders that affect children and adolescents. Bipolar disorder is a very serious, highly impactful disorder that significantly affects mood, behavior, and thinking. While bipolar disorder is listed as a type of mood disorder in *DSM* (APA, 2000), it has unique characteristics that are unlike other mood disorders and requires a special approach to intervention. Accordingly, I have afforded a special section of this chapter to bipolar disorder.

Foundational Information

Originally called manic-depressive disorder, bipolar disorder is differentiated from the other mood disorders by the presence of *manic episodes.* A manic episode is defined by *DSM* (APA, 2000) as a distinct period of at least one week during which unusually and persistently elevated, expansive, or irritable mood is present. In addition, a specified number of other symptoms must be present from a list including inflated self-esteem or grandiosity, racing thoughts, decreased need for sleep, physical agitation, and increased engagement in pleasurable activities with a high risk of negative consequences (e.g., going on a spending spree when on a limited budget). While it is possible to have bipolar disorder without a depressive component (since the presence of mania is the defining characteristic), in the majority of cases, individuals cycle between mania and major depression.

The stereotypical bipolar pattern for adults—a period of manic, high-energy behavior, followed by a period of normal behavior, followed by a period of depression—is rare among children. Children with bipolar disorder generally have more long-standing problems and fewer periods of wellness (Papolos & Papolos, 2002). Furthermore, while adults characteristically cycle between mood phases over a course of months or years, children can cycle between the ups and downs of bipolar disorder over a period of weeks or may even fluctuate between one mood state and another within a single day (termed *ultradian cycling*). One study of children with bipolar disorder seen in outpatient pediatric and child psychiatry clinics, in fact, found that 77% of the children had at least one mood cycle per day, averaging over three cycles per day (Geller, Craney, et al., 2002).

Children with bipolar disorder tend to be inflexible, highly irritable, and prone to rageful outbursts (Papolos & Papolos, 2002). While children's manic episodes generally include adultlike symptoms such as racing thoughts and grandiosity (Staton, Volness, & Beatty, 2008), the episodes also frequently consist of extreme mood swings and severe irritability (Kowatch et al., 2005). The difference between the "look" of bipolar disorder in adults and that in children and adolescents is reflected in the results of a study of youth diagnosed as having bipolar disorder (Biederman et al., 2004). As illustrated in Figure 6.5, these children and adolescents were much more likely to display severe irritability than the type of euphoria that is often associated with an adult manic episode. Indeed, about four out of five of the group exhibited severe irritability.

While in some cases children with bipolar disorder may be able to hide these difficult behaviors at school, families bear the full brunt of the disorder. Adolescents with bipolar disorder may display features of both the adult expression of the disorder, with periods in which they feel energetic, overconfident, and special, and features of the childhood expression of the disorder, with highly irritable and oppositional behavior and rages. Children and adolescents with bipolar disorder have high rates of psychosis and hospitalization, as well as poor psychosocial functioning (Birmaher & Axelson, 2006). They also are prone to hypersexual behavior—inappropriate sexual behaviors such as children with bipolar disorder under the age of 10 drawing pictures of naked people in

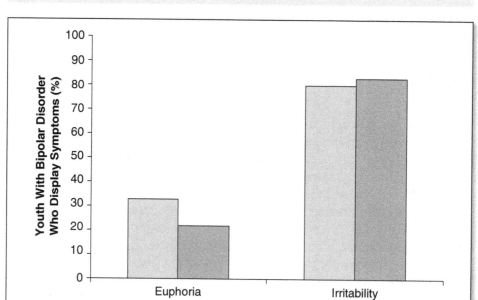

Figure 6.5 Percentages of Youth With Bipolar Disorder Who Display Symptoms of Euphoria or Irritability

Source: Biederman et al. (2004).

Note: Males, $n = 224$; Females, $n = 77$

public, using sexually explicit language in restaurants, and propositioning classmates (Geller, Zimerman, et al., 2002). Finally, youth with bipolar disorder are at high risk for suicidal ideation and attempts (Birmaher & Axelson); 10% to 15% of people with bipolar disorder commit suicide (APA, 2000).

Bipolar disorder has several main subtypes: *bipolar I, bipolar II,* and *cyclothymic disorder.* Bipolar I is the most severe subtype, with a diagnosis requiring the display of a full manic episode and, typically, also including one or more major depressive episodes. Bipolar II requires a major depressive episode, but only a less-severe type of manic episode called a *hypomanic episode.* The final subtype, cyclothymic disorder, consists of at least one year's duration (two years for adults) of mood fluctuations that include both manic and depressive symptoms, though neither rise to the level of a full manic episode or full major depressive episode (APA, 2000).

Just as with most other mental disorders, bipolar disorder typically does not occur alone, but rather co-occurs with one or more additional disorders. Youth with bipolar disorder are particularly likely to also have ADHD; ADHD is present in about 70% to 90% of children with bipolar disorder and 30% to 40% of adolescents with bipolar disorder (Kowatch et al., 2005).

Prevalence

It is extremely difficult to obtain accurate data on the prevalence of bipolar disorder among youth. Epidemiological studies differ in the types of assessments that are used, the level of training of the evaluators, and the criteria employed. Furthermore, the assessment of bipolar disorder in children and adolescents is exceedingly complex, and skilled clinicians can disagree about whether a young client does or does not have bipolar disorder. There is even professional disagreement about whether DSM criteria are overly restrictive and may not accurately reflect the core elements of bipolar disorder (Pavuluri, Birmaher, & Naylor, 2005). All this being said, though, research indicates that bipolar disorder is uncommon among children and adolescents, with prevalence estimates hovering around 1% in studies using strict DSM definitions of the disorder (Kessler et al., 2001). Bipolar I, the most serious type of bipolar disorder, has prevalence estimates of well below 1% (Kessler et al.). It does seem indisputable that the past decade has seen a dramatic increase in the number of children and adolescents with a diagnosis of bipolar disorder. One study of the types of diagnoses assigned to children and adolescents discharged from psychiatric facilities found that in the nine years from 1996 to 2004, bipolar disorder went from being one of the least frequent diagnoses to the most frequently assigned diagnosis (Blader & Carlson, 2007).

Gender Considerations

Gender differences in the prevalence of bipolar disorder are evident neither among adults (APA, 2000) nor among children and adolescents (Biederman et al., 2004). While there are no apparent gender differences in the prevalence of bipolar disorder, there is some evidence that there may be some subtle differences in the way the disorder plays out. Initial episodes for men tend to be manic episodes, while initial episodes for women tend to be major depressive episodes. Over time, manic episodes tend to predominate in men, while the reverse is true for women (APA).

INTERVENTION GUIDELINES FOR STUDENTS WITH BIPOLAR DISORDER

Bipolar disorder presents unique and formidable intervention challenges due to the frequent presence of highly volatile and unpredictable behavior associated with the manic component of the disorder. Unfortunately, there is minimal research on effective psychosocial treatments for children and adolescents with bipolar disorder (Pavuluri et al., 2005) and virtually none on school-based interventions. This would, however, not be a very useful section of this chapter if it described the difficulty of the problem without suggesting some solutions. So I will combine extrapolations from the skimpy professional intervention literature with a dose of common sense and suggest some school-based intervention guidelines for children with bipolar disorder.

INTERVENTION GUIDELINES FOR BIPOLAR DISORDERS

1. Educate the student, teachers, and families about bipolar disorder.
2. Collaborate, collaborate, collaborate.
3. Provide structure and consistency.
4. Plan the day.
5. Think "big picture."
6. Don't expect consistent behavior.
7. Ride out the storms.
8. Look past the irritability.
9. Don't forget about problems *not* associated with the disorder.

Guideline 1: Educate the Student, Teachers, and Families About Bipolar Disorder

Put yourself in the place of a child or adolescent with bipolar disorder. You never know from day to day—and sometimes from hour to hour—how you will feel or whether you will be holding things together or feeling as though your life is falling apart. You often feel at the mercy of your emotions, which buffet you throughout the day. You find yourself saying and doing things that, upon reflection, embarrass you and that don't seem like the real you. You see that your friends and classmates don't have the kind of trouble you do. You believe you are crazy, or inherently bad, or both.

Now imagine that a helpful adult—perhaps a school counselor—sits down with you and talks to you about what bipolar disorder is and how it affects mood and behavior. You learn that there is a reason you feel and act the way you do, and you discover that there are other young people who have the same disorder you do and that they understand your life. You no longer feel alone.

Education about bipolar disorder can provide that kind of relief and can help reduce self-blame among students with bipolar disorder. Education can also be enormously helpful to parents and families. There is some evidence that parents with children with bipolar disorder respond to their child with less blame and more understanding if they receive education about the disorder—learning to view bipolar disorder as a "no fault" illness, the development of which is the fault of neither the child nor the parents (Fristad, 2006). Teachers, too, can become more understanding and supportive if they learn more about bipolar disorder. Clearly, helping students, families, and teachers learn more about bipolar disorder has important benefits.

An easy-to-read and helpful book that can be recommended to both parents and school personnel is *The Bipolar Child* by Demitri and Janice Papolos (2002). Websites of the Child and Adolescent Bipolar Foundation (www.bpkids.org) and the National Institute of Mental Health (www.nimh .nih.gov/health/topics/bipolar-disorder/index.shtml) are other good places to start.

Guideline 2: Collaborate, Collaborate, Collaborate

Bipolar disorder is a very complex, high-impact disorder that is best addressed among youth with a coordinated treatment approach that includes specialized medical care (preferably from a child psychiatrist), individual and family therapy, and school-based support. Collaboration among the various service providers, as well as the family, is essential for optimal outcomes. School counselors can be very helpful in insuring that the family members and multiple professionals involved are all talking to each other (Bardick & Bernes, 2005).

Another advantage of a highly collaborative approach is that it provides some emotional support for each of the professionals involved. Working with students with bipolar disorder can be very stressful, for multiple reasons. The characteristics of the disorder—volatile, unpredictable moods with highly irritable and reactive behavior—test the patience and equanimity of even the most grounded and competent school counselor. It can be very trying for school counselors who are invested in the well-being of students with bipolar disorder to watch the very difficult ups and downs the students experience. For these reasons, a collaborative approach that provides a supportive team not just for the student but also for the service providers is essential.

Guideline 3: Provide Structure and Consistency

There are some similarities between children and adolescents with disruptive behavior disorders and those with bipolar disorder. For both sets of youth, their inner experience is often chaotic and they struggle with regulating their emotions and behavior. Consequently, just as youth with disruptive behavior disorders need added structure, so too do students with bipolar disorder. The unpredictable and erratic nature of the moods and actions of students with bipolar disorder makes it even more crucial for school counselors and teachers to respond with even-keel, consistent behavior. Calm, collected, and predictable adult behavior can be like a rudder on a ship in high seas—the waves may be crashing down, but the ship is slowly going in the right direction.

Guideline 4: Plan the Day

It is easy for teachers and school counselors to become reactive when working with students with bipolar disorder, due to the unpredictable and often dramatic behavior that is a part of the disorder. A goal for these key adults, therefore, should be to make every effort to be proactive and prepared, to be in a better position to respond effectively to behaviors or issues that arise. One way to do this is to plan the day. There are two ways in which this can be done. First, teachers and other school staff who interact with students with bipolar disorder can mentally review the upcoming day, think about activities or transitions that may be particularly likely to trigger behavioral issues, and make some tentative plans for how to manage any problems that develop. In this way, teachers will be less likely to be caught off guard and are more apt to respond in ways that are helpful if behavior problems do occur.

The second way to plan the day is for the school counselor to meet with the student at the beginning of the day and review the daily schedule. This allows the counselor to make a connection with the student and settle the student into the day. It also allows the counselor and the student to review any parts of the day that have been particularly challenging in the past and do some proactive problem solving about ways to help those times go smoothly. While school counselors are generally in the best position to do this morning planning, in some schools it may work best to have a classroom teacher or special education teacher make this daily connection.

Guideline 5: Think "Big Picture"

One of the keys to effectively helping students with bipolar disorder has nothing to do with strategies or interventions but, rather, consists of cultivating an attitude and belief system that is most conducive to doing good work with students. The next several guidelines will speak to elements of that kind of attitude and belief system. The recommendation to think "big picture" is designed to serve as a counterweight to the typical pattern of students with bipolar disorder of having many peaks and valleys in their day-to-day behavior and adjustment. There is a danger that teachers and school staff will overhaul effective intervention packages because the student is experiencing a short-term run of bad days. While it is appropriate to make minor day-to-day modifications to stay on top of burgeoning emotional or behavioral issues, school counselors and teachers should determine whether the general trend line over the course of recent weeks and months is positive or negative. It is the longer-term trend lines that serve as better indicators of the need for substantial change in intervention plans.

Talking in big-picture terms can also be helpful in fostering a more-realistic and hopeful attitude in both students with bipolar disorder and their families. With students, an example of a helpful big-picture statement is, "I know it is discouraging to have the kind of tough days you've had lately, but it still seems like eighth grade has been much better than seventh grade." An example of a similar statement that could be shared with parents is, "I agree that Mario's behavior has been worse in the past two weeks, but remember how much he was struggling last year? Things have gotten so much better. I still think we are basically doing the right things to help him, but we just need to tweak his program."

Guideline 6: Don't Expect Consistent Behavior

Part of the unspoken belief system of many adults is that children and adolescents should behave well—and behave well consistently. If we dig a little deeper into this belief, we find that it is based on a more-fundamental belief that children and adolescents can control their behavior if they choose. A corollary of this belief is that young people who misbehave are making conscious choices to misbehave. Moreover, adults who believe that children and adolescents *choose* to misbehave typically respond to young people's misbehavior with anger and negative judgments: "Why can't Billy just behave?"

Let's take a deep breath and see if there is another way to think about this. We know that bipolar disorder, by definition, leads to emotional turmoil and behavioral volatility. For students with bipolar disorder, unpredictability and inconsistency is the norm. If teachers and other school staff expect consistent behavior, more often than not they will be frustrated and disappointed. It makes more sense, and leads to a more helpful attitude, if teachers, school counselors, and others *expect* ups and downs.

None of this means that students with bipolar disorder should not be held accountable for their actions. Students with bipolar disorder should not be exempt from experiencing the consequences of their behavior. But these consequences should not include being the recipients of anger and disdain from the adults who are working with them at school. Limit setting is best done in a calm and matter-of-fact manner (Fristad, 2006).

Guideline 7: Ride Out the Storms

Many students with bipolar disorder experience emotional and behavioral storms. The storm clouds can build quickly, and suddenly the storm is at full force, often engulfing not just the student but also classmates and teachers. The good thing about storms, though, is that they end.

Teachers and school counselors can help students weather these storms and perhaps even hasten the end of the storms, if they stay calm and solid and resolute in the face of the storm. There can be value in talk-ing to students about the choices they made and about how to make bet-ter choices in the future, but these discussions should take place *after* the storm. During the storm, adults should work to stay calm, to insure that the student is safe, and to defuse the student's emotions.

Guideline 8: Look Past the Irritability

It is no fun to be around a student who is irritable and whose mood often seems black, and there is a tendency for adults faced with this type of demeanor to either stop interacting with the student or become irritable themselves. For teachers and school counselors working with students with bipolar disorder, though, it is important to neither withdraw nor begin linking their own moods to the dysphoric moods of the students. One way teachers and school counselors can maintain a helpful and sup-portive stance is to clearly understand that irritability is a symptom of bipolar disorder and be able to look past it. Think about the experience of looking at a beautiful centuries-old painting that is covered with dust and grime. Just as the experience of viewing the painting is enhanced by look-ing past the dust and grime and appreciating the beauty of the painting, work with students with bipolar disorder is enhanced by looking past the irritability and seeing the struggling person underneath who needs sup-port and understanding. It may be helpful in talking to teachers and other school staff about a student with bipolar disorder to say clearly that the student is not a bad person but has a bad illness (Mackinaw-Koons & Fristad, 2004).

Looking past the irritability may also help teachers and school coun-selors respond to students with bipolar disorder with greater empathy and warmth. Displaying warmth may be particularly important. One study that tracked youth with bipolar disorder over a two-year period found that, of the students who had recovered during that time period, those whose mothers treated them with little warmth were four times more likely to relapse than students with high-warmth mothers (Geller, Craney, et al., 2002).

Guideline 9: Don't Forget About
Problems *Not* Associated With the Disorder

When working with students who have bipolar disorder, it is easy to focus only on the symptoms of the disorder, because those symptoms are so severe and pervasive. There are many ways, however, that school coun-selors can be helpful that have nothing to do with the disorder. Students with bipolar disorder also face the problems and challenges that all stu-dents face, such as needing to figure out postsecondary career and educa-tional plans. Sometimes school counselors can be most helpful by assisting students with bipolar disorder with these sorts of problems. Given that students with bipolar disorder are particularly vulnerable to stress, helping them with developmentally appropriate stresses and issues may often be the best way of helping them manage their disorder.

SUMMARY POINTS

- Mood disorders have core symptoms of disruptions of mood and affect. Youth with mood disorders may look sad and depressed but are as likely to come across as touchy and irritable.
- Mood disorders are linked to negative patterns of thinking, negative patterns of isolative or irritable behavior, and social problems.
- Youth with mood disorders may be unaware of why they are feeling the way they are, or they may even be unable to identify the feelings they are experiencing. School counselors can help these students expand their awareness of their feelings.
- Students with mood disorders can benefit from learning that they can feel better by changing the way they think about the events that happen to them. Strategies such as use of a thought diary can assist with this process.
- The social lives of students with mood disorders can be improved by the use of strategies such as role-playing, building a social vocabulary, and creating a network of support at school.
- Increased physical activity and increased engagement in pleasant events can be of major benefit to students with mood disorders.
- Bipolar disorder is a special subset of mood disorders characterized by the presence of disruptive manic episodes with wide mood swings and periods of rage.
- School counselors and teachers can assist students with bipolar disorder by remaining calm during emotional storms and providing consistency and structure.

7

Anxiety Disorders

Emily's parents have sought help for her because they are concerned about her constant worrying. They report that Emily, a fourth grader, has an array of worries, including worrying about doing well in school, worrying about what other children think of her, and worrying about getting sick. Emily also is prone to frequent stomachaches, which her doctor has said are probably stress related. School reports indicate that Emily does well academically but seems to put a great deal of pressure on herself and, in the words of one teacher, "seems to have the weight of the world on her shoulders." Emily describes herself as a "worrywart" and reports that she often thinks about what would happen if she doesn't pass fourth grade and what would happen if she gets a bad disease.

High school has been an ordeal for Ethan. He has always been shy, but now in the midst of his sophomore year he finds that he feels anxious virtually all the time at school, but particularly when he must do something that draws the attention of others. Talking in front of the class feels terrifying to him, and even talking to a group of boys at lunch feels hard for him. He would like to have a girlfriend, but the thought of talking to girls feels much too scary for him. Ethan is embarrassed and ashamed of his anxiety and tries to hide it as much as he can. He likes his school counselor but can't imagine talking to his counselor about his anxiety.

Emily and Ethan have anxiety disorders, a group of internalizing disorders that affect large numbers of children and adolescents and that, if untreated, create much distress and suffering. In addition to the pain and distress caused by the disorder itself, the excessive amount of emotional energy students with anxiety disorders must devote to managing their anxiety takes away from their ability to focus on both school tasks and social development.

RESEARCH FINDINGS

Research suggests that between 10% and 20% of youth may experience an anxiety disorder at some point during their childhood and adolescence (Costello, Mustillo, Erkanli, Keeler, & Angold, 2003; Vasa & Pine, 2004). Research has provided a range of prevalence figures for youth experiencing an anxiety disorder at any one point in time. One study from the mid-1990s found approximately 7% of youth aged 9 to 17 had some type of anxiety disorder with at least moderate impairment in the past six months (Shaffer et al., 1996), while a more-recent study found slightly lower rates, with a three-month prevalence of 2.3%. What is clear is that numerous students in K–12 schools are impacted by anxiety disorders and that, at any particular time, school counselors can expect to have at least a handful of students with active anxiety disorders in their caseload.

While the numbers of students with problematic anxiety are substantial, there is some good news. Research studies have found a variety of intervention models to be effective in reducing symptoms and improving functioning in children and adolescents with anxiety disorders (Bernstein, Layne, Egan, & Tennison, 2005; McLoone, Hudson, & Rapee, 2006; Santucci, Ehrenreich, Trosper, Bennett, & Pincus, 2009; Warner, Fisher, Shrout, Rathor, & Klein, 2007). The areas positively impacted by intervention include school performance; one study found that high-anxiety students whose anxiety was reduced by participation in a cognitive-behavioral intervention displayed improvements in both academic performance and social functioning (Wood, 2006).

TYPES OF ANXIETY DISORDERS

The family of anxiety disorders includes a number of specific disorders, all of which have at their core the experience of excessively high and often-debilitating anxiety. The nine anxiety disorders most relevant to children and adolescents are presented in Figure 7.1. (The disorders are presented as completely distinct entities in Figure 7.1, but that probably oversimplifies reality. It is more likely that there is overlap among many of the specific disorders.) It is beyond the scope of this chapter to provide a thorough discussion of each specific disorder, but what I will attempt to do is present a brief overview of each of the nine disorders and then describe some

Figure 7.1   Anxiety Disorders Most Relevant to Children and Adolescents

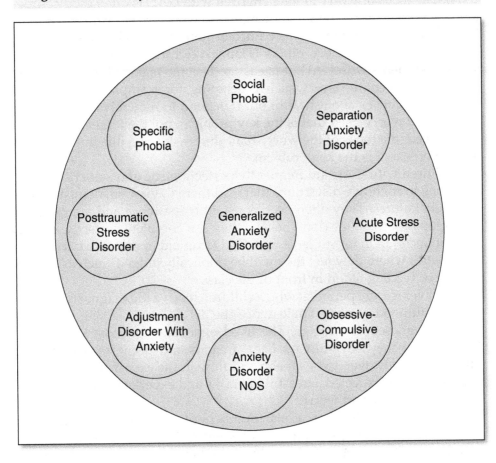

general school-based intervention guidelines that can be useful for most, if not all, anxiety disorders.

Generalized Anxiety Disorder

Diagnostic and Statistical Manual of Mental Disorders (*DSM*, APA, 2000) criteria indicate that *generalized anxiety disorder* (GAD) is characterized by excessive anxiety and worry occurring more days than not and focused on a broad range of events or activities. For children's anxiety to meet DSM criteria for GAD, the worry must be accompanied by at least one other symptom, such as restlessness, concentration difficulty, muscle tension, irritability, or frequent fatigue and sleep problems, and the symptoms must persist for at least six months (APA).

The defining feature of GAD is excessive worry (Beidel & Turner, 2005). While worry is a normal part of everyone's experience, in comparison to the general population the worry experienced by individuals with

GAD is more intense, frequent, and uncontrollable (Flannery-Schroeder, 2004). The focus of worry among children with GAD is often their competence or performance, though they may also worry excessively about their health, the future, and their safety. Furthermore, they may worry about the health and safety of close others (Flannery-Schroeder). When trying to support students with GAD, it is easy to become engaged in discussions about the target of the worry, such as debating, for example, the validity of a student's worries about health. But it is good to remember that it is the anxiety and worry itself that is the key problem, not the target of the worries. Indeed, the focus of the worry may shift over time, illustrating that it is the worry that is the key problem.

Children with GAD are frequently perfectionistic and self-critical and are prone to cognitive distortions that lead them to view small mistakes as complete failures. They often need constant reassurance and are prone to giving up on tasks they don't believe they can complete perfectly. In fact, it is not uncommon for students with GAD to avoid or refuse to participate in activities where they feel they will be publically judged, such as a choir concert or reading aloud in front of the class.

The average age period at which children receive the diagnosis of GAD is late childhood or early adolescence (Beidel & Turner, 2005), though it can be diagnosed at any age. The lived experience of most youth with GAD is that they have always been anxious and prone to over worry. There tends, however, to be an ebb and flow in the experience of anxiety, and as could be expected, stressful life tasks and experiences tend to exacerbate the anxiety and worry.

Research indicates that similar numbers of young boys and girls are diagnosed with GAD, but more adolescent girls are diagnosed as compared to adolescent boys. It is unclear whether this represents a true difference in the prevalence of the disorder or a reflection of adolescent girls' greater willingness to disclose symptoms of anxiety.

Social Phobia

The essential feature of *social phobia* is a "marked and persistent fear of social or performance situations in which embarrassment may occur" (APA, 2000, p. 450). Prevalence data are scant, but the existing research suggests between 1% and 2% of youth have social phobia (Beidel, Morris, & Turner, 2004). Children and adolescents with social phobia experience great anxiety when they are in situations where they perceive that others may judge or evaluate them, such as giving a speech in class or being at a party. Much of the distress centers on a fear that others will judge them to be weak, anxious, or crazy (APA). For example, an adolescent with social phobia might detest public speaking because of a fear that others could see him trembling or hear his voice shake, and know he was anxious. As you can see, the perception of being negatively evaluated is a key component of the disorder. These children appear socially inhibited and timid to others (Beidel et al.).

Exposure to feared situations provokes an immediate anxiety response (APA, 2000). One study of children with social phobia found that, while in distressing social situations, over half of the children experienced heart palpitations, shakiness, flushes, sweating, and nausea (Beidel et al., 2004). Moreover, there often is much anticipatory worry and anxiety leading up to a feared event. Social avoidance is present in most cases (Beidel et al.). While youth with social phobia typically attempt to avoid the feared situation—staying home "sick" on the day they are scheduled to do a class presentation, for example—they alternately may endure the situation with a feeling of dread. The dreaded events themselves tend to occur frequently; children with social phobia report experiencing a distressing event approximately every other day (Beidel et al.). Furthermore, most of those events occur at school. The most feared event for adolescents, according to one study, was talking to peers.

In youth, symptoms of anxiety and fear must persist for six months to be diagnosable (APA, 2000). Youth with social phobia also are prone to be hypersensitive to criticism or rejection, to have low self-esteem, and to be plagued by feelings of inferiority. Underachievement in school due to test anxiety or unwillingness to participate in class discussions is possible; school refusal is possible (APA). It is also important to remember that comorbidity is the rule for individuals with social phobia. Other disorders that are frequently comorbid include other anxiety disorders, mood disorders, and ADHD (Beidel et al., 2004).

The typical age of onset is in the midteens, though social phobia has been diagnosed as early as age 8 (Beidel et al., 2004). Even when diagnosed at a later age, social phobia is often preceded by a childhood history of shyness and social reluctance (APA, 2000). Social phobia can be a lifelong problem, but with some individuals, it does recede in adulthood. Part of the variation in the expression of symptoms is due to changing social demands and life stressors. For example, if a high school student with social phobia graduates and takes a job in a warehouse with few social demands, the phobic symptoms may remit. But in a few years, if the individual receives a promotion to a position requiring considerable interaction and some public speaking, the symptoms may recur.

Cognitive factors are intertwined with the emotional and behavioral symptoms of social phobia. In addition to chronic anticipatory worry about social embarrassment, students with social phobia tend to underestimate their abilities on feared tasks (Beidel & Turner, 2005). In the behavioral realm, youth with social phobia generally have deficiencies in social skills (Beidel et al., 2004). This creates a vicious cycle for students with social phobia where they avoid social situations, thereby missing the chance to further develop their social skills and reinforcing their belief that they are socially inadequate (see Figure 7.2).

Figure 7.2   Cycle of Social Skills and Social Avoidance

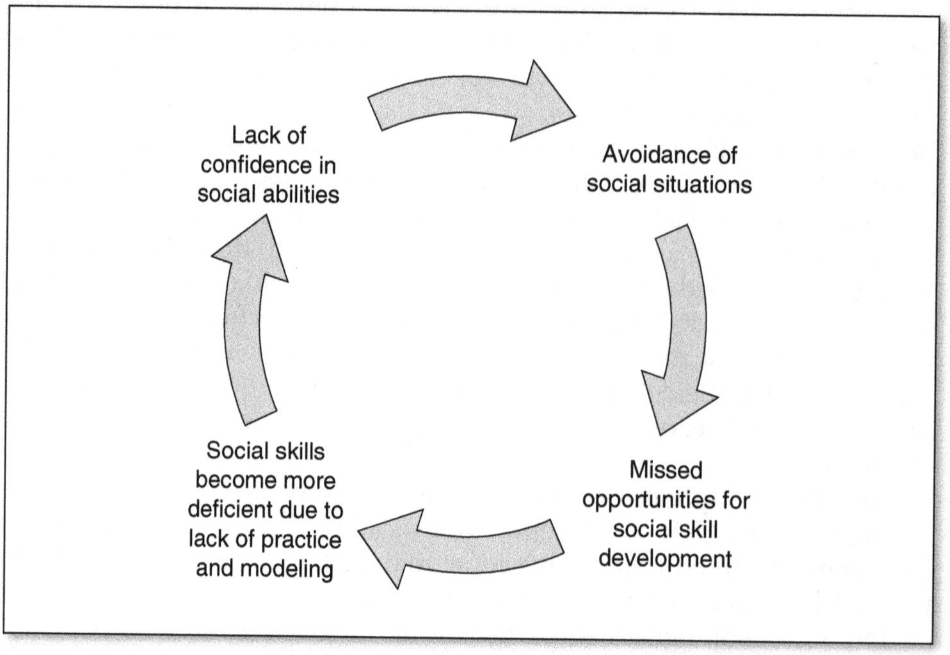

Lack of
confidence in
social abilities

Avoidance of
social situations

Social skills
become more
deficient due to
lack of practice
and modeling

Missed
opportunities for
social skill
development

Finally, it is good to keep in mind that children differ both in their level of comfort in social situations and in their desire to socialize with peers (Beidel et al., 2004; see Figure 7.3). Some children may not be comfortable in social situations, but don't find that distressing, as they aren't all that interested in connecting socially with peers. The children who find social phobia most distressing are those who feel intensely uncomfortable in social situations but who also want to have friends and interact socially.

Specific Phobia

DSM notes that the essential feature of a *specific phobia* is a "marked and persistent fear of clearly discernable, circumscribed objects or situations" (APA, 2000, p. 443). As opposed to generalized fears or anxiety associated with GAD or social phobia, in specific phobia the feared object or situation is narrow and specific. Among adults, there are two sources of distress connected with a specific phobia: the fear of the object or situation itself (such as getting bit by a dog) and the fear of experiencing the symptoms of fear, such as panicking or losing control. The intensity of fear and distress seems to be related to one's proximity to the feared object or situation and the perceived ability to escape. Part of the fear of flying, for example, is the inability to escape the situation once the plane is on the runway.

Figure 7.3   Sociability Versus Social Comfort

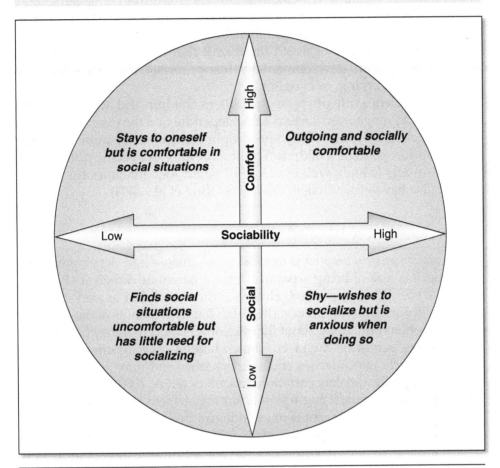

Source: Adapted from concepts in Beidel and Turner (2005).

Among children, common specific phobias are of animals, thunderstorms, darkness, and medical or dental procedures (King, Muris, & Ollendick, 2004). When evaluating children's fears, however, caution is advised because fears are so common among children. Normal fears, however, are not excessive, do not persist, and do not significantly impair functioning. The fears associated with specific phobia, on the other hand, are persistent, maladaptive, and cause much distress (King et al.). Unlike developmentally normal fears, specific phobia often persists for a period of years. Researchers following children with specific phobia for periods of two to five years have found between 20% and 40% met diagnostic criteria at the end of the follow-up period (Beidel & Turner, 2005). Symptoms must persist for six months to meet diagnostic criteria (APA, 2000).

Similar to social phobia, the specific feared stimulus elicits an immediate anxiety response in those with specific phobia. The anxiety involves three response systems: cognitive, physiological, and behavioral. In the cognitive domain, the response includes self-statements about being scared, about not being able to cope, and about the situation being personally harmful. The physiological response includes increased heart rate, sweating, and upset stomach. Behaviorally, children with specific phobia typically attempt to escape or avoid the fear. If that is not possible, children often respond with developmentally inappropriate fear behaviors like thumb sucking, crying, or clinging.

The prevalence rate of specific phobia in children and adolescents has been found to range from 2.6% to 4.5%, depending on the exact population studied (Beidel & Turner, 2005). Specific phobia tends to be more prevalent in girls and in younger children. The comorbidity of specific phobia with other disorders is high; well over half of youth seen in clinics for Specific phobia also have other anxiety disorders (King et al., 2004).

Separation Anxiety Disorder

Separation anxiety disorder is marked by an intense and developmentally inappropriate fear of being separated from a parent or caregiver (Beidel & Turner, 2005). When separated, children with separation anxiety disorder become very anxious and preoccupied with the whereabouts of the parent or caregiver, often ruminating about illnesses or accidents that may befall themselves or the parent or caregiver. These children may experience somatic symptoms such as headaches and stomachaches and may also experience sadness or apathy and concentration difficulties (APA, 2000). To be diagnosable, the symptoms must cause significant impairment and last at least four weeks; the latter requirement is to exclude children who display the kind of short-term separation problems that are within developmental expectations.

Separation anxiety disorder can have a significant impact on overall functioning. Children with the disorder may refuse to go to school or may attend with extreme reluctance and much distress. Expected attendance at camps or sleepovers can elicit a similar reaction. These children may also have trouble at bedtime and insist that someone stay with them until they fall asleep. Children with separation anxiety disorder often come from close-knit families and are often seen as excessively demanding and in need of constant attention (APA, 2000).

The peak age of onset for separation anxiety disorder is seven to nine (Beidel & Turner, 2005). While separation anxiety disorder is relatively common, with prevalence rates estimated at between 3% and 5%, it also has a high recovery rate (Beidel & Turner). There may be some ebb and flow to the symptoms, but well over half of children with separation anxiety disorder are free of anxiety disorders at long-term follow-up (Beidel & Turner). Two caveats, however, are necessary. First, for some children separation anxiety disorder is chronic and leads to significant negative life consequences (Silverman & Dick-Niederhauser, 2004). Second, comorbidity is common, with about half of children having a co-occurring anxiety disorder (Silverman & Dick-Niederhauser).

Finally, it is worth having a brief discussion about the relationship between separation anxiety disorder and school refusal. It is generally true that elementary-aged children who refuse to go to school (the old term for this was *school phobia*) are in fact expressing their anxiety at separating from their parents or caregivers. These children can give reasons why they do not want to go to school, such as being bullied or having a mean teacher. But these reasons tend to be red herrings, as the true dynamic is a fear of leaving their parents or caregivers. Nevertheless, while this is generally true, it is not *always* true. In fact, school refusal may be a symptom of separation anxiety disorder, but there are many other possible causes of school refusal, including specific phobias, disruptive behavior disorders, and family issues. It is also possible to have separation anxiety disorder without school refusal (Silverman & Dick-Niederhauser, 2004).

Posttraumatic Stress Disorder

Posttraumatic stress disorder (PTSD) is a complex disorder, as can be seen by its description in *DSM* (APA, 2000):

> The development of characteristic symptoms following exposure to an extreme traumatic stressor involving direct personal experience of an event that involves actual or threatened death or serious injury or other threat to one's physical integrity; or witnessing an event that involves death, injury, or a threat to the physical integrity of another person; or learning about unexpected or violent death, serious harm, or threat of death or injury experienced by a family member or other close associate. (p. 463)

In addition to exposure to life-threatening stressors, the individual's response must also involve intense fear, helplessness, or horror (in children, the response must involve disorganized or agitated behavior). PTSD also cannot be diagnosed until a month has passed since exposure to the stressor.

A broad array of events can serve as the traumatic stressor that elicits PTSD. Much of the original work in understanding what PTSD is and how it affects people was done with soldiers who had experienced traumatic military combat. But it is now well-known that anyone—certainly including children and adolescents—can experience life events that are sufficiently traumatic to lead to PTSD. Examples of these events include being physically assaulted, being in a severe automobile accident, experiencing a natural disaster, or being a victim of sexual abuse. In general, the most important factor in determining whether PTSD develops is the intensity and duration of the traumatic event, as well as the individual's proximity to the traumatic event (APA, 2000). In addition, the PTSD may be particularly severe if the trauma is inflicted by humans, as in the case of sexual or physical assault. Trauma inflicted by humans not only can cause physical and emotional wounds, but these events also can involve a devastating loss of trust in others.

It is important to note that traumatic events are not an infrequent occurrence among children and adolescents. One study, for example, found that approximately 40% of adolescents in a community sample experienced a significant traumatic event by age 18 (Gianconia et al., 1995). Immigrants from war-torn countries may be particularly likely to have been exposed to traumatic events. It is also important to note, however, that not every individual who experiences a traumatic event develops PTSD. Indeed, just a fraction of both children and adults who experience a trauma go on to have PTSD (Beidel & Turner, 2005; Gianconia et al.). It is unclear exactly what differentiates those who develop PTSD and those who do not, but preexisting anxiety or mental health problems and low social support may confer a vulnerability to PTSD. Regardless, it is clear that people's responses to traumatic events tend to involve recovery and resilience more often than psychopathology (Beidel & Turner). The actual prevalence of PTSD in children and adolescents is unclear (Beidel & Turner).

Individuals who do develop PTSD display a constellation of three main symptom domains: *reexperiencing, avoidance,* and *arousal* (APA, 2000). Reexperiencing can include intrusive thoughts, memories, and nightmares. In children, reexperiencing can take the form of traumatic play and repetitive behavioral reenactments of the traumatic event (McKnight, Compton, & March, 2004). Diagnostic acumen is required to judge whether play-based reenactments of the traumatic event represent a true PTSD symptom, as it is normal and healthy for children to work out their fears through play. When these reenactments become concerning is when they seem to be performed in a joyless and forced manner.

The second domain of symptoms, avoidance, can involve both a physical and a psychological element. The avoidance can involve avoiding thoughts or conversations about the trauma, avoiding physical reminders of the trauma, and being frightened of events that occurred before or during the trauma, such as yelling or alcohol use. It can also involve emotional numbing, which is a way of psychologically avoiding the trauma. The third symptom domain, arousal, can include irritability, hypervigilance, and difficulty concentrating. Children are often on alert for more traumatic events and may make a habit of scanning their surroundings in an attempt to stay safe (Beidel & Turner, 2005). Sleep problems are common.

The course of PTSD is variable. About half of adults with PTSD see symptoms recede within three months (APA, 2000). There is not sufficient research with youth to have a clear understanding of how PTSD develops, but it is known that PTSD among children and adolescents is associated with increased risk of a host of other anxiety disorders and mood disorders, as well as substance-abuse problems (APA).

Acute Stress Disorder

Acute stress disorder is closely related to PTSD; similar to PTSD, its essential feature is the development of anxiety (or dissociative) symptoms following exposure to an extremely traumatic event (APA, 2000). The key difference between the two disorders is the amount of time that has passed since exposure to the traumatic event. Recall that PTSD cannot be diagnosed in the first month after exposure to a traumatic stressor. It is during that first month that a diagnosis of acute stress disorder may be made. There is actually a very specific window of time in which acute stress disorder can be diagnosed. It cannot be diagnosed until two days after a trauma (since stress reactions are normal and expected in those first two days) and cannot exist longer than four weeks after the trauma. If anxiety symptoms persist for more than four weeks, PTSD may be considered.

Acute stress disorder is precipitated by the same kinds of traumas that precipitate PTSD. In addition to PTSD-like symptoms of reexperiencing, avoidance, and arousal, acute stress disorder also causes dissociative symptoms such as a sense of emotional numbing, absence of emotional reactions, and depersonalization. People with acute stress disorder may feel detached from their bodies and experience life as a dream state (APA, 2000). Helplessness and despair may also be present.

Given the close connection between acute stress disorder and PTSD, it is easy to assume that they are really just different names for the same thing, with one name being used early in the life of the disorder and the other name being used as the disorder progresses. But this may not be true. In fact, some research indicates that relatively few children who are diagnosed with acute stress disorder go on to have PTSD, and most children who have PTSD did not have a preceding diagnosis of acute stress disorder (Beidel & Turner, 2005).

Obsessive-Compulsive Disorder

As the name implies, *obsessive-compulsive disorder* (OCD) is a disorder in which the individual is plagued by persistent obsessions and compulsions. *Obsessions* are "persistent ideas, thoughts, impulses, or images that are experienced as intrusive and inappropriate and that cause marked anxiety or distress" (APA, 2000, p. 457). Typically, obsessions are experienced as being foreign to one's thought process; in other words, they are not thoughts that are welcome or are consciously chosen. The most common obsessions among adults are repetitive thoughts of contamination, repeated doubts about things like having left the oven on, a need to have things in a certain rigid order, aggressive impulses, or sexual imagery. These are not simply repetitive worries about real-life problems. In fact, *DSM* (APA) criteria dictate that the obsessions or compulsions (or both) consume more than one hour a day and cause significant impairment. Individuals with OCD often try to manage the obsessions by ignoring or suppressing them. Most people with OCD also try to manage the obsessions by performing some act to neutralize them, such as repeatedly checking the oven to make sure it is turned off. These behaviors are *compulsions.*

The formal *DSM* (APA, 2000) definition of compulsions is "repetitive behaviors (e.g., hand washing, ordering, checking) or mental acts (e.g., praying, counting, repeating words silently) the goal of which is to prevent or reduce anxiety or distress, not to provide pleasure or gratification" (p. 457). Compulsions can be viewed as rituals people with OCD use to alleviate their anxiety (Beidel & Turner, 2005). The compulsions are either clearly excessive (such as washing hands multiple times per hour in an attempt to rid them of germs) or not related in any realistic way to what they are intended to prevent (such as repeatedly counting to keep some sort of imagined danger at bay). There is a forced quality to these behaviors, and people feel driven to perform the behaviors even though they often realize the compulsions are excessive or unreasonable. OCD can be very disruptive to healthy functioning. The obsessions and compulsions can consume a tremendous amount of mental energy, leaving little left over for work or social tasks. In addition, people with OCD often avoid situations that provoke the symptoms, such as avoiding situations where they would have to shake hands or be around dirt, which further disrupts functioning.

It is worth mentioning that it is not necessarily problematic for children to display some obsessions and compulsions. Repeating thoughts and behaviors is a part of developing mastery, and most, if not all, children and adolescents will have periods where they exhibit what may look like obsessions and compulsions in the mastery process (March, Franklin, Leonard, & Foa, 2004). Developmentally normal obsessions and compulsions, however, have a different look, feel, and outcome than the obsessions and compulsions connected with OCD. The former do not seem dysfunctional or distressing and lead to mastery. The latter are performed with a sense of anxiety and lead to dysfunction rather than accomplishment. Indeed, OCD typically disrupts school, social, and vocational functioning (March et al.). The symptoms typically wax and wane, with more-severe symptoms generally being experienced during periods of greater life stress (APA, 2000).

OCD is a relatively rare disorder, with about 7 out of 1,000 children and adolescents estimated to experience OCD in the course of a year (APA, 2000). Nevertheless, it is also a disorder that is significantly undertreated. One study examined 18 children with OCD and found that only 4 were receiving treatment (March et al., 2004). Part of the reason for the lack of treatment might be the secretiveness that tends to surround the disorder; research suggests that, in approximately three-fourths of cases of childhood OCD, the parents are unaware of the OCD symptoms (Rapoport et al., 2000). Youth with OCD are almost always embarrassed by their symptoms, and because they do not wish others to be aware of their symptoms, they typically hide their obsessions and compulsions.

It is also important to be aware of the high degree of comorbidity seen with OCD. As many as 74% of youth with OCD may have another mental health disorder (Beidell & Turner, 2005), with tic disorders, other anxiety disorders, and Tourette disorder often being co-occurring disorders (APA, 2000; March et al., 2004). OCD is more prevalent in boys (APA).

Anxiety Disorder Not Otherwise Specified (NOS)

The diagnosis of *anxiety disorder NOS* is made when the individual displays significant anxiety symptoms but does not meet specific criteria for any of the other DSM anxiety disorders (APA, 2000). For example, it may be an appropriate diagnosis in cases where there is a mix of depressive and anxious symptoms but the person does not meet criteria for any mood or anxiety disorder.

Adjustment Disorder With Anxiety

As discussed in earlier chapters, adjustment disorders are emotional or behavioral problems, or both, that occur within three months of exposure to an identifiable stressor. One of the subtypes is *adjustment disorder with anxiety*, which is for individuals who are exposed to a significant stressor and respond with substantial anxiety symptoms. You may wonder how this differs from acute stress disorder and PTSD. The major difference is the severity of the stressor. With the latter two disorders, the precipitating event must be a major life-threatening trauma. In the case of adjustment disorder with anxiety, the stressor may be much less severe.

INTERVENTION GUIDELINES

As with virtually all mental health disorders, symptomatology in the anxiety domain can rise to the level of a diagnosable anxiety disorder but can also exist in the form of subclinical symptoms that are distressing but that do not meet criteria for a full disorder. In other words, even students without diagnosable anxiety disorders can have anxiety symptoms worth addressing. Many of the following guidelines are applicable to both diagnosable and lower-level anxiety problems. Some of the guidelines involve relatively advanced clinical techniques, so counselors should assess their own training and experience and use good judgment in deciding whether they have the competence to implement the guideline they are considering. If the severity or complexity of the anxiety disorder seems beyond the competence of the counselor, then a referral to a qualified mental health practitioner is in order.

INTERVENTION GUIDELINES FOR ANXIETY DISORDERS

1. Seek collaboration.

2. Teach relaxation.

3. For specific fears, try gentle exposure.

4. Work on cognitions.

5. Develop coping strategies.

6. Expect comorbidity.

Guideline 1: Seek Collaboration

The previous section of this chapter makes it clear that, while the multiple types of anxiety disorders are bound together by the common thread of anxiety, each disorder is also unique in important ways. Given the varieties and complexities of anxiety disorders, a prime intervention guideline for school counselors is to do whatever possible to help connect students and families with community mental health professionals who have experience and expertise working with childhood anxiety disorders.

Furthermore, pharmacological treatment is often a part of comprehensive treatment for anxiety disorders. In particular, consideration of the use of psychotropic medication has been recommended for older children and adolescents and for youth who have not responded to previous psychosocial interventions (Stein & Seedat, 2004). While school counselors should not be in the position of offering opinions about the use of medication in the treatment of anxiety, the reality is that a student with anxiety may be taking medication for the anxiety, and school counselors are wise to develop a working relationship with the prescribing physician (with parental consent to do so, of course). One specific way counselors can be of assistance is to coordinate observations from teachers and other school staff to determine whether the medication is helping and to relay any signs of side effects.

Guideline 2: Teach Relaxation

A major component of many forms of anxiety is a high state of arousal (Beidell & Turner, 2005). Consider your own experience. Think of times when you were completely physically relaxed—sitting in the warm sun on a beach, perhaps, or reading a book in front of a fire. Did you feel any anxiety during those times? And think about times you felt very anxious, such as before a public speaking function. Do you remember your muscles being tensed and your heart racing? Your answers to these questions probably illustrate a key point: Anxiety and deep physical relaxation are incompatible states. As people become more relaxed physically, their anxiety diminishes. To take advantage of this relationship, most intervention packages for anxiety prominently feature relaxation training as a component.

Relaxation training is typically conducted by means of progressive muscle relaxation, which is a technique of tensing and relaxing muscle groups in a systematic manner (Himle, Fischer, Van Etten Lee, & Muroff, 2006). Each muscle group, in turn, is moderately tensed for approximately 5 seconds, followed by 15 to 20 seconds of letting go of the tension. In the initial stages, students are led through the progressive muscle-relaxation procedure using a specific script. An excellent script for use with older children and adolescents is provided in Merrell's (2008) book *Helping Students Overcome Depression and Anxiety*. Throughout the procedure, students should be encouraged to notice the differences they feel in their body in the tensing phase versus the release phase, to help them identify the sensations that accompany a physically relaxed state (Himle et al.).

One goal of the technique is to help students become aware of when their bodies are tense and learn how to rapidly apply a relaxation procedure to relieve that tension. To this end, a three-stage process can be used to first introduce the relaxation technique and then fade its use as the student becomes able to independently initiate the relaxation response (Himle et al., 2006). The first stage is to introduce the muscle-relaxation technique via a script, and then have students practice the technique on a daily basis. After a week or two of daily practice, the students move to the second stage, which is dropping the tension part of the procedure and only practicing the relaxation component. Cuing, linked to breathing, is also added to this stage (Ost, 1987). As the student inhales, the counselor says "inhale," and as the student exhales, the counselor says "relax." After the student has mastered this breath-linked relaxation process, daily use of the technique is prescribed as homework for one or two weeks. The third stage is to teach the student to take several deep breaths, think "relax" before each exhale, and scan the body for tension to be released through the breath (Ost). This final stage should be practiced multiple times per day—and easily can, since it is simple and brief.

School counselors using relaxation training with students should bear in mind several important points. One is to use a clear, relaxed, calm voice (Merrell, 2008). In addition, the physical environment is important. The space should be comfortable (hard-backed desk chairs are not conducive to relaxation!) and as private as is possible. Finally, the script that is used should be appropriate to the developmental level of the students. An example of a relaxation script that is developmentally targeted at children is provided in Box 7.1.

BOX 7.1   RELAXATION SCRIPT FOR ELEMENTARY-AGED STUDENTS

Introduction

Today we're going to do some special exercises called *relaxation exercises*. These exercises help you learn how to relax when you're feeling worried and tense and help you get rid of those butterflies-in-your-stomach feelings. They're also kind of cool, because you can do some of them in the classroom without anybody even noticing.

In order for you to get the best feelings from these exercises, there are some rules you must follow. First, do exactly what I say, even if it seems kind of silly. Second, try hard to do what I say. Third, be sure to pay attention to your body. During these exercises, pay attention to how your muscles feel when they are tight and when they are loose and relaxed. And, fourth, you must practice. The more you practice, the more relaxed you can get. Does anyone have any questions?

Are you ready to begin? Okay, great. First, get as comfortable as you can in your chair. Sit back, get both feet on the floor, and just let your arms hang loose. That's fine. Now, close your eyes and don't open them until I say to. Remember to follow my instructions very carefully, try hard, and pay attention to your body. Here we go.

Hands and Arms

Pretend you have a whole lemon in your left hand. Now squeeze it hard. Try to squeeze all the juice out. Feel the tightness in your hand and arm as you squeeze. Now drop the lemon. Notice how your muscles feel when they are relaxed. Take another lemon and squeeze it. Try to squeeze this one harder than you did the first one. That's right. Really hard. Now, drop your lemon and relax. See how much better your hand and arm feel when they are relaxed. One more time, take a lemon in your left hand and squeeze all the juice out. Don't leave a single drop. Squeeze hard. Good. Now, relax and let the lemon fall from your hand. (Repeat the process for the right hand and arm.)

Arms and Shoulders

Pretend you are a furry, lazy cat. You want to stretch. Stretch your arms out in front of you. Raise them up high over your head. Way back. Feel the pull on your shoulders. Stretch higher. Now, just let your arms gently drop back to your side. Okay, kittens, let's stretch again. Pull them back, way back. Pull hard. Now let them drop. Good. Notice how your shoulders feel more relaxed. This time let's have a great big stretch. Try to touch the ceiling. Stretch your arms way out in front of you. Raise them way up high over your head. Push them way, way back. Notice the tension and pull in your arms and shoulders. Hold tight, now. Great. Let them drop quickly and feel how good it is to be relaxed. It feels good and warm and lazy.

Shoulder and Neck

Now, pretend you are a turtle. You're sitting out on a rock by a nice peaceful pond, just relaxing in the warm sun. It feels nice and warm and safe here. Uh-oh! You sense danger. Pull your head into your shell. Try to pull your shoulders up to your ears and push your head down into your shoulders. Hold it tight. It isn't easy to be a turtle in a shell. The danger is past now. You can come out into the warm sunshine, and once again, you can relax and feel the warm sunshine. Watch out now! More danger. Hurry, pull your head back into your shell and hold it tight. You have to be closed in tight to protect yourself. Okay, you can relax now. Bring your head out and let your shoulders relax. Notice how much better it feels to be relaxed than to be all tight. One more time now. Danger! Pull your head in. Push your shoulders way up to your ears and hold tight. Don't let even a tiny piece of your head show outside your shell. Hold it. Feel the tenseness in your neck and shoulders. Okay. You can come out now. It's safe again. Relax and feel comfortable in your safety. There's no more danger. Nothing to worry about. Nothing to be afraid of. You feel good.

Jaw

You have a giant jawbreaker bubble gum in your mouth. It's very hard to chew. Bite down on it. Hard! Let your neck muscles help you. Now relax. Just let your jaw hang loose. Notice how good it feels to just let your jaw drop. Okay, let's tackle that jawbreaker again now. Bite down. Hard! Try to squeeze it out between your teeth. That's good. You're really tearing that gum up. Now relax again. Just let your jaw drop off your face. It feels so good just to let go and not have to fight that bubble gum. Okay, one more time. We're really going to tear it up this time. Bite down. Hard as you can. Harder. Oh, you're really working hard. Good. Now relax. Try to relax your whole body. You've beaten the bubble gum. Let yourself go as loose as you can.

Face and Nose

Here comes a pesky old fly. He has landed on your nose. Try to get him off without using your hands. That's right, wrinkle up your nose. Make as many wrinkles in your nose as you can. Scrunch your nose up real hard. Good. You've chased him away. Now, you can relax your nose. Oops, here he comes back again. Right back in the middle of your nose. Wrinkle up your nose again. Shoo him off. Wrinkle it up hard. Hold it just as tight as you can. Okay, he flew away. You can relax your face. Notice that when you scrunch up your nose that your cheeks and your mouth and your forehead and your eyes all help you; they get tight, too. So when you relax your nose, your whole face relaxes too, and that feels good. Uh-oh. This time that old fly has come back, but this time he's on your forehead. Make lots of wrinkles. Try to catch him between all those wrinkles. Hold it tight, now. Okay, you can let go. He's gone for good. Now you can just relax. Let your face go smooth, no wrinkles anywhere. Your face feels nice and smooth and relaxed.

(Continued)

(Continued)

Stomach

Hey! Here comes a cute baby elephant. But he's not watching where he's going. He doesn't see you lying on your back in the grass, and he's about to step on your stomach. Don't move. You don't have time to get out of the way. Just get ready for him. Make your stomach very hard. Tighten up your stomach muscles really tight. Hold it. It looks like he is going the other way. You can relax now. Let your stomach go soft. Let it be as relaxed as you can. That feels so much better. Oops, he's coming this way again. Get ready. Tighten up your stomach. Really hard. If he steps on you when your stomach is hard, it won't hurt. Make your stomach into a rock. Okay, he's moving away again. You can relax now. Kind of settle down, get comfortable and relax. Notice the difference between a tight stomach and a relaxed one. That's how we want it to feel—nice and loose and relaxed. Uh-oh . . . this time the baby elephant is really coming your way and not turning around. He's headed straight for you. Tighten up. Tighten hard. Here he comes. This is really it. You've got to hold on tight. He's stepping on you. He's stepped over you. Now he's gone for good. You can relax completely. You're safe. Everything is okay, and you can feel nice and relaxed.

This time, imagine that you want to squeeze through a narrow fence and the boards have splinters on them. You'll have to make yourself very skinny if you're going to make it through. Suck your stomach in. Try to squeeze it up against your backbone. Try to be as skinny as you can. You've got to get through. Now relax. You don't have to be skinny now. Just relax and feel your stomach being warm and loose. Okay, let's try to get through that fence now. Squeeze up your stomach. Make sure it touches your backbone. Get it real small and tight. Get as skinny as you can. Hold tight now. You've got to squeeze through. You got through that skinny little fence and no splinters. You can relax now. Settle back and let your stomach come back out where it belongs. You can feel really good now.

Legs and Feet

Now, pretend that you are standing barefoot in a big, fat mud puddle. Squish your toes down deep into the mud. Try to get your feet down to the bottom of the mud puddle. You'll probably need your legs to help you push. Push down, spread your toes apart, and feel the mud squish up between your toes. Now, step out of the mud puddle. Relax your feet. Let your toes go loose and feel how nice that is. It feels good to be relaxed. Back into the mud puddle. Squish your toes down. Let your leg muscles help you push your feet down. Push your feet. Hard. Try to squeeze that mud puddle dry. Okay. Come back out now. Relax your feet, relax your legs, relax your toes. It feels so good to be relaxed. No tenseness anywhere. You feel kind of warm and tingly.

Conclusion

Stay as relaxed as you can. Let your whole body go limp and feel all your muscles relax. In a few minutes, I will ask you to open your eyes, and that will be the end of this session. As you go through the day, remember how good it feels to be relaxed. Sometimes you have to make yourself tighter before you can be relaxed, just as we did in these exercises. Practice these exercises every day to get more and more relaxed. A good time to practice is at night, after you have gone to bed and the lights are out and you won't be disturbed. It will help you get to sleep. Then, when you are a really good relaxer, you can help yourself relax here at school. Just remember the elephant, or the jaw-breaker, or the mud puddle, and you can do our exercises and nobody will know. Now, you are ready to go back to class feeling very relaxed. You've worked hard in here, and it feels good to work hard. Very slowly, now, open your eyes and wiggle your muscles around a little. You've done a great job. You're going to be a super relaxer.

Source: Adapted from Koeppen (1974, pp. 16–20).

While relaxation training is well suited to individual sessions, it can also be modified for use in counseling groups and even whole classrooms. Even students who will never experience an anxiety disorder can benefit from a tool to help them manage their normal fears and anxieties. Relaxation training is a nice option for students with ongoing generalized anxiety but is less helpful for students with very specific fears and phobias (Himle et al., 2006). Exposure strategies, as discussed in the next guideline, are generally better choices for these issues.

Guideline 3: For Specific Fears, Try Gentle Exposure

One of the major approaches to helping people conquer specific fears is to gradually expose them to the feared object or situation until they begin to feel less fearful (King, Heyne, & Ollendick, 2005). Most people use some variation of this approach to deal with their normal fears and anxieties, such as forcing themselves to board a plane when flying feels scary or pushing themselves to get up in front of others to speak when they are afraid of public speaking. Students with anxiety disorders or excessive fears, however, have not been successful in managing their anxieties and often have developed avoidance behaviors or other maladaptive responses to manage their feelings. For these students, a well-planned, systematic, graduated, gentle exposure to the feared situation or object may be a useful intervention.

Figure 7.4 Systematic Desensitization Steps

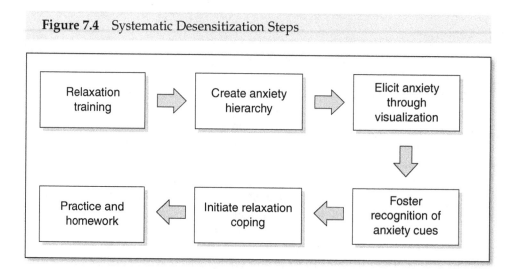

Perhaps the best known exposure technique is *systematic desensitization*. As illustrated in Figure 7.4, systematic desensitization involves a series of steps in which the anxiety associated with the specific feared object or situation is removed by employing relaxation techniques. The process of systematic desensitization consists of six steps or components. The first two steps lay the groundwork for the desensitization process. The first step is to teach the student how to relax using a technique such as progressive muscle relaxation. This is key—the process will not work unless the student is able to effectively relax. The second step is to create an anxiety hierarchy, which is a graduated list of anxiety-producing events or stimuli (see Box 7.2 for an example). With relaxation training complete and an anxiety hierarchy in hand, it is time to move to the third step, which is the actual desensitization process. This involves making sure the student is comfortable and then asking the youth to visualize being in the least anxiety-producing situation described in the anxiety hierarchy. For example, for a fear of spiders, this might be visualizing a spider in a covered jar sitting nearby. As the student visualizes this, anxiety will predictably arise. At this point, the counselor talks to the student about what bodily sensations are evident, in an attempt to help the student better recognize the bodily sensations that signal the presence of anxiety. Next, the counselor asks the student to employ relaxation techniques to calm the anxiety. The process of visualizing anxiety-producing scenes, then employing relaxation techniques to repel anxious feelings, is repeated as often as needed to get to the point where the student can visualize the scene without feeling anxiety or worry. Then, the process is repeated with the next step on the hierarchy. To be fully effective, regular practice and homework is necessary as a final step.

BOX 7.2   CONSTRUCTING ANXIETY HIERARCHIES

Listed is a sample anxiety hierarchy for a 10th-grade student we will call Tanishia who has severe test anxiety. Specifically, Tanishia experiences a racing heart, sweating, and feelings of panic as an important test looms. During the test itself, she feels intensely anxious and finds it virtually impossible to think clearly. Not surprisingly, her performance on tests is quite poor.

In constructing the anxiety hierarchy, the counselor talks with Tanishia about the progression of anxiety, asking Tanishia to describe the moment when anxiety for an upcoming test first appears, and then they talk in detail about how the anxiety builds leading up to the test. In collaboration with Tanishia, the counselor then lists a series of events leading up to the test that involve an escalating sense of anxiety, from the least anxiety-producing event to the most anxiety-producing event. The number of steps in the hierarchy is somewhat arbitrary, but younger children will have fewer steps than adolescents. If the counselor gets the sense that the anxiety is severe and will not be easily overcome, it is wise to include a greater number of steps, as this allows more relaxation work to be done. The anxiety hierarchy for Tanishia follows:

Step 1:   Tanishia walks into her math class and sees a note on the board that a major exam is scheduled in three days.

Step 2:   Tanishia's math teacher talks about the exam in the days leading up to test day.

Step 3:   Tanishia opens up her math book to study the night before the exam.

Step 4:   Tanishia rides the bus to school on the morning of the exam, thinking about the test.

Step 5:   Tanishia walks down the hall to her math class.

Step 6:   Tanishia enters her class, sits in her seat, and sees large block letters on the board saying *test today*.

Step 7:   Tanishia's teacher walks around the room, passing out the exam.

Step 8:   Tanishia begins working on the exam.

Step 9:   Several items into the exam, Tanishia reaches a problem she is not sure she knows the answer to.

Once the anxiety hierarchy is jointly constructed by the student and the school counselor, the counselor then begins sessions in which the student uses relaxation techniques to become deeply relaxed. The counselor asks the student to visualize the event depicted in the least anxiety-producing step in the hierarchy. As the anxiety level rises, the student is asked to use relaxation techniques to "relax away" the anxiety. Once relaxation is achieved, the counselor and student move to the next step on the hierarchy.

The process described above uses visualization to elicit the specific fears and anxieties. It is also possible to build in an in vivo component to the desensitization process. For example, when working with a student with test anxiety, a school counselor might want to have the student take an exam in the counselor's office and walk through the desensitization process using a real exam to elicit anxiety. A true in vivo training session would involve going to the setting where the fear exists, such as a classroom or a playground. While this has the advantage of treating the anxiety as it happens in the student's environment, there are issues of privacy to be considered—most adolescents, for example, would be uncomfortable having a school counselor shadow them in the lunchroom to work on social anxieties.

Guideline 4: Work on Cognitions

The previous guideline focused on addressing the physical arousal that tends to be associated with severe anxiety. Cases of significant anxiety, though, involve more than just physical arousal. They invariably also involve distorted or maladaptive thought processes or belief systems. Thus the basis of an intervention guideline focused on addressing cognitions.

There are some characteristic cognitions that tend to be held by students with high anxiety. One frequent cognition is unrealistic worry: "It will be *awful* if I fail." "If I don't get into Stanford, my life will be over." A related pattern of thinking is exaggerating the risks and dangers of life: "I'll definitely fail if I take Advanced English." "I'm sure the plane will crash if I get on it." These two related thought processes combine to lead anxious students to believe both that bad things will happen to them and that, when the bad things do happen, they will be truly calamitous. A final cognitive tendency is to have an excessive sense of self-consciousness: "Everyone noticed when I tripped walking up the steps, and now they all think I'm a dork."

The example of test anxiety used earlier offers a good illustration of the role of cognitions in anxiety. While severe test anxiety certainly includes physiological symptoms such as a racing heart and sweaty palms, it also includes distorted patterns of thinking. Students with test anxiety tend to have excessively high achievement goals, underestimate their ability to successfully meet those goals, and overestimate the degree of calamity that will befall them if they do not do well on the test. All of these beliefs and perceptions are amenable to examination and reflection in a counseling session. In some cases, it may be helpful to provide factual information to correct students' misperceptions. It might help a student who is convinced her grade point average will plummet if she does not get an A on the final exam to calculate how much her overall grade point average would change if she got a B instead of an A in the class. A student who believes he must get a 36 on the ACT to get into Stanford could benefit from hearing about the actual ACT scores of students who were admitted to Stanford.

The cognitive intervention strategies presented in Chapter 6 also can be useful with anxiety disorders. Identifying thinking errors, encouraging alternate interpretations, reviewing and rehearsing thoughts, and developing positive self-statements are all techniques that can be used with students with high anxiety.

Guideline 5: Develop Coping Strategies

This guideline encompasses many of the other intervention ideas we have already talked about in this chapter. Being able to mobilize a quick relaxation response is certainly a coping strategy, as is the use of positive self-statements in anxiety-producing situations. But it never hurts to have a comprehensive discussion about coping strategies with students plagued by anxiety. The value of having such a discussion is that it allows students with anxiety to talk out loud about what they fear and what they worry may happen to them in situations that frighten them. Sometimes just verbalizing the fear in the presence of an empathic listener can relieve anxiety. It also provides an opportunity to talk about coping strategies to use in feared situations.

Let's look at an example. Assume you are the school counselor for a seventh-grade student named Lizzy who has struggled with shyness and social phobia for much of her life. Her immediate problem is a presentation she needs to give in English class. Thinking of the presentation terrifies her. As you probe to discover exactly what it is about the presentation that is frightening to Lizzy, you find that she is most afraid of being completely unable to talk, either because her mouth becomes so dry that she is physically unable to talk or because she forgets everything she plans to say. At this point, the natural tendency of most adults would be to try to reassure Lizzy—trying to reason with her that the chances of either of these things happening are remote. While "reassurance therapy" may be effective with some children, for many students with anxiety this approach does not reassure, as they still worry about the feared event even if statistically there is a very small chance that event will become reality.

What is often more effective is to talk to anxious students about what they can do if the feared event *does* occur. In Lizzy's case, a coping plan might include asking her teacher if it is okay to have a water bottle with her during the presentation in case of dry mouth and preparing detailed notes to refer to if her mind goes blank.

It is possible, of course, to focus on coping strategies *and* to provide some reality-based reassurance. Useful phrases to accomplish this include "This seems very, very unlikely to happen, but if it ever does, let's talk about how you could manage it" and "This has never happened to a student in my 20 years of being a school counselor, but if it feels better to come up with a plan for dealing with it anyway, we can definitely do that."

Guideline 6: Expect Comorbidity

A clear theme running through the literature on all types of childhood mental health disorders is that, rather than striking individuals in isolation, mental disorders more typically come in bunches. This is very true for anxiety disorders. Students with one anxiety disorder are likely to experience one or more additional mental disorders over the course of their lives. For example, one large-scale study of high school students found that more than two-thirds of students with an anxiety disorder also had a past or current history of another mental disorder (Lewinsohn, Zinbarg, Seeley, Lewinsohn, & Sack, 1997).

School counselors who work with students with anxiety disorders should be aware of the likelihood that these students will also experience other disorders. This reality further supports the importance of developing individualized intervention packages rather than using cookie-cutter interventions matched to a certain disorder. One student with GAD may also be dealing with major depressive disorder, while another student who shares the GAD diagnosis may be depression free but may have a substance-abuse problem. Clearly, being aware of the potential for comorbidity and the importance of individualizing intervention approaches is critical.

SUMMARY POINTS

- Anxiety disorders are a family of disorders that include specific disorders such as generalized anxiety disorder, social phobia, and obsessive-compulsive disorder. The core feature of all anxiety disorders is excessive and often-debilitating anxiety.
- Between 10% and 20% of youth may experience an anxiety disorder at some point during their childhood and adolescence.
- When working with students with anxiety disorders, school counselors should seek to collaborate with mental health professionals and medical professionals.
- Anxiety cannot coexist with deep physical relaxation, so a good intervention for students with anxiety disorders is to teach them a relaxation procedure such as progressive muscle relaxation.
- Gentle exposure techniques such as systematic desensitization can assist students with specific fears.
- Address cognitions that contribute to anxiety, such as worrying excessively and exaggerating the risks and dangers of life.

8

Autism Spectrum Disorders

James's fifth-grade year has been very challenging. He struggles academically; while he is intellectually capable, his daily work is messy and often undone, and assignments that require planning and organization are very hard for him. James has the most trouble, though, with social relationships. His teacher describes him as being "different . . . not unpleasant or mean, but just different." James stays to himself, and when he does interact with peers, he tends to say and do things that come across as odd and inappropriate. Part of James's oddness is his strong interest in the Titanic. A number of adults at school have reported that James has cornered them and talked nonstop for well over 20 minutes about the Titanic. His social behavior has brought him to the point where his classmates either shun him or tease him.

Nicole, an eighth grader, has struggled throughout her school career with friendships and with school performance. She comes across as being friendly but socially awkward, and close observation of her social interactions shows that she talks only about things that interest her and does not respond to conversational topics brought up by others. Consequently, her peers tend to either humor her by listening to her monologues for a short period of time or, more typically, by staying away from her. Nicole's main area of interest is Barbie dolls, a topic about which she has a wealth of detailed facts. Yet she seems unaware that other girls her age have little interest in Barbie dolls. In addition to her social problems,

> *Nicole has a history at school of having angry outbursts during which she shouts, refuses to follow directions, and at times, flees the classroom. These outbursts seem to occur most often with substitute teachers or on days when the daily schedule is disrupted for some reason.*

The cases of James and Nicole are examples of *autism spectrum disorders,* or ASD. While both James and Nicole have mild cases, their cases still illustrate the pervasiveness of the social difficulties associated with ASD, as well as the potential impact of the disorder on school performance and behavior. ASD, particularly in its more-severe forms, can affect multiple areas of functioning and can limit both career choices and the ability to live independently. The students with ASD that most school counselors will be involved with, though, will have less-severe forms of the disorder and can function in regular education schools with proper support.

TYPES OF AUTISM SPECTRUM DISORDERS

It is easy to get confused with the various labels related to ASD. *Diagnostic and Statistical Manual of Mental Disorders* (*DSM,* APA, 2000) uses an alternate term, *pervasive developmental disorder* (PDD). This chapter is actually a departure from the previous chapters, where DSM terminology was used for the major disorders. In this chapter, I am electing to use the term *autism spectrum disorder,* as ASD is the term more commonly used in schools. As implied by the word *spectrum,* ASD refers to a family of disorders that share some common features. These disorders are portrayed in Figure 8.1. As a group, these disorders are described in *DSM* (APA, 2000), as being characterized by "severe and pervasive impairment in several areas of development: reciprocal social interaction skills, communication skills, or the presence of stereotyped behavior, interests, and activities" (p. 69). Clearly, the gravity of this description reflects the severe nature of the disorders.

While the term that will be used throughout this chapter will be *ASD,* implying a treatment of all five of the specific disorders subsumed under that umbrella term, I will use the term to primarily address just two of the disorders: *autistic disorder* and *Asperger disorder.* Two of the three other disorders in the ASD family, *Rett disorder* and *childhood disintegrative disorder,* are quite rare and involve the kind of impairment that typically means school support is provided by special education staff rather than school counselors. The last of the five disorders, *pervasive developmental disorder— not otherwise specified* (PDD-NOS), is a nonspecific diagnosis for children who display some PDD symptoms but do not meet full criteria for any of the other four disorders. In this next section, we'll examine the characteristics and defining features of the two most prominent disorders in the ASD family, autistic disorder and Asperger disorder.

Figure 8.1   Autism Spectrum Disorders (Also Called *Pervasive Developmental Disorders*)

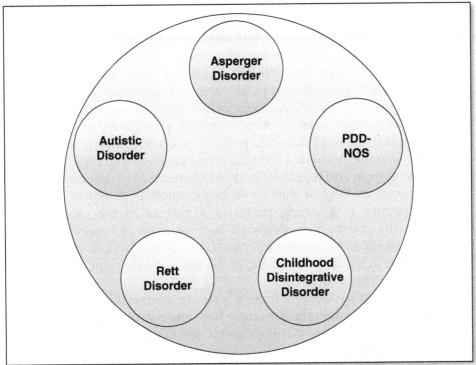

Autistic Disorder

Autistic disorder is relatively rare. According to *DSM* (APA, 2000), the estimated prevalence of autistic disorder is 5 per 10,000, though more-recent epidemiological studies suggest the rate may be as high as 19 per 10,000 (Chakrabarti & Frombonne, 2005). Mapping these prevalence rates onto a school of 1,000 students, we could predict that no more than two students at that school would have autistic disorder. The essential features of autistic disorder are "the presence of markedly abnormal or impaired development in social interaction and communication and a markedly restricted repertoire of activity and interests" (APA, 2000, p. 70). In contrast to disorders such as depression and anxiety that can be considered "hidden" disorders because people suffering from them usually do not appear different from others, individuals with autistic disorder tend to be immediately recognizable as being severely disabled. In the social domain, students with autistic disorder are characteristically unresponsive to social cues and typically do not respond to social overtures from others. Nonverbal behavior is a mystery to them. In more-severe cases, students seem completely unaware of the presence of other people; in less-severe cases, there may be an awareness of others but a lack of understanding of the needs and interests of others. They appear to be in their own world, with that inner world being inaccessible to others.

In addition to these deficits in social behavior, students with autistic disorder have significantly impaired communication skills. The level of impairment can range from total absence of spoken language to language that includes ample vocabulary but lacks social reciprocity and often is odd and idiosyncratic. Along with impairment of social and communication skills comes the other essential feature of autistic disorder, a significantly restricted and stereotypical range of activities and interests. Examples noted in *DSM* (APA, 2000) include being preoccupied with narrow interests such as dates or phone numbers, repetitively mimicking the actions of a television actor, taking precisely the same route to school each day, and becoming fascinated with movement such as a spinning wheel on a toy. Stereotypical and repetitive body movements may occur, such as finger flicking or rocking of the whole body. Another common feature of autistic disorder is a strong need for sameness in the environment. Students with autistic disorder may become very distressed by trivial changes in their environment such as a slight change in desk placement, a minor change in the daily schedule, or the use of a new color of marker on the classroom whiteboard.

It is important to note that there is a strong relationship between autistic disorder and mental retardation. In fact, one recent study of preschool children with pervasive developmental disorders found that 67% of children with autistic disorder also had mental retardation (Chakrabarti & Frombonne, 2005).

Developmental Course and Gender Considerations

DSM criteria specify that the onset of autistic disorder occurs before age 3. Over the course of childhood and adolescence, some developmental progress is generally evident, but significant impairment continues to exist in comparison to age-mates. In the social realm, individuals with autistic disorder may progress from near total social unawareness to being able to interact socially, though the nature of those interactions often remains unusual. Most individuals with autistic disorder, despite modest progress, never reach the point of being able to live independently; it has been estimated that only about a third of people with autistic disorder achieve a degree of independence as adults (APA, 2000). Autistic disorder is much more likely to be seen in males than in females (APA).

Asperger Disorder

There is professional debate about whether *Asperger disorder* is truly a distinct entity from autistic disorder or whether they can be considered to lie on a continuum of autistic behavior. If we agree with some recent evidence supporting the view that the two disorders exist on a continuum rather than as separate and unique conditions (Macintosh & Dissanayake, 2006), then Asperger disorder (also called *Asperger syndrome* by some experts) can be viewed as a milder version of autism that includes less-severe behaviors and less-debilitating outcomes than autistic disorder. According to *DSM* (APA, 2000), the essential features of Asperger disorder are "severe and sustained impairment in social interaction . . . and the development of restricted, repetitive patterns of behavior, interests, and activities" (p. 80). Similar to individuals with autistic disorder, children and adolescents with Asperger disorder struggle with social relationships and social skills. The exact nature of this struggle varies with each student. Some students with Asperger disorder may appear disinterested in any social interaction. Others may shun contact with classmates but seek out conversations with adults in the building, almost behaving as miniadults. Others may appear interested in connecting socially with peers but do so in an odd and one-sided manner, tending to speak in monologues and not understanding the reciprocal nature of appropriate social relationships.

The lack of reciprocity in social interaction that is characteristic of students with Asperger disorder is worth examining further. Particularly with students with mild cases of Asperger's, it sometimes takes awhile to appreciate the inappropriateness of the social behavior and the way it interferes with genuine friendships. It is like listening to a band where the drummer goes on an extended solo and refuses to stop—it can take some time to finally realize not only that none of the other band members are getting a chance to play but also that you are getting tired of listening to the drums. In the case of students with Asperger's, often adults are initially impressed and even charmed when listening to the student talk about a topic with passion and apparently strong knowledge. Peers are often keener judges of the appropriateness of the social behavior. They quickly realize that the student with Asperger's is neither displaying an interest in others nor talking about a topic that is very interesting.

This segues into the other essential feature of Asperger disorder, which is a restricted and repetitive pattern of interests and behaviors. Of course, it is normal for children and adults to have hobbies and areas of special interest. But students with Asperger disorder tend to have areas of interest that seem qualitatively different (i.e., eccentric or unusual) and developmentally off. Attwood (2007) gave the example of an eight-year-old girl who had a special interest in lawn mowers and spent her time reading lawn mower catalogues and talking in detail about lawn mowers. Of course, there is nothing wrong with being interested in lawn mowers—except that most other eight-year-olds don't share that interest, so talking about it at length will push others away instead of bring them closer. It is not just the unusualness of the area of interest that is different for students with Asperger's, but it is also the intensity of the focus on the area. Whether the interest is *Star Wars*, the *Titanic*, refrigerators, or evergreen trees, students with Asperger's tend to focus on their area of interest with such intensity that, while they amass many facts about the topic, they have little time remaining for other age-appropriate activities and interests (APA, 2000). Furthermore, the factual information gathered about the topic seems impressive, but a close examination typically shows that the student with Asperger's lacks the kind of deep understanding that can make a person truly expert in an interest area. For example, a high school student might be able to recite endless facts about Civil War battles but have no awareness of the larger cultural, social, political, and historical forces that served as a backdrop to the Civil War.

In addition to the core features of social impairments and restricted areas of interest, many students with Asperger disorder display other key characteristics. Movement and coordination is often immature (Attwood, 2007). Students with Asperger's can appear clumsy and poorly coordinated, lacking an age-appropriate fluidity when walking, running, throwing, and participating in games and sports. This makes it clear why participating in PE class and in team sports can be so challenging for these students, as they have the double whammy of struggling with both the social and the physical demands those activities entail. Students with Asperger disorder are also inclined to have pronounced preferences and sensitivities to various sensory experiences (Attwood). Most students with Asperger's have definite dislikes when it comes to food—due to both the taste and the texture of the food—and often have only a small range of foods they will eat. Tactile sensitivity is common. Students may be particularly sensitive to the feel and fit of clothes; things such as the labels on the inside of shirts can be experienced as very bothersome. Sensitivities to light and sound are often seen as well. Students with Asperger disorder often feel overwhelmed by loud noise and may be seen putting their hands over their ears in attempts to protect themselves from the noise. Some specific sounds, such as from garbage disposals or vacuum cleaners, can seem almost painful.

While there are a number of areas in which students with Asperger disorder struggle, it is important to also note an area where they usually do *not* have problems. Development in the cognitive and language domains is generally age appropriate. A main factor that distinguishes Asperger and autistic disorder is language development; by definition, the language skills of persons with autistic disorder are impaired. This is not to say that students with Asperger disorder have mastered all aspects of language at an age-appropriate level. Indeed, while their vocabulary can be extensive and their diction can be very precise, there are also typically unusual aspects of their language. Students with Asperger's may communicate in an overly formal manner, sometimes with a flat tone of voice. Initiating, maintaining, and ending conversations at an age-appropriate level is a challenge. It is almost as though they are reading a script and cannot deviate from the script even when the person they are conversing with isn't interested in the topic or tries to signal a change in the conversation. Following the natural back-and-forth flow of conversation is difficult for students with Asperger's.

Prevalence

DSM (APA, 2000) does not even hazard a guess about the prevalence rate of Asperger disorder, stating that definitive prevalence data are lacking. A recent study of over 26,000 children in the U.K. found a prevalence of Asperger's of 9.5 per 10,000, or an average of approximately 1 student in a school of 1,000 (Chakrabarti & Frombonne, 2005). Other experts suggest that DSM criteria for Asperger's may be overly restrictive and that, if more-liberal criteria are used, the prevalence rates increase to 36 to 48 children per 10,000, or about 3 to 5 students with Asperger disorder in a school of 1,000 (Attwood, 2007). It is also worth mentioning that different states have surprisingly different rates of identification of ASD. In fact, data from the 2008–2009 school year indicate that the number of public school eight-year-olds who were classified as ASD ranged from a high of 1 in 67 students (Minnesota) to 1 in 781 (Iowa), with a national average of 1 in 143 ("Autism State Rankings," 2010).

Gender Considerations and Developmental Course

Similar to autistic disorder, Asperger disorder is more likely to be seen in males, with boys at least five times as likely to have a diagnosis as girls are (APA, 2000). Asperger disorder is a lifelong condition, and individuals do not grow out of it. Nevertheless, the fit between the characteristics of the disorder and the surrounding environment, coupled with the way the individual adapts to the disorder, can make some degree of difference in how disabling the disorder is. For example, the tendency of children with Asperger's to use adultlike vocabulary and diction can make them seem odd in comparison with age-mates in elementary school, but as those children move into adulthood, their language style naturally stands out less. On the other hand, the impressive vocabulary of some children with Asperger's can mask their social difficulties and make adults less likely to fully recognize their social deficits (APA).

Some older children and adolescents with Asperger's can also begin to adapt to the disorder and figure out ways to minimize their social impairments. Students come to understand that, in order to learn social behavior, they must study it almost like a school subject. They tend to learn social behavior through an analytical thought process, painstakingly examining facial expressions, ways to initiate conversations, and so forth. It is almost as though they become anthropologists, studying the behavior of peers to figure out how to behave themselves. This does not happen in isolation; the efforts of teachers and families to work with students with Asperger's certainly contribute to their gains. Yet these gains come with great effort for students with Asperger's, and as the social skills of their peers become more sophisticated, it becomes increasingly more difficult to match the social fluency of peers. Furthermore, as adolescent students with Asperger's make gains in social awareness, they can become more aware of their social deficits and the way they do not fit in with their classmates, increasing the risk they will suffer from depression and discouragement.

The good news is that as adults many individuals with Asperger disorder are able to construct a life that fits them and the way they think and behave. Adults with Asperger's often choose careers that take advantage of their intense interest in a topic while minimizing social demands on them, such as a research scientist, a computer programmer, or a park ranger. Job promotions often pose a risk to occupational success for individuals with Asperger's, as they can involve less work of the kind that they find so fascinating and more of the kind of management and people work with which they struggle. Adults with Asperger disorder who are successful in management positions often have a good administrative assistant who can buffer some of the social and organizational demands of management (Attwood, 2007).

INTERVENTION GUIDELINES

The following guidelines are intended primarily for students at the milder end of the autism spectrum, given that these are the students most likely to be seen by school counselors. Students with more-severe cases of autism tend to receive service in either special programs or special schools and are well served by special education staff.

INTERVENTION GUIDELINES FOR STUDENTS WITH AUTISM SPECTRUM DISORDERS

1. Seek to understand rather than judge.
2. Provide intense and comprehensive social-skill instruction.
3. Make the daily school experience as clear and predictable as possible.
4. Help students with ASD manage stress and anxiety.
5. Teach to strengths.
6. Provide organizational assistance.
7. Support areas of special interest—to a point.
8. Protect students with ASD from bullying and teasing.

Guideline 1: Seek to Understand Rather Than Judge

Think about how you would feel if you went to a party and met a man who cornered you and talked incessantly about his favorite hobby, with no apparent interest in anything you had to say and no apparent awareness of the little signals you were sending that you wished to exit the conversation. And on top of that, he commented that the host of the party had gained weight and didn't look good. How would you feel? Frustrated? Annoyed . . . even angry? How would you describe him when talking later to your friends? Inconsiderate? Selfish? Boring? Insensitive? Chances are that you wouldn't have kind things to say about the man, and you wouldn't want to be near him again. If it was an older child or adolescent who displayed that behavior, you would certainly cut the youth some slack, but you would still likely feel irritated and see the child as being self-involved and rude.

This is the reaction students with ASD tend to elicit from peers and adults. They *are* self-involved. But rather than being reflective of a character flaw or an intentional disregard for the thoughts and feelings of others, the self-involvement is simply the way the minds of ASD children work. To expect them to naturally and easily consider the needs and desires of others is to expect them to do something they are not cognitively able to do. While children with ASD are self-focused, they are not selfish in the way we generally think of that word. And they can make socially insensitive comments, but not because they are intentionally hurtful or rude. Rather, they make socially inappropriate comments because they don't fully understand the rules that govern social conversation.

The first thing that school counselors and teachers can do, then, is to strive not to make negative judgments about students with ASD based on the students' lack of awareness of social rules and the needs and interests of others. Rather than judge the social behavior of students with ASD, we should seek to understand the behavior, and then teach the behavior we want to see. For example, rather than becoming irritated with a high school student with ASD who talks endlessly about trucks, understand that this reflects a lack of social awareness. Teach the student to limit speeches about trucks and to periodically ask a question of conversational partners.

Guideline 2: Provide Intense and Comprehensive Social-Skill Instruction

A strong focus on building social skills and awareness is a necessity for students with ASD in light of the significant social deficits that, by definition, accompany ASD. There is evidence that social-skill instruction of moderate duration and frequency has minimal impact on students with ASD (Bellini, Peters, Benner, & Hopf, 2007), which indicates that social-skill instruction should be intense and should permeate the students' school experiences.

There are a number of ways that social skills and social awareness can be fostered in students with ASD. But social-skill instruction should be carefully planned and provided with an awareness of the scope and sequence of social-skill development, since students with ASD may be lacking fundamental social skills that must be addressed before more-complex skills are taught (Myles, 2005). An example of a well-developed sequence of social skills for ASD students can be found in Baker's (2003) book *Social Skills Training for Children and Adolescents with Asperger Syndrome and Social Communication Problems.*

Social-skill instruction with students with ASD typically needs to address some very basic skills. This may include teaching students how to make appropriate eye contact, teaching the "rules" of play, and explicitly teaching which kind of facial expressions reflect various feelings. In addition, social-skill instruction should include the *rationale* for the skill being taught—why it is important, how to use the skill, and how the skill fits in with other skills the student already knows (Myles, 2005). Knowing why a skill is important deepens the learning of the skill. Some additional ideas for fostering the social skills of students with ASD follow:

- *Model and rehearse common social situations.* Modeling and rehearsal will be an integral part of formal social-skills classes or groups for students with ASD. But it is also possible to incorporate modeling and rehearsal in small counseling groups, in individual sessions, and even during classroom instruction. Many school counselors find that they are already doing considerable work with social skills in their practice. For example, school counselors are adept at conducting role plays, which are really a form of modeling and rehearsal. But an intentional focus on modeling and rehearsal of social skills can benefit students with ASD.
- *Use social stories.* Social stories are brief personalized narratives written specifically for a student with ASD to help the student learn appropriate social behavior in a certain situation. More information about social stories is provided in the accompanying text box.

SOCIAL STORIES

Social stories are brief, individually designed stories that are used to provide a specific and personal social-skill lesson to a student with ASD. Carol Gray, who has trademarked the phrase "Social Story" and has developed a set of procedures for writing the stories, has an informative website worth viewing (www.thegraycenter.org). According to Gray (2010), the goal of a social story is to share accurate social information in a reassuring manner easily understood by the audience.

Let's take the example of Lindsey, a sixth-grade student with ASD, to illustrate. Lindsey has been having a hard time socializing with her classmates at lunch. She talks a great deal about her fascination with hummingbirds and never displays interest in the conversational topics brought up by others at her table. Consequently, the other students either tease or ignore her.

In an attempt to address some of Lindsey's social-skill deficits that are contributing to this situation, her school counselor wrote the following social story:

At lunch, I like to talk to the other kids about hummingbirds. But I also want to listen to what they are talking about, since good friends listen to each other. So when I sit down at my table at lunch, I'll look at the other kids and listen to what they are talking about. I'll nod my head and try to think of a question I can ask about the thing they are talking about. That will make them feel good because they will know I am listening to them.

Social stories can be used to teach and reinforce a variety of social behaviors. While the effectiveness of social stories with students with ASD is equivocal, research does suggest that the stories are more effective when implemented correctly (Reynhout & Carter, 2009).

- *Use social scripts.* Social scripts are written or videotaped statements or phrases that students with ASD can use in social situations (Myles, 2005). The statements can be very simple: "Hi, can I sit here?" "I have to go, bye," or "Can you help me?" These need to be used prudently, as rigid overuse of scripts can lead the student to appear unnatural and robotic. But they can be helpful in providing students with a way to begin to communicate appropriately with others. Students can be taught different scripts for interacting with adults and with children—in fact, an important social skill is learning the difference between what is appropriate language with adults and what is appropriate language with children. Scripts aimed at conversations with peers should be written in child-friendly language (Myles).
- *Teach the student how to be a social observer.* A helpful technique for many students with ASD is to select a socially skilled peer to model, and then carefully observe how that peer behaves in social situations. If a student with ASD is having problems making friends, for example, the school counselor could ask that student to pick out a classmate who has many friends. The student could then watch how the classmate behaves around other students. Teaching students with ASD to be social observers can also help them handle new situations. For example, remind a student with ASD who is going to a professional baseball game for the first time, and is nervous about how to behave, to watch how other people nearby behave and do what they do.

- *Review the student's social behavior and talk about what could be done differently (and why).* Much like professional sports teams look at film of previous games to identify mistakes that can be corrected, students with ASD can review previous social situations to identify unsociable behaviors that can be replaced. Then, follow up with a discussion of what other behaviors they could have chosen that would have been more effective. Ideally, this review would cover a class or other time period that the school counselor observed, so both the student and the counselor could describe what happened. For example, the school counselor might observe the student during lunchtime and then that afternoon meet with the student and review the social behavior displayed. But social experiences that were not observed by the counselor can certainly also be reviewed during individual sessions.

- *Encourage selective participation in community and extracurricular groups.* Participation in community groups and extracurricular activities can be wonderful opportunities for social-skill development, but the social demands that come with participation can be overwhelming for students with ASD. School counselors, along with teachers and parents, should be thoughtful and prudent when deciding whether a particular group or activity is right for a student with ASD. In the sports domain, for example, a sport like basketball that requires fluid and spontaneous decision making may seem confusing and indecipherable for a student with ASD. On the other hand, a sport that involves careful planning and execution like golf or archery may work fine. In addition to the social, physical, and cognitive demands of the activity itself, it is important to consider how much adult support the student will have. It is always a good idea to consult with the adult in charge of the activity beforehand and discuss the needs and preferences of the student with ASD.

Guideline 3: Make the Daily School Experience as Clear and Predictable as Possible

Students with ASD hate ambiguity. Not knowing how they are supposed to behave in school is highly anxiety producing. Part of the reason for this is that students with ASD are not adept at figuring out what Myles (2005) called the "hidden curriculum," which is a set of rules and expectations in school that are not stated out loud but that everyone knows— except for students with ASD. Students are most comfortable and most successful when they know just what is expected of them. The following are some ideas for making their school experience as clear and predictable as possible. Most of these ideas are for the classroom; school counselors can work with teachers to implement them:

- *Be consistent.* As much as possible, all aspects of the daily class environment should be the same day after day. This includes the daily routine, the expectations of students, and the behavior of the teacher. It is particularly helpful to post class rules and a daily schedule. In addition, the physical environment of the room should also be well organized and predictable (Silverman & Weinfeld, 2007).
- *Signal upcoming transitions.* A brief mention should be made to students with ASD shortly before normal transitions such as the end of a class period or the end of the school day, so these transition points do not come as a surprise. It is particular helpful to attend to transitions when something out of the ordinary is happening during the day, such as a change in the normal schedule. In that case, it can be helpful for some students with ASD to meet briefly at the beginning of the day and go over the revised daily schedule, previewing what will happen.
- *Illuminate the hidden curriculum.* Think about all the unwritten rules that can exist in a classroom: *When the teacher stops talking and stands quietly, she expects the class to stop talking and listen. When the teacher raises his voice and gets red in the face, he is angry. It is okay to hand in homework a day late but not more than a day late. It is not okay to say out loud that someone is wearing an ugly shirt.* That is a lot to learn! Students with age-appropriate levels of social awareness can have trouble with the hidden curriculum; students with ASD find it confusing and distressing. One thing school counselors can do to minimize the confusion created by the hidden curriculum is to work with teachers to be more explicit in expressing their expectations and corrections. For example, most teachers have a "look" they give when they are upset with the class. A suggestion could be to accompany the look with clear and explicit words about the class behavior they are bothered by and what they would like the class to do differently. School counselors can also work individually with students with ASD to examine the hidden curriculum and better understand it.
- *Make adult language clear and simple.* Students with ASD often take language literally and have trouble deciphering figures of speech and metaphors (Silverman & Weinfeld, 2007). Accordingly, school counselors and teachers should strive to use clear and descriptive language and minimize the use of metaphors and figures of speech—or explain what they mean. For example, one of my favorite elementary school teachers had a habit of responding to incorrect student answers by saying, "Swing and a miss!" As much as the class enjoyed the teacher's style, this is just the kind of expression that would be baffling to many students with ASD and would need explanation. Adults working with students with ASD should also be aware that attempts at humor may not always be understood. In particular, sarcasm should be avoided.

Guideline 4: Help Students With ASD Manage Stress and Anxiety

It is stressful and scary to constantly be in a social world that seems unpredictable and indecipherable. Students with ASD are prone to feelings of anxiety and can benefit from efforts to help them manage their stress and anxiety. The first step in this process is to teach students how to identify their own feelings. It often helps to explore the physical sensations that may signal the presence of different feelings. A school counselor might help a student discover, for example, that a tight feeling in the stomach signals nervous.

School counselors can also help students with ASD develop strategies to manage stressful feelings. Calming techniques might include using a rocking chair in a corner of the classroom, doing some deep breathing, or putting on a weighted vest (Silverman & Weinfeld, 2007). It can be helpful to create a "home base" that feels safe (Myles & Hubbard, 2005). During times of stress, going to the home base can serve as a calming strategy. The strategies that are developed can be put on a laminated index card that can be kept on the student's desk. Finally, the school counselor can work with teachers to identify signs of stress and overstimulation that a student with ASD may display in the classroom. Once these signs are identified, teachers can then intervene as soon as the signs are shown and encourage the student to use the calming techniques or to go to a home base (Silverman & Weinfeld).

Guideline 5: Teach to Strengths

While it is critical to address the social deficits of students with ASD, it is also important to focus on and teach to their strengths (Silverman & Weinfeld, 2007). Students with ASD often have a strong fund of knowledge, a good to excellent vocabulary, a desire to learn and share what they know, and strong reading decoding skills. Teachers can capitalize on these skills to help students connect with the curriculum and feel successful. For example, a student who is in a cooperative learning group might be given the unofficial role of being the group fact checker. In addition to the benefit of using strengths to better access the curriculum, a focus on strengths also helps students with ASD feel like valued members of the class community (Silverman & Weinfeld).

Guideline 6: Provide Organizational Assistance

Alert readers will notice that this exact guideline was offered in Chapter 5 for students with ADHD. Indeed, poor organizational skills are characteristic of students with several types of mental health problems, including ASD. The strategies presented in Chapter 5, which included using an assignment notebook, trying color-coded folders, having a study buddy, and having an adult assigned to periodically help with locker and desk cleanups, are also very useful for students with ASD. It can be particularly useful to help students break large assignments into component parts, as they tend to get overwhelmed by big assignments.

Guideline 7: Support Areas of Special Interest—to a Point

One dilemma faced by teachers who have students with ASD is how much to allow those students to focus on their special area of interest. Many students would spend most of the school day reading or drawing or talking about their area of interest if they were allowed to do so. A balance needs to be struck between communicating respect for the special interest on the one hand and communicating the expectation that other work also needs to be done on the other hand (Silverman & Weinfeld, 2007). One way to strike that balance is to provide a specific, and limited, time of the school day when the student can focus on the special interest. The special interest may also be used as a bridge to other topics ("Max, do any of the characters in this book resemble the kind of hero that Luke Skywalker was in *Star Wars*?"), as well as a vehicle for connecting socially with other students ("Anne, did you know that Evan knows a lot about satellites? I bet if you two sat next to each other at lunch you would have a good conversation about that."). In many cases, the special interest can be used as a reinforcer, for example, allowing a student with ASD to read a book related to a special interest during the last 15 minutes of school if work is done. Finally, it is a good idea for teachers and school counselors to always be thinking about ways that the special interest might relate to a career area and pursue any possible connections.

Guideline 8: Protect Students With ASD From Bullying and Teasing

This final guideline is a reminder for educators that students with ASD come across to peers as being different and odd, thereby becoming natural targets for bullying and teasing. It is the school's responsibility to keep students with ASD safe and protect them from bullying. All adults in the school need to be vigilant in watching for episodes of bullying and intervening swiftly when that happens. In addition, school counselors might consider developing disability awareness lessons to present as part of the developmental guidance program. These lessons could include segments where all students are educated about ASD, focusing particularly on acceptance of students with ASD and how to be a friend to them. The choice of whether to deliver lessons like this should be made carefully, though, based on a judgment about how receptive the class would be to the lesson. Obviously, the lesson should not be presented if there is a risk that it could further stigmatize students with ASD.

SUMMARY POINTS

- Autism spectrum disorders (ASDs), which include autistic disorder and Asperger disorder, have as their core feature pervasive impairment of social interaction skills and the presence of stereotyped behavior, interests, and activities.
- The stereotyped interests of students with ASD are typically eccentric and are not the kinds of interests that appeal to their peers.
- A natural tendency is to view the behavior of students with ASD as being selfish and rude, but teachers and counselors should understand that self-involved behavior is a manifestation of the disorder.
- The primary intervention for students with ASD is to provide intense and comprehensive social-skills instruction through techniques such as modeling and rehearsal of social behavior and the use of social stories.
- Students with ASD benefit when their daily school experience is as clear and predictable as possible.
- Provide students with ASD with organization assistance.
- It is important for the adults at school to protect students with ASD from bullying and teasing.

9

Communicating With Teachers and Families About Students' Mental Health Needs

$\mathbf{E}$ffective school counselors realize the critical importance of communicating clearly and frequently with teachers and parents and are adept at doing just that. Indeed, communicating, collaborating, and consulting are key functions of school counselors. School counselors are wise to view themselves as members in a partnership with teachers and families (and students!), with the shared goal of fostering student achievement and adjustment. Counselors, teachers, and parents[1] working together can be a formidable positive force in students' lives.

These partnerships, however, are easier to write about in a book than they are to create and maintain in real life. Classroom teachers are faced with large numbers of students, increasing demands for accountability and high student-test scores, and the need to educate students with increasingly complex social and mental health problems. Because of these

---

[1]Throughout this chapter I have elected to use the term *parents* rather than the cumbersome *parents/guardians* simply to facilitate concise writing. This should not obscure the fact that many students live with non-parental adult guardians.

multiple factors, even well-intentioned teachers may not be inclined to give up more of their time to engage in a collaborative process with the school counselor. Creating partnerships with parents is also challenging. Almost 20 years ago, Lombana (1983), reflecting on the state of home-school communication, wrote, "the two institutions that most influence the growth and development of young people—the home and the school—are generally at odds with each other. At best, parents and school personnel conduct an uneasy and superficial alliance" (p. 2). This statement still rings true. Some parents, due to their own negative experiences when attending school, may fear and resist communicating with teachers. Teachers, on the other hand, may hold the view that the reason students misbehave and have other problems is because parents are not doing their job—and perhaps also because the parents share some of the negative behavior traits exhibited by their children (Seligman, 2000). These dynamics are clearly not conducive to positive, honest, trusting communication.

In addition to the challenges inherently faced by school counselors who wish to communicate and partner with teachers and parents, the presence of mental health problems adds another significant layer of challenge. From the preceding chapters, it is clear that mental health problems impact large numbers of children and adolescents and that these problems can disrupt school functioning, hinder peer relationships, and cause discouragement and pain for both the students and their families. The complexity and intractability of many mental health problems adds substantial stress to the affected students, teachers, and families and can make communication among all parties even more difficult. At the same time, though, these challenges must not deter school counselors from doing whatever possible to foster quality communication with teachers and families, since the magnitude of the challenge is even more reason why the power of an integrated counselor-teacher-parent team is so necessary.

BARRIERS AND OPPORTUNITIES

While the basics of clear and respectful communication are the same regardless of whether counselors are communicating with teachers or parents, each group of stakeholders has its own unique set of circumstances that serve to facilitate communication in some ways and hinder communication in other ways. Among the unique circumstances that facilitate communication between school counselors and teachers is that they are both conversant in the "language of school" and are both generally aware of the areas of freedom and areas of limitation associated with each respective position. For example, counselors understand that teachers have high numbers of students and cannot be expected to implement interventions that require massive amounts of time and individual student attention. Likewise, teachers tend to understand that school counselors have large caseloads that preclude long-term, individual counseling with numbers of students. There are, of course, exceptions to the rule: school counselors who are not fully aware of the myriad demands faced by classroom teachers and classroom teachers who have the fanciful notion that school counselors are swimming in free time. But teachers and school counselors certainly have fewer misconceptions about their counterparts' jobs than are held by parents or the general public.

As nice as it can be for school counselors to communicate with fellow school professionals who understand the school environment and have much experience with youth, there are also some factors that can serve as barriers to good counselor-teacher communication. One factor is that teachers can, understandably, become overwhelmed by the high numbers of students and student needs, and become more focused on finding ways to have difficult students removed from their classes than on looking at ways to intervene with problem behaviors. In addition, teachers may hold the belief that they are the unquestioned leaders of their classrooms (Epstein & Sanders, 2006) and resist efforts of others that they perceive might question that leadership. Finally, because teachers may see the behavioral manifestations of mental health problems but not the full picture of symptoms and emotional struggles—such as seeing the irritability and lack of work production of a student with dysthymic disorder without seeing the depressed mood—they may have trouble understanding why they should not take a hard-line approach with the student.

School counselors also face unique challenges and opportunities when communicating with parents about students' mental health issues. Some of the challenges, such as possible language barriers and the sense of confusion and mistrust some parents may feel when they hear one version of how school is going from their child and a very different version from school staff, have nothing to do with the mental health component. The presence of mental health issues can both exacerbate these communication barriers and add additional challenges. For one, dealing with a child's mental health problems can be emotionally overwhelming and physically exhausting for parents, leaving them with neither the time nor the emotional resources to effectively communicate with the school. Furthermore, given the genetic link and familial contribution to some mental health disorders, it is possible that parents of students with mental health disorders have their own mental health concerns, perhaps as well as a history of negative school experiences. It is also possible that parents of students with mental health problems are involved with mental health professionals and systems outside the school that may be providing intervention messages that conflict with similar messages from the school.

While significant communication barriers can exist between school counselors and parents of children with mental health problems, there are factors that contribute to unique opportunities for forging trusting and open lines of communication. One such factor is that parents of children with mental health problems are often desperate for help. These parents have often received liberal doses of parenting advice from friends, family members, and even other professionals, much of which may have come in the form of "get tough" messages or simplistic, cookie-cutter parenting strategies. While parents may be leery of receiving more unhelpful or even blaming advice from school counselors, once they realize that the counselor will not judge, is an expert on problem solving, and can serve as an excellent liaison with teachers and administrators, they may begin to see the counselor as one of their biggest allies.

GUIDELINES FOR COMMUNICATING WITH TEACHERS AND PARENTS

Communication with teachers and parents regarding children's mental health issues can involve difficult and emotion-laden conversations. While the dialogue can be challenging, being willing to have the discussion can be critical to developing a team approach that can ultimately enhance the welfare of students with mental health problems. The following guidelines are provided to assist school counselors as they engage in these critical conversations.

GUIDELINES FOR COMMUNICATING WITH TEACHERS AND PARENTS

1. Listen and empathize.
2. Give the message that unique children need unique interventions.
3. Avoid premature reassurance.
4. Provide realistic hope.
5. Don't overwhelm parents in team meetings.
6. Share difficult news with care.
7. Follow up after important communications or meetings.

Guideline 1: Listen and Empathize

The importance of listening is not a new concept for school counselors. Listening as a core counseling skill is emphasized at every level of training and should be second nature to practicing school counselors. Nonetheless, this chapter would not be complete without emphasizing the need for focused and skilled listening when communicating with teachers and parents about students' mental health problems. Being the teacher or parent of a child with mental health problems can be extraordinarily difficult, and providing teachers and parents with an opportunity to share their stories and stresses in an atmosphere of nonjudgmental listening can be therapeutic in its own right.

The best kind of listening is empathic listening. There are two components of empathic listening, each of which is equally necessary. The first component is listening well enough to understand the experience of the teachers or parents from their point of view—being able to see the world through their eyes and understand, as much as possible, what it would be like to be in their shoes. This is more than just listening to the words that are spoken. It is also listening to the nonverbal messages that are being sent and "hearing" what is *not* being said. In all, this involves gaining a deep understanding of what the person is going through. The second component of empathic listening is to communicate this understanding back to the teacher or parent. By doing this, you let the teacher or parents know you have listened to them and understand what they are experiencing. Let's look at two examples of statements to emphasize this point:

Statement 1: It sure sounds like you have been through the wringer. I'm sorry to hear that.

Statement 2: You feel sad and hopeless because you fear your son's life will be limited because of his mental health problems, and you are angry with the school because no one seems to understand how serious your son's problems are.

The first statement reflects average listening—surface-level listening that is better than nothing but doesn't communicate true empathy. The second statement reflects a much deeper understanding of the parent's perspective and would likely lead the parent to feel much more understood.

Another important aspect of effective listening is to listen for unused opportunities and strengths (Egan, 2010). It is easy for teachers and parents to become overwhelmed with the number and severity of problems experienced by children with mental health problems. School counselors can help by listening for strengths or underused resources that the teachers and parents may not even be aware of. For example, a teacher might talk about the excellent drawing skills of a student with oppositional defiant disorder and could benefit from a suggestion to use free time for drawing as a reward for work completion. A parent might talk about the strong relationship between her child and the child's grandfather and could benefit from a suggestion to try to increase the amount of involvement the grandfather has with the child.

Guideline 2: Give the Message That Unique Children Need Unique Interventions

A tendency seen with some teachers is to assume that intervention methods that work with most students should work for all students. If a stern approach and taking away privileges for misbehavior is an effective behavior-management approach for most students, why shouldn't it work with all students? It is easy to understand this reasoning. After all, if a tried-and-true approach works 95% of the time, does it make sense to try anything else? The answer, of course, is yes. If the current approach in the classroom is not working, then trying something new is both reasonable and necessary. So the challenge is persuading reluctant teachers to try a new approach for students whose mental health problems prevent the standard intervention strategies from working.

One way to help teachers see the value of new and unique intervention approaches is to emphasize that the mental health needs of the student are unique and require an equally unique approach on the part of the teacher. The counselor can support the teacher by emphasizing that the teacher's typical intervention approach is fine for most students and should be retained—but just not for the student with mental health problems who is not responding to the approach.

Emphasizing the unique behavior-management requirements of children with mental health problems can also be a valuable technique with parents. It is a particularly appropriate strategy for parents who have older children who are not experiencing the kinds of difficulties that the child with mental health problems is experiencing. It is natural for parents to become frustrated and discouraged if the parenting strategies they used effectively with older children do not work with the younger child. Counselors can validate the parents' overall competence while also helping them see that the unique needs of the child with mental health problems necessitate a different parenting approach.

Guideline 3: Avoid Premature Reassurance

Conversations with parents of students with mental health problems can be emotionally wrenching, as the parents struggle with feelings of sadness, anger, blame, pain, and guilt surrounding the problems their child is having. These conversations, understandably, pull at counselors' desire to help people feel better and to take away people's pain. And that is as it should be. The problem that this may create, though, is that it may lead school counselors to offer false and premature reassurance, which has the opposite of the intended effect. Premature reassurance does not reassure.

Here are two examples of statements a school counselor could make after two parents talk about the problems they are having with a daughter who has recently been diagnosed with bipolar disorder:

Statement 1:   I'm sure this is not as bad as you think. We just need to think positively about this.

Statement 2:   I can tell from the looks on your faces that it feels scary and distressing to think about what this may mean for your daughter.

The first statement is premature reassurance. This response would likely lead the parents to question not only the counselor's understanding of the situation but also the credibility and helpfulness of the counselor. The second statement is not one of reassurance, but it demonstrates to the parents that the counselor heard both their words and the feelings underlying the words. This sets the stage for an effective working relationship between the counselor and the parents.

Guideline 4: Provide Realistic Hope

While it is important not to give premature reassurance, it is also important to provide parents and teachers with realistic hope. Indeed, one of the complaints parents have when faced with situations where they must receive troubling information from professionals about their child is that the professionals do not present the difficult news in a manner that provides hope for the future (Cottrell & Summers, 1990). Providing hope does not mean sugarcoating the truth or ignoring reality. Rather, it means not only acknowledging the present concerns in a realistic manner but also highlighting areas of strength and providing helpful strategies for dealing with the problem areas. Even in very difficult situations, there are some hopeful aspects. For example, in a case where a student has recently received a diagnosis of Asperger disorder, the parents might find it hopeful to be reminded that now at least they know what they are dealing with and can connect with other parents who have children with the same disorder. It can also help foster a sense of hopefulness to emphasize to parents and teachers that they are not alone in having to deal with the student; now there is a team of professionals who can help. Using unifying language (*we, us, together*) in conversations with parents and teachers can help in this regard (Ramsey, 2002).

Guideline 5: Don't Overwhelm Parents in Team Meetings

Convening face-to-face meetings where parents, teachers, school counselors, and other involved parties can get together and talk directly about how best to create a positive school plan for students with mental health problems can be one of the most powerful and effective interventions possible. But these meetings can also be terribly stressful and discouraging to parents, and it is easy for parents to feel ganged up on and overwhelmed by the school personnel at the meeting. Luckily there are a few specific guidelines that can help team meetings feel much less overwhelming for parents.

First, it is important to attend to the physical environment in which the meeting will take place. The physical environment should provide both comfort and privacy (Fallowfield, 1993), with tissues discreetly available. If the meeting will take place around a rectangular table, it is helpful to avoid a seating arrangement where parents are on one side of the table and a number of professionals are on the other side. This arrangement visibly reinforces an us-against-them feeling and can feel isolating to some parents. The school counselor can modify this arrangement by choosing to sit across a corner of the table from the parents. In addition to attending to the physical arrangements, it is also important to schedule sufficient time for the meeting (Fallowfield). Parents should be given ample opportunity to ask questions (Sloper & Turner, 1993) and should not feel unnecessarily rushed or pressured due to time constraints.

In general, the fewer the number of school personnel at a team meeting with parents the better. This is particularly important if there has been a tenuous relationship between home and school. The reason for having fewer school professionals at the meeting, of course, is to avoid having parents feel ganged up on and outnumbered. In most cases, for example, an entire grade-level team of teachers need not attend; rather, having a representative from the team is usually sufficient. There may be cases where an entire grade-level team should attend, as would be the case if all members of the team have unique information about the student or will have the student in class. But if possible, fewer is better. It is also important for parents' comfort level to make sure all the participants attending the meeting introduce themselves and state their relationship to the child (Fallowfield, 1993).

Guideline 6: Share Difficult News With Care

A stressful and unfortunate part of communicating with parents about children with mental health problems occurs on occasions when school counselors or other school professionals must deliver difficult and troubling news to the parents. Whether it involves telling parents that their child is being referred for a special education evaluation, or is being suspended for fighting, or is becoming increasingly socially isolated, there are times when school professionals must share information with parents that may be profoundly troubling. Indeed, hearing difficult news about their children can result in both emotional and physical distress for parents (Heiman, 2002). The difficult nature of the communications can lead to behaviors and reactions in both the school professionals and the parents that impede productive communication and make it more difficult for parents to deal with the news in a proactive manner (Auger, 2006). This makes it imperative that difficult news be shared with care.

Fortunately, there are a number of ways that school professionals can conduct these difficult conversations that enhance parents' ability to hear the news and make sense of what they are hearing (Buckman, 1992). It is helpful to think of these conversations as consisting of three parts (see Figure 9.1). The first part is asking parents to share their perceptions of how school is going for their child and whether they have concerns about the meeting itself. Questions such as "Have you had any concerns about your son's academic performance?" and "Are you worried

Figure 9.1   Process for Sharing Difficult Information With Parents

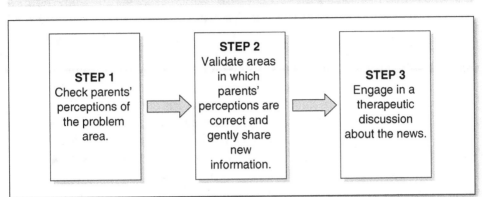

about what you may hear today?" can elicit parents' perceptions. This is helpful because it provides a sense of how differently parents and the school see the problem area; if there is a large discrepancy, it will be even more important to share information with care, as it will likely feel more distressing to the parents.

The second part of the process is validating the elements of the parents' perceptions that are accurate and then gently sharing any new information that differs from the parents' perceptions. An affirming and clarifying statement might be offered at this stage: "You are right in saying that your son is just like other boys his age in many respects. But we are seeing some areas where his development does appear out of the ordinary."

There are a number of specific strategies that can be helpful when actually delivering the troubling news. Recipients of difficult news may fail to retain as much as half of what they hear, so it is important both to avoid giving too much information at one time and to frequently check parents' understanding of the information. Accordingly, the information is best provided in chunks (Buckman, 1992) and followed by minisummaries ("I know I've been throwing a lot of information at you, so let me summarize some of the main points . . ."). It can also be helpful to periodically ask parents if they can share what they have heard the main points to be ("Just to make sure I'm being clear, would you be willing to tell me the main points that you've understood from what I've said?"). While difficult news is best offered in a respectful and gentle manner, it is also important to be direct and honest (Sloper & Turner, 1993). Parents tend to feel angry and frustrated when they sense that school personnel are withholding information and using polite but evasive language (Lawrence-Lightfoot, 2003). A final reminder for the information-providing stage is to avoid educational or mental health jargon. Words or acronyms such as *EBD, RTI, FBA, LRE, self-contained, NCLB, para, meds, ADHD, Ritalin, case manager,* or *resource room* may be part of the everyday vocabulary of school professionals, but they may be foreign to parents.

After the troubling information is shared with parents, it is time for the third and final stage of the process, which is engaging parents in a therapeutic dialogue about the information. This stage includes identifying areas of agreement between parents and school personnel, open discussion of areas of disagreement, joint problem solving and development of any needed intervention steps, and provision of resources to the parents. Perhaps what is most important, though, is helping parents process the emotions arising from what they have heard. Parents will display a wide range of reactions when hearing difficult news about their child. It is important to give parents much latitude in how they express their emotions (Buckman, 1992). This is a time to listen and empathize rather than to judge whether parents are responding in the "correct" manner. Occasionally, parents may not respond and may almost appear to be in shock from what they have heard. This is an understandable reaction to distressing news and is best treated with patience and empathy: "This must be overwhelming for you. I'll just let you process this for a minute or two, and then we'll go over the main findings once more to make sure you are clear about them."

Clearly, the manner in which school professionals share difficult news with parents is extremely important. It is worth remembering that the way the information is presented, and the manner in which parents feel treated and listened to by the school participants, not only impacts how well parents can hear and process the information but also affects the tone of future communications.

Guideline 7: Follow Up After
Important Communications or Meetings

It is typical for parents and teachers to have questions and concerns after important meetings or conferences. This is even more likely after a difficult meeting or conference where emotions were running high. It is common, for example, for parents to realize that they heard something about a math score, or a behavior incident, but be unable to remember any of the specifics. It is also common for parents to wish either that they had said things they didn't in the meeting or that they had *not* said some things they did.

Rumination after important meetings or conferences is the rule. School counselors can be instrumental in helping parents with these ruminations and memory lapses by making contact following meetings and conferences. Even a quick phone call or e-mail affords parents a chance to have questions answered and also provides them someone to process the meeting with. In addition, these contacts are great relationship builders.

In addition to getting into the habit of making follow-up contact with parents, school counselors are wise to make a habit of making similar contact with teachers. These contacts serve a number of purposes, including providing an opportunity for responding to questions, summarizing the main points of the meeting or conference, and verifying any action steps that were decided upon. Furthermore, regular follow-up serves as a demonstration of the professionalism of the school counselor.

SUMMARY POINTS

- The stress associated with having children with mental health problems compounds the inherent challenges to effective home-school communication. But counselors must overcome these challenges because clear and productive communication between home and school is critical to the success of students with mental health problems.
- Counselors can build relationships with parents of students with mental health problems by using empathic listening.
- Effective listening includes listening for unused opportunities and strengths.
- Communicate to parents that typical parenting strategies may not work with children with mental health problems. These unique children may need unique parenting approaches.
- Provide realistic hope to parents of students with mental health problems. Let them know they are not alone.
- Share difficult information with parents with care and sensitivity, using techniques such as presenting information in chunks, summarizing frequently, and soliciting parents' perceptions of the problems.

References

Abramson, L. Y., Metalsky, G. I., & Alloy, L. Y. (1989). Hopelessness depression: A theory-based subtype of depression. *Psychological Review, 96*, 358–372.

American Psychiatric Association. (1994). *Diagnostic and statistical manual of mental disorders* (4th ed.). Washington, DC: Author.

American Psychiatric Association. (2000). *Diagnostic and statistical manual of mental disorders* (Revised 4th ed.). Washington, DC: Author.

American School Counselor Association. (2009). *The professional school counselor and student mental health* [Position statement]. Retrieved from http://asca2.timberlake publishing.com//files/StudentMentalHealth.pdf

Angold, A., Erkanli, A., Farmer, E. M. Z., Fairbank, J. A., Burns, B. J., Keeler, G., . . . Costello, E. J. (2002). Psychiatric disorder, impairment, and service use in rural African American and White youth. *Archives of General Psychiatry, 59*, 893–901.

Attwood, T. (2007). *The complete guide to Asperger's syndrome.* London: Jessica Kingsley.

Auger, R. W. (2006). Delivering difficult news to parents: Guidelines for school counselors. *Professional School Counseling, 10*, 139–145.

Autism State Rankings Prevalence. (2010). Available from http://www.fightingautism .org/idea/autism-state-rankings-prevalence.php

Baker, J. E. (2003). *Social skills training for children and adolescents with Asperger syndrome and social communication problems.* Shawnee Mission, KS: Autism Asperger.

Bardick, A. D., & Bernes, K. B. (2005). A closer examination of bipolar disorder in school-age children. *Professional School Counseling, 9*, 72–77.

Barkley, R. A. (1995). *Taking charge of ADHD: The complete authoritative guide for parents.* New York: Guilford Press.

Barkley, R. A. (1998). *Attention-deficit hyperactivity disorder: A handbook for diagnosis and treatment* (2nd ed.). New York: Guilford Press.

Barkley, R. A., Fischer, M., Smallish, L., & Fletcher, K. (2006). Young adult outcome of hyperactive children: Adaptive functioning in major life activities. *Journal of the American Academy of Child and Adolescent Psychiatry, 45*, 192–202.

Beck, A. T., Rush, J., Shaw, B., & Emery, G. (1979). *Cognitive therapy of depression.* New York: Guilford Press.

Beidel, D. C., Morris, T. L., & Turner, M. W. (2004). Social phobia. In T. L. Morris & J. S. March (Eds.), *Anxiety disorders in children and adolescents* (pp. 141–163). New York: Guilford Press.

Beidel, D. C., & Turner, S. M. (2005). *Childhood anxiety disorders: A guide to research and treatment.* New York: Routledge.

Bellini, S., Peters, J. K., Benner, L., & Hopf, A. (2007). A meta-analysis of school-based social skills interventions for children with autism spectrum disorders. *Remedial and Special Education, 28,* 153–162.

Bennett, D. S., Ambrosini, P. J., Kudes, D., Metz, C., & Rabinovich, H. (2005). Gender differences in adolescent depression: Do symptoms differ for boys and girls? *Journal of Affective Disorders, 89,* 35–44.

Bernstein, G. A., Layne, A. E., Egan, E. A., & Tennison, D. M. (2005). School-based interventions for anxious children. *Journal of the American Academy of Child and Adolescent Psychiatry, 44,* 1118–1127.

Bernstein, N. (1996). *Treating the unmanageable adolescent: A guide to oppositional defiant and conduct disorders.* Northvale, NJ: Jason Aronson.

Biederman, J., Kwon, A., Wozniak, J., Mick, E., Markowitz, S., Fazio, V., . . . Faraone, S. V. (2004). Absence of gender differences in pediatric bipolar disorder: Findings from a large sample of referred youth. *Journal of Affective Disorders, 83,* 207–214.

Biederman, J., Petty, C. R., Dolan, C., Hughes, S., Mick, E., Monuteaux, M. C., . . . Faraone, S. V. (2008). The long-term longitudinal course of oppositional defiant disorder and conduct disorder in ADHD boys: Findings from a controlled 10-year prospective longitudinal follow-up study. *Psychological Medicine, 38,* 1027–1036.

Birmaher, B., & Axelson, D. (2006). Course and outcome of bipolar spectrum disorder in children and adolescents: A review of the existing literature. *Development and Psychopathology, 18,* 1023–1035.

Birmaher, B., Ryan, N. D., Williamson, D. E., Brent, D. A., Kaufman, J., Dahl, R. E., . . . Nelson, B. (1996). Childhood and adolescent depression: A review of the past 10 years. Part I. *Journal of the American Academy of Child and Adolescent Psychiatry, 35,* 1427–1439.

Blader, J. C., & Carlson, G. A. (2007). Increased rates of bipolar disorder diagnoses among U.S. child, adolescent, and adult inpatients, 1996–2004. *Biological Psychiatry, 62,* 107–114.

Bloomquist, M. L., & Schnell, S. V. (2002). *Helping children with aggression and conduct problems: Best practices for intervention.* New York: Guilford Press.

Bongers, I. L., Koot, H. M., van der Ende, J., & Verhulst, F. C. (2004). Developmental trajectories of externalizing behaviors in childhood and adolescence. *Child Development, 75,* 1523–1537.

Brigman, G., & Earley, B. (1991). *Group counseling for school counselors: A practical guide.* Portland, ME: J. Weston Walch.

Brown, K. S., & Parsons, R. D. (1998). Accurate identification of childhood aggression: A key to successful intervention. *Professional School Counseling, 2,* 135–140.

Buckman, R. (1992). *How to break bad news: A guide for health care professionals.* Baltimore: Johns Hopkins University Press.

Budman, C. L., Rockmore, L., Stokes, J., & Sossin, M. (2003). Clinical phenomenology of episodic rage in children with Tourette's syndrome. *Journal of Psychosomatic Research, 55,* 59–65.

Burns, D. D., & Nolen-Hoeksema, S. (1992). Therapeutic empathy and recovery from depression in cognitive-behavioral therapy: A structural equation model. *Journal of Consulting and Clinical Psychology, 60,* 441–449.

Burns, M. O., & Seligman, M. E. P. (1991). Explanatory style, helplessness, and depression. In C. R. Snyder & D. R. Forsyth (Eds.), *Handbook of social and clinical psychology: The health perspective* (pp. 267–284). Elmsford, NY: Pergamon Press.

Cartledge, G., Kea, C., & Simmons-Reed, E. (2002). Serving culturally diverse children with serious emotional disturbance and their families. *Journal of Child and Family Studies, 11,* 113–126.

Cauce, A. M., Domenech-Rodriquez, M., Paradise, M., Cochran, B. N., Shea, J. M., Srebnik, D., . . . Baydar, N. (2002). Cultural and contextual influences in mental health help seeking: A focus on ethnic minority youth. *Journal of Consulting and Clinical Psychology, 70,* 44–55.

Centers for Disease Control and Prevention. (2006, June). Youth risk behavior surveillance: United States, 2005. Surveillance summaries (No. SS-5). *MMWR, 55.* Retrieved from http://www.cdc.gov/mmwr/PDF/SS/SS5505.pdf

Chakrabarti, S., & Frombonne, E. (2005). Pervasive developmental disorders in preschool children: Confirmation of high prevalence. *American Journal of Psychiatry, 162,* 1133–1141.

Chan, Y., Dennis, M. L., & Funk, R. R. (2008). Prevalence and comorbidity of major internalizing and externalizing problems among adolescents and adults presenting to substance abuse treatment. *Journal of Substance Abuse Treatment, 34,* 14–24.

Christensen, L., & Duncan, K. (1995). Distinguishing depressed from nondepressed individuals using energy and psychosocial variables. *Journal of Consulting and Clinical Psychology, 63,* 495–498.

Clare, S. K., Jenson, W. R., Kehle, T. J., & Bray, M. A. (2000). Self-modeling as a treatment for increasing on-task behavior. *Psychology in the Schools, 37,* 517–522.

Cole, D. A., Martin, J. M., Powers, B., & Truglio, R. (1996). Modeling causal relations between academic and social competence and depression: A multitrait-multimethod longitudinal study of children. *Journal of Abnormal Psychology, 105,* 258–270.

Colman, I., Wadsworth, M. E. J., Croudace, T. J., & Jones, P. B. (2007). Forty-year psychiatric outcomes following assessment for internalizing disorder in adolescence. *American Journal of Psychiatry, 164,* 126–133.

Copeland, M. E., & Copans, S. (2002). *Recovering from depression: A workbook for teens* (Rev. ed.). Baltimore: Paul H. Brookes.

Costello, E. J., Erkanli, A., & Angold, A. (2006). Is there an epidemic of child or adolescent depression? *Journal of Child Psychology and Psychiatry, 47,* 1263–1271.

Costello, E. J., Mustillo, S., Erkanli, A., Keeler, G., & Angold, A. (2003). Prevalence and development of psychiatric disorders in childhood and adolescence. *Archives of General Psychiatry, 60,* 837–844.

Cottrell, D. J., & Summers, K. (1990). Communicating an evolutionary diagnosis of disability to parents. *Child: Care, Health and Development, 16,* 211–218.

Craft, L. L., & Landers, D. M. (1998). The effect of exercise on clinical depression and depression resulting from mental illness: A meta-analysis. *Journal of Sport & Exercise Psychology, 20,* 339–357.

Dimmitt, C., Carey, J. C., & Hatch, T. (2007). *Evidence-based school counseling: Making a difference with data-driven practices.* Thousand Oaks, CA: Corwin.

Dishion, T. J., McCord, J., & Poulin, F. (1999). When interventions harm: Peer groups and problem behavior. *American Psychologist, 54,* 755–764.

DuPaul, G. J., Jitendra, A. K., Tresco, K. E., Vile Junod, R. E., Volpe, R. J., & Lutz, J. G. (2006). Children with attention deficit hyperactivity disorder: Are there gender differences in school functioning? *School Psychology Review, 35,* 292–308.

Egan, G. (2010). *The skilled helper* (9th ed.). Belmont, CA: Brooks/Cole.

Elkins, I. J., McGue, M., & Iacono, W. G. (2007). Prospective effects of attention-deficit/hyperactivity disorder, conduct disorder, and sex on adolescent substance use and abuse. *Archives of General Psychiatry, 64,* 1145–1152.

Embry, D. D. (2002). The Good Behavior Game: A best practice candidate as a universal behavioral vaccine. *Clinical Child and Family Psychology Review, 5,* 273–297.

Embry, D. D., & Straatemeier, G. (2001). *The PAX Act Game manual: How to apply the Good Behavior Game.* Tucson, AZ: PAXIS Institute.

Endo, T., Shiori, T., Someya, T., Toyabe, S., & Akazawa, K. (2007). Parental mental health affects behavioral changes in children following a devastating disaster: A community survey after the 2004 Niigata-Chuetsu earthquake. *General Hospital Psychiatry, 29,* 175–176.

Epstein, J. L., & Sanders, M. C. (2006). Prospects for change: Preparing educators for school, family, and community partnerships. *Peabody Journal of Education, 81,* 81–120.

Evans, J. R., Van Velsor, P., & Schumacher, J. E. (2002). Addressing adolescent depression: A role for school counselors. *Professional School Counseling, 5,* 211–219.

Ezpeleta, L., Keeler, G., Erkanli, A., Costello, E. J., & Angold, A. (2001). Epidemiology of psychiatric disability in childhood and adolescence. *Journal of Child Psychology and Psychiatry, 42,* 901–914.

Fabiano, G. A., Pelham, W. E., Coles, E. K., Gnagy, E. M., Chronis-Tuscano, A., & O'Conner, B. C. (2009). A meta-analysis of behavioral treatments for attention-deficit/hyperactivity disorder. *Clinical Psychology Review, 29,* 129–140.

Fallowfield, L. (1993). Giving sad and bad news. *Lancet, 341,* 476–478.

Ferguson, D. M., Horwood, L. J., & Ridder, E. M. (2005). Show me the child at seven: The consequences of conduct problems in childhood for psychosocial functioning in adulthood. *Journal of Child Psychology and Psychiatry, 46,* 837–849.

Field, T., Diego, M., & Sanders, C. (2001a). Adolescent depression and risk factors. *Adolescence, 36,* 491–498.

Field, T., Diego, M., & Sanders, C. E. (2001b). Exercise is positively related to adolescents' relationships and academics. *Adolescence, 36,* 105–110.

Flannery-Schroeder, E. C. (2004). Generalized anxiety disorder. In T. L. Morris & J. S. March (Eds.), *Anxiety disorders in children and adolescents* (pp. 125–140). New York: Guilford Press.

Fontaine, R. G., Burks, V. S., & Dodge, K. A. (2002). Response decision processes and externalizing behavior problems in adolescents. *Development and Psychopathology, 14,* 107–122.

Freedenthal, S. (2007). Racial disparities in mental health service use by adolescents who thought about or attempted suicide. *Suicide and Life-Threatening Behavior, 37,* 22–34.

Frey, A., & George-Nichols, N. (2003). Intervention practices for students with emotional and behavioral disorders: Using research to inform school social work practice. *Children & Schools, 25,* 97–104.

Frick, P. J. (1994). Family dysfunction and the disruptive behavior disorders: A review of recent empirical findings. *Advances in Clinical Child Psychology, 16,* 203–226.

Fristad, M. A. (2006). Psychoeducational treatment for school-aged children with bipolar disorder. *Development and Psychopathology, 18,* 1289–1306.

Gable, R. A., Hendrickson, J. M., & Van Acker, R. (2001). Maintaining the integrity of FBA-based interventions in schools. *Education and Treatment of Children, 24,* 248–260.

Garber, J., Weiss, B., & Shanley, N. (1993). Cognitions, depressive symptoms, and development in adolescents. *Journal of Abnormal Psychology, 102,* 47–57.

Garland, E. J. (1997). *Depression is the pits, but I'm getting better: A guide for adolescents.* Washington, DC: Magination Press.

Garrison, C. Z., Waller, J. L., Cuffee, S. P., McKeown, R. E., Addy, C. L., & Jackson, K. L. (1997). Incidence of major depressive disorder and dysthymia in young adolescents. *Journal of the American Academy of Child and Adolescent Psychiatry, 36,* 458–465.

Geller, B., Craney, J. L., Bolhofner, K., Nickelsburg, M. J., Williams, M., & Zimerman, B. (2002). Two-year prospective follow-up of children with a prepubertal and early adolescent bipolar disorder phenotype. *American Journal of Psychiatry, 159,* 927–933.

Geller, B., Zimerman, B., Williams, M., DelBello, M., Frazier, J., & Beringer, L. (2002). Phenomenology of prepubertal and early adolescent bipolar disorder: Examples of elated mood, grandiose behaviors, decreased need for sleep, racing thoughts and hypersexuality. *Journal of Child and Adolescent Psychopharmacology, 12,* 3–9.

Gershon, J. (2002). A meta-analytic review of gender differences in ADHD. *Journal of Attention Disorders, 5,* 143–154.

Gianconia, R. M., Reinherz, H. Z., Silverman, A. B., Pakiz, B., Frost, A. K., & Cohen, E. (1995). Traumas and posttraumatic stress disorder in a community population of older adolescents. *Journal of the American Academy of Child and Adolescent Psychiatry, 34,* 1369–1380.

Gladstone, T. R. G., & Kaslow, N. J. (1995). Depression and attributions in children and adolescents: A meta-analytic review. *Journal of Abnormal Child Psychology, 23,* 597–606.

Goh, M., Herting Wahl, K., Koch McDonald, J., Brissett, A. A., & Yoon, E. (2007). Working with immigrant students in school: The role of school counselors in building cross-cultural bridges. *Journal of Multicultural Counseling and Development, 35,* 66–79.

Gray, C. (2010). *What are social stories?* Retrieved from http://www.thegraycenter .org/social-stories/what-are-social-stories

Greenberg, K. R. (2003). *Group counseling in K–12 schools: A handbook for school counselors.* Boston: Allyn & Bacon.

Greene, R. W., Biederman, J., Faraone, S. V., Monuteaux, M. C., Mick, E., DuPree, E. P., . . . Goring, J. C. (2001). Social impairment in girls with ADHD: Patterns, gender comparisons, and correlates. *Journal of the American Academy of Child and Adolescent Psychiatry, 40,* 704–710.

Hanson, R. F., Self-Brown, S., Fricker-Elhai, A., Kilpatrick, D. G., Saunders, B. E., & Resnick, H. (2006). Relations among parental substance use, violence exposure and mental health: The national survey of adolescents. *Addictive Behaviors, 31,* 1988–2001.

Heiman, T. (2002). Parents of children with disabilities: Resilience, coping, and future expectations. *Journal of Developmental and Physical Disabilities, 14,* 159–171.

Hilarski, C. (2004). Victimization history as a risk factor for conduct disorder behaviors: Exploring connections in a national sample of youth. *Stress, Trauma, and Crisis, 7,* 47–59.

Hillenmeier, M. M., Foster, E. M., Heinrichs, B., & Heier, B. (2007). Racial differences in parental reports of attention-deficit/hyperactivity disorder behaviors. *Journal of Developmental & Behavioral Pediatrics, 28,* 353–361.

Himle, J. A., Fischer, D. J., Van Etten Lee, M., & Muroff, J. R. (2006). Childhood anxiety disorders. In R. J. Waller (Ed.), *Fostering child & adolescent mental health in the classroom* (pp. 77–98). Thousand Oaks, CA: Sage.

Hogue, A., Henderson, C. E., Dauber, S., Barajas, P. C., Fried, A., & Liddle, H. A. (2008). Treatment adherence, competence, and outcome in individual and family therapy for adolescent behavior problems. *Journal of Consulting and Clinical Psychology, 76,* 544–555.

Horvath, A. O., & Symonds, B. D. (1991). Relation between working alliance and outcome in psychotherapy: A meta-analysis. *Journal of Counseling Psychology, 38,* 139–149.

House, A. E. (2002). *DSM-IV diagnosis in the schools.* New York: Guilford Press.

Hoven, C. W., Duarte, C. S., Lucas, C. P., Wu, P., Mandell, D. J., Goodwin, R. D., . . . Susser, E. (2005). Psychopathology among New York City public school children 6 months after September 11. *Archives of General Psychiatry, 62,* 545–552.

Individuals With Disabilities Education Act, 20 U.S.C § 1400 et. seq.

Joiner, T. E., Lewinsohn, P. M., & Seeley, J. R. (2002). The core of loneliness: Lack of pleasurable engagement—more so than painful disconnection—predicts social impairment, depression onset, and recovery from depressive disorders among adolescents. *Journal of Personality Assessment, 79,* 472–491.

Jones, W. P. (1997). *Deciphering the diagnostic codes: A guide for school counselors.* Thousand Oaks, CA: Corwin.

Kehle, T. J., Clark, E., Jenson, W. R., & Wampold, B. E. (1986). Effectiveness of self-observation with behavior disordered elementary school children. *School Psychology Review, 15,* 289–295.

Kehle, T. J., Owen, S. V., & Cressy, E. T. (1990). The use of self-modeling as an intervention in school psychology: A case study of an elective mute. *School Psychology Review, 19,* 115–121.

Kessler, R. C., Avenevoli, S., & Merikangas, K. R. (2001). Mood disorders in children and adolescents: An epidemiologic perspective. *Biological Psychiatry, 49,* 1002–1014.

Kessler, R. C., Berglund, P., Demler, O., Jin, R., & Walters, E. E. (2005). Lifetime prevalence and age-of-onset distributions of DSM-IV disorders in the National Comorbidity Survey Replication. *Archives of General Psychiatry, 62,* 593–602.

King, N. J., Heyne, D., & Ollendick, T. H. (2005). Cognitive-behavioral treatments for anxiety and phobic disorders in children and adolescents: A review. *Behavioral Disorders, 30,* 241–257.

King, N. J., Muris, P., & Ollendick, T. H. (2004). Specific phobia. In T. L. Morris & J. S. March (Eds.), *Anxiety disorders in children and adolescents* (pp. 263–279). New York: Guilford Press.

Koeppen, A. S. (1974). Relaxation training for children. *Elementary School Guidance and Counseling, 9,* 14–21.

Kovacs, M., Obrosky, D. S., Gastonis, C., & Richards, C. (1997). First-episode major depressive and dysthymic disorder in childhood: Clinical and sociodemographic factors in recovery. *Journal of American Academy of Child and Adolescent Psychiatry, 36,* 777–784.

Kovaleski, J. R. (2007). Response to intervention: Considerations for research and systems change. *School Psychology Review, 36*, 638–646.

Kowatch, R. A., Fristad, M., Birmaher, B., Dineen Wagner, K., Findling, R. L., Hellander, M., . . . Child Psychiatric Workgroup on Bipolar Disorder. (2005). Treatment guidelines for children and adolescents with bipolar disorder. *Journal of the American Academy of Child and Adolescent Psychiatry, 44*, 213–235.

Langberg, J. M., Epstein, J. N., Urbanowicz, C. M., Simon, J. O., & Graham, A. J. (2008). Efficacy of an organizational skills intervention to improve the academic functioning of students with attention-deficit/hyperactivity disorder. *School Psychology Quarterly, 23*, 407–417.

Lau, A. S., Garland, A. F., Yeh, M., McCabe, K. M., Wood, P. A., & Hough, R. L. (2004). Race/ethnicity and inter-informant agreement in assessing adolescent psychopathology. *Journal of Emotional and Behavioral Disorders, 12*, 145–156.

Lauer, R. E., Giordani, B., Boivin, M. J., Halle, N., Glasgow, B., Alessi, N. E., . . . Berent, S. (1994). Effects of depression on memory performance and metamemory in children. *Journal of the American Academy of Child and Adolescent Psychiatry, 33*, 679–685.

Lawrence-Lightfoot, S. (2003). *The essential conversation: What parents and teachers can learn from each other.* New York: Ballantine Books.

Lee, C. (2007). Hispanics and the death penalty: Discriminatory charging practices in San Joaquin County, California. *Journal of Criminal Justice, 35*, 17–27.

Lewinsohn, P. M. (1974). A behavioral approach to depression. In R. J. Friedman & M. M. Katz (Eds.), *The psychology of depression: Contemporary theory and research* (pp. 157–185). New York: John Wiley.

Lewinsohn, P. M., Clarke, G. N., Seeley, J. R., & Rohde, P. (1994). Major depression in community adolescents: Age of onset, episode duration, and time to recurrence. *Journal of the American Academy of Child and Adolescent Psychiatry, 33*, 809–818.

Lewinsohn, P. M., & Gotlib, I. H. (1995). Behavioral theory and treatment of depression. In E. E. Beckham & W. R. Leber (Eds.), *Handbook of depression* (2nd ed., pp. 352–375). New York: Guilford Press.

Lewinsohn, P. M., Zinbarg, R., Seeley, J. R., Lewinsohn, M., & Sack, W. H. (1997). Lifetime comorbidity among anxiety disorders and between anxiety disorders and other mental disorders in adolescents. *Journal of Anxiety Disorders, 11*, 377–394.

Livingston, R. B., Stark, K. D., Haak, R. A., & Jennings, E. (1996). Neuropsychological profiles of children with depressive and anxiety disorders. *Child Neuropsychology, 2*, 48–62.

Lombana, J. H. (1983). *Home-school partnerships: Guidelines and strategies for educators.* New York: Grune & Stratton.

Lovejoy, M. C., Graczyk, P. A., O'Hare, E., & Neuman, G. (2000). Maternal depression and parenting behavior: A meta-analytic review. *Clinical Psychology Review, 20*, 561–592.

Macintosh, K., & Dissanayake, C. (2006). A comparative study of the spontaneous social interactions of children with high-functioning autism and children with Asperger's disorder. *Autism, 10*, 199–220.

Mackinaw-Koons, B., & Fristad, M. A. (2004). Children with bipolar disorder: How to break down barriers and work effectively together. *Professional Psychology: Research and Practice, 35*, 481–484.

Mann, E. M., Ikeda, Y., Mueller, C. W., Takahashi, A., Tao, K. T., Humris, E., . . . Chin, D. (1992). Cross-cultural differences in rating hyperactive-disruptive behaviors in children. *American Journal of Psychiatry, 149,* 1539–1542.

March, J. S., Franklin, M. E., Leonard, H. L., & Foa, E. B. (2004). Obsessive-compulsive disorder. In T. L. Morris & J. S. March (Eds.), *Anxiety disorders in children and adolescents* (pp. 212–240). New York: Guilford Press.

Markus, H., & Nurius, P. (1986). Possible selves. *American Psychologist, 41,* 954–969.

Masi, G., Tomaiuolo, F., Sbrana, B., Poli, P., Baracchini, G., Pruneti, C. A., . . . Marcheschi, M. (2001). Depressive symptoms and academic self-image in adolescence. *Psychopathology, 34,* 57–61.

McConaughy, S. H., Kay, P. J., & Fitzgerald, M. (2000). How long is long enough? Outcomes for a school-based prevention program. *Exceptional Children, 67,* 21–34.

McGee, R., Anderson, J., Williams, S., & Silva, P. A. (1986). Cognitive correlates of depressive symptoms in 11-year-old children. *Journal of Abnormal Child Psychology, 14,* 517–524.

McKnight, C. D., Compton, S. N., & March, J. S. (2004). Posttraumatic stress disorder. In T. L. Morris & J. S. March (Eds.), *Anxiety disorders in children and adolescents* (pp. 241–262). New York: Guilford Press.

McLaughlin, K. A., Hilt, L. M., & Nolen-Hokesema, S. (2007). Racial/ethnic differences in internalizing and externalizing symptoms in adolescents. *Journal of Abnormal Child Psychology, 35,* 801–816.

McLoone, J., Hudson, J. L., & Rapee, R. M. (2006). Treating anxiety disorders in a school setting. *Education and Treatment of Children, 29,* 219–242.

McMiller, W. P., & Weisz, J. R. (1996). Help-seeking preceding mental health clinic intake among African-American, Latino, and Caucasian youths. *Journal of the American Academy of Child and Adolescent Psychiatry, 35,* 1086–1094.

Mennen, F. E., & Trickett, P. K. (2007). Mental health needs of urban children. *Children and Youth Services Review, 29,* 1220–1234.

Merrell, K. W. (2008). *Helping students overcome depression and anxiety: A practical guide* (2nd ed.). New York: Guilford Press.

Mesman, J., & Koot, H. M. (2000). Child-reported depression and anxiety in preadolescence: I. Associations with parent- and teacher-reported problems. *Journal of the American Academy of Child and Adolescent Psychiatry, 39,* 1371–1378.

Miller, T. W., Nigg, J. T., & Miller, R. L. (2009). Attention deficit hyperactivity disorder in African American children: What can be concluded from the past ten years? *Clinical Psychology Review, 29,* 77–86.

Minnesota Department of Health. (2007). *2007 Minnesota Student Survey: Statewide tables.* St. Paul, MN: Author.

Molina, B. S. G., Hinshaw, S. P., Swanson, J. M., Arnold, L. E., Vitiello, B., Jensen, P. S., . . . MTA Cooperative Group. (2009). The MTA at 8 years: Prospective follow-up of children treated for combined-type ADHD in a multisite study. *Journal of the American Academy of Child and Adolescent Psychiatry, 48,* 484–500.

Murthy, R. S. (2007). Mass violence and mental health: Recent epidemiological findings. *International Review of Psychiatry, 19,* 183–192.

Myles, B. S. (2005). *Children and youth with Asperger syndrome: Strategies for success in inclusive settings.* Thousand Oaks, CA: Corwin.

Myles, B. S., & Hubbard, A. (2005). Environmental modification. In B. S. Myles (Ed.), *Children and youth with Asperger syndrome: Strategies for success in inclusive settings* (pp. 15–34). Thousand Oaks, CA: Corwin.

Nguyen, L., Huang, L. N., Arganza, G. R., & Liao, Q. (2007). The influence of race and ethnicity on psychiatric diagnoses and clinical characteristics of children and adolescents in children's services. *Cultural Diversity and Ethnic Minority Psychology, 13*, 18–25.

Nock, M. K., Kazdin, A. E., Hiripi, E., & Kessler, R. C. (2007). Lifetime prevalence, correlates, and persistence of oppositional defiant disorder: Results from the National Comorbidity Survey Replication. *Journal of Child Psychology and Psychiatry, 48*, 703–713.

Ollendick, T. H., Jarrett, M. A., Grills-Taquechel, A. E., Hovey, L. D., & Wolff, J. C. (2008). Comorbidity as a predictor and moderator of treatment outcome in youth with anxiety, affective, attention deficit/hyperactivity disorder, and oppositional/conduct disorders. *Clinical Psychology Review, 28*, 1447–1471.

Ost, L. (1987). Applied relaxation: Description of a coping technique and review of controlled studies. *Behaviour Research and Therapy, 25*, 397–409.

Osterlind, S. J., Koller, J. R., & Morris, E. F. (2007). Incidence and practical issues of mental health for school-aged youth in juvenile justice detention. *Journal of Correctional Health Care, 13*, 268–277.

Ostrander, R. (2004). Oppositional defiant disorder and conduct disorder. In F. M. Kline & L. B. Silver (Eds.), *The educator's guide to mental health issues in the classroom* (pp. 267–286). Baltimore: Paul H. Brookes.

Ostrander, R., Weinfurt, K. P., & Nay, W. R. (1998). The role of age, family support, and negative cognitions in the prediction of depressive symptoms. *School Psychology Review, 27*, 121–137.

Paige, L. Z., Kitzis, S. N., & Wolfe, J. (2003). Rural underpinnings for resiliency and linkages (RURAL): A Safe Schools/Healthy Students project. *Psychology in the Schools, 40*, 531–547.

Paone, T. R., & Douma, K. B. (2009). Child-centered play therapy with a seven-year-old boy diagnosed with intermittent explosive disorder. *International Journal of Play Therapy, 18*, 31–44.

Papolos, D. F., & Papolos, J. (2002). *The bipolar child.* New York: Broadway Books.

Pastor, P. N., & Reuben, C. A. (2008). Diagnosed attention deficit hyperactivity disorder and learning disability: United States, 2004–2006. National Center for Health Statistics. *Vital Health and Statistics, 10*(237).

Pavuluri, M. N., Birmaher, B., & Naylor, M. W. (2005). Pediatric bipolar disorder: A review of the past 10 years. *Journal of the American Academy of Child and Adolescent Psychiatry, 44*, 846–871.

Pfiffner, L. J., & Barkley, R. A. (1998). Treatment of ADHD in school settings. In R. A. Barkley (Ed.), *Attention-deficit hyperactivity disorder: A handbook for diagnosis and treatment* (2nd ed., pp. 458–490). New York: Guilford Press.

Pierangelo, R., & Giuliani, G. (2008). *Classroom management techniques for students with ADHD: A step-by-step guide for educators.* Thousand Oaks, CA: Corwin.

Prelow, H. M., Danoff-Burg, S., Swenson, R. R., & Pulgiano, D. (2004). The impact of ecological risk and perceived discrimination on the psychological adjustment of African American and European American youth. *Journal of Community Psychology, 32*, 375–389.

Quay, H. C. (1993). The psychobiology of undersocialized aggressive conduct disorder: A theoretical perspective. *Development and Psychopathology, 5*, 165–180.

Ramsey, R. D. (2002). *How to say the right thing every time: Communicating well with students, staff, parents, and the public.* Thousand Oaks, CA: Corwin.

Rao, U., Weissman, M. M., Martin, J. A., & Hammond, R. W. (1993). Childhood depression and risk of suicide: A preliminary report of a longitudinal study. *Journal of the American Academy of Child and Adolescent Psychiatry, 32,* 21–27.

Rapoport, J. L., Inoff-Germain, G., Weissman, M. M., Greenwald, S., Narrow, W. E., Jensen, P. S., . . . Canino, G. (2000). Childhood obsessive-compulsive disorder in the NIMH MECA study: Parent versus child identification of cases. *Journal of Anxiety Disorders, 14,* 535–548.

Rehabilitation Act of 1973, 29 U.S.C. § 701 et seq.

Reynhout, G., & Carter, M. (2009). The use of social stories by teachers and their perceived efficacy. *Research in Autism Spectrum Disorders, 3,* 232–251.

Rinaldi, C. M., & Heath, N. L. (2006). An examination of the conflict resolution strategies and goals of children with depressive symptoms. *Emotional and Behavioural Difficulties, 11,* 187–204.

Ritchie, M. H., & Huss, S. N. (2000). Recruitment and screening of minors for group counseling. *Journal for Specialists in Group Work, 25,* 145–156.

Rohde, P., Lewinsohn, P. M., & Seeley, J. R. (1994). Are adolescents changed by an episode of major depression? *Journal of the American Academy of Child and Adolescent Psychiatry, 33,* 1289–1298.

Rowley, S. J., Burchinal, M. R., Roberts, J. E., & Zeisel, S. A. (2008). Racial identity, social context, and race-related social cognition in African Americans during middle childhood. *Developmental Psychology, 44,* 1537–1546.

Santucci, L. C., Ehrenreich, J. T., Trosper, S. E., Bennett, S. M., & Pincus, D. B. (2009). Development and preliminary evaluation of a one-week summer treatment program for separation anxiety disorder. *Cognitive and Behavioral Practice, 16,* 317–331.

Schraedley, P. K., Gotlib, I. H., & Hayward, C. (1999). Gender differences in correlates of depressive symptoms in adolescents. *Journal of Adolescent Health, 25,* 98–108.

Schwab-Stone, M., Ruchkin, V., Vermeiren, R., & Leckman, P. (2001). Cultural considerations in the treatment of children and adolescents. *Child and Adolescent Psychiatric Clinics of North America, 10,* 729–743.

Sciutto, M. J., Nolfi, C. J., & Bluhm, C. (2004). Effects of child gender and symptom type on referral for ADHD by elementary school teachers. *Journal of Emotional and Behavioral Disorders, 12,* 247–253.

Seligman, M. (2000). *Conducting effective conferences with parents of children with disabilities: A guide for teachers.* New York: Guilford Press.

Seligman, M. E. P. (1995). *The optimistic child.* Boston: Houghton Mifflin.

Shaffer, D., Fisher, P., Dulcan, M. K., Davies, M., Piacentini, J., Schwab-Stone, M. E., . . . Regier, D. A. (1996). The NIMH Diagnostic Interview Schedule for Children Version 2.3 (DISC-2.3): Description, acceptability, prevalence rates, and performance in the MECA Study. Methods for the Epidemiology of Child and Adolescent Mental Disorders Study. *Journal of the American Academy of Child and Adolescent Psychiatry, 35,* 865–877.

Shields, A., & Cicchetti, D. (2001). Parental maltreatment and emotional dysregulation as risk factors for bullying and victimization in middle childhood. *Journal of Clinical Child Psychology, 30,* 349–363.

Shirk, S. R., & Karver, M. (2003). Prediction of treatment outcomes from relationship variables in child and adolescent therapy: A meta-analytic review. *Journal of Consulting and Clinical Psychology, 71,* 452–464.

Silverman, S. M., & Weinfeld, R. (2007). *School success for kids with Asperger's syndrome*. Waco, TX: Prufrock Press.

Silverman, W. K., & Dick-Niederhauser, A. (2004). Separation anxiety disorder. In T. L. Morris & J. S. March (Eds.), *Anxiety disorders in children and adolescents* (pp. 164–188). New York: Guilford Press.

Sloper, P., & Turner, S. (1993). Determinants of parental satisfaction with disclosure of disability. *Developmental Medicine and Child Neurology, 35,* 816–825.

Smith, T. E. C. (2002). Section 504: What teachers need to know. *Intervention in School and Clinic, 37,* 259–266.

Stanley, M. J., Canham, D. L., & Cureton, V. Y. (2006). Assessing prevalence of emotional and behavioral problems in suspended middle school students. *Journal of School Nursing, 22,* 40–47.

Stark, K. D. (1990). *Childhood depression: School-based intervention.* New York: Guilford Press.

Stark, K. D., Ostrander, R., Kurowski, C. A., Swearer, S., & Bowen, B. (1995). Affective and mood disorders. In M. Herson & R. T. Ammerman (Eds.), *Advanced abnormal child psychology* (pp. 253–282). Hillsdale, NJ: Lawrence Erlbaum.

Stark, K. D., Rouse, L. W., & Kurowski, C. (1994). Psychological treatment approaches for depression in children. In W. M. Reynolds & H. R. Johnston (Eds.), *Handbook of depression in children and adolescents* (pp. 275–307). New York: Plenum Press.

Staton, D., Volness, L. J., & Beatty, W. W. (2008). Diagnosis and classification of pediatric bipolar disorder. *Journal of Affective Disorders, 105,* 205–212.

Stein, M. B., & Seedat, S. (2004). Pharmacotherapy. In T. L. Morris & J. S. March (Eds.), *Anxiety disorders in children and adolescents* (2nd ed., pp. 329–354). New York: Guilford Press.

Substance Abuse and Mental Health Services Administration. (2007). *Results from the 2006 National Survey on Drug Use and Health: National findings* (Office of Applied Studies, NSDUH Series H-32, DHHS Publication No. SMA 07–4293). Rockville, MD: Author.

Szalacha, L. A., Erkut, S., Coll, C. G., Alarcon, O., Fields, J. P., & Ceder, I. (2003). Discrimination and Puerto Rican children's and adolescents' mental health. *Cultural Diversity and Ethnic Minority Psychology, 9,* 141–155.

Todd, R. D., Huang, H., & Henderson, C. A. (2008). Poor utility of the age of onset criterion for DSM-IV attention deficit/hyperactivity disorder: Recommendations for DSM-IV and ICD-11. *Journal of Child Psychology and Psychiatry, 49,* 942–949.

Turner, H. A., Finkelhor, D., & Ormrod, R. (2006). The effect of lifetime victimization on the mental health of children and adolescents. *Social Science & Medicine, 62,* 13–27.

U.S. Department of Education, Office of Special Education and Rehabilitative Services, Office of Special Education Programs. (2004). *Teaching children with attention deficit hyperactivity disorder: Instructional strategies and practices.* Washington, DC: Author.

U.S. Department of Health and Human Services. (1999). *Mental health: A report of the Surgeon General.* Rockville, MD: Author. Retrieved from http://www.surgeon general.gov/library/mentalhealth/home.html

Vanneman, A., Hamilton, L., Baldwin Anderson, J., & Rahman, T. (2009). *Achievement gaps: How Black and White students in public schools perform in mathematics and reading on the National Assessment of Educational Progress* (NCES 2009–455). Washington, DC: National Center for Education Statistics, Institute of Education Sciences, U.S. Department of Education.

Vasa, R. A., & Pine, D. S. (2004). Neurobiology. In T. L. Morris & J. S. March (Eds.), *Anxiety disorders in children and adolescents* (pp. 3–26). New York: Guilford Press.

Vitaro, F., Pelletier, D., Gagnon, C., & Baron, P. (1995). Correlates of depressive symptoms in early adolescence. *Journal of Emotional and Behavioral Disorders, 3,* 241–251.

Wade, T. J., Cairney, J., & Pevalin, D. J. (2002). Emergence of gender differences in depression during adolescence: National panel results from three countries. *Journal of the American Academy of Child and Adolescent Psychiatry, 41,* 190–198.

Wall, T. N., & Hayes, J. A. (2000). Depressed clients' attributions of responsibility for the causes of and solutions to their problems. *Journal of Counseling and Development, 78,* 81–86.

Wampold, B. E. (2001). *The great psychotherapy debate: Models, methods, and findings.* Mahwah, NJ: Lawrence Erlbaum.

Warner, C. A., Fisher, P. H., Shrout, P. E., Rathor, S., & Klein, R. G. (2007). Treating adolescents with social anxiety disorder in school: An attention control trial. *Journal of Child Psychology and Psychiatry, 48,* 676–686.

Weiner, B. (1985). An attributional theory of achievement motivation and emotion. *Psychological Review, 92,* 548–573.

Weissman, M. M., Wolk, S., Goldstein, R. B., Moreau, D., Adams, P., Greenwald, S., . . . Wickramaratne, P. (1999). Depressed adolescents grown up. *Journal of the American Medical Association, 281,* 1707–1713.

Weist, M. D., & Evans, S. W. (2005). Expanded school mental health: Challenges and opportunities in an expanding field. *Journal of Youth and Adolescence, 34,* 3–6.

White Kress, V. E., Eriksen, K. P., Rayle, A. D., & Ford, S. J. W. (2005). The DSM-IV-TR and culture: Considerations for counselors. *Journal of Counseling & Development, 83,* 97–104.

Wierzbicki, M., & Rexford, L. (1989). Cognitive and behavioral correlates of depression in clinical and nonclinical populations. *Journal of Clinical Psychology, 45,* 872–877.

Wood, J. (2006). Effect of anxiety reduction on children's school performance and social adjustment. *Developmental Psychology, 42,* 345–349.

Wood, P. A., Yeh, M., Pan, D., Lambros, K. M., McCabe, K. M., & Hough, R. L. (2005). Exploring the relationship between race/ethnicity, age of first school-based services utilization, and age of first specialty mental health care for at-risk youth. *Mental Health Services Research, 7,* 185–196.

Wu, P., Hoven, C. W., Bird, H. R., Moore, R. E., Cohen, P., Alegria, M., . . . Roper, M. T. (1999). Depressive and disruptive disorders and mental health service utilization in children and adolescents. *Journal of the American Academy of Child and Adolescent Psychiatry, 38,* 1081–1092.

Wyn, J., Cahill, H., Holdsworth, R., Rowling, L., & Carson, S. (2000). MindMatters, a whole-school approach promoting mental health and wellbeing. *Australian and New Zealand Journal of Psychiatry, 34,* 594–601.

Yeh, M., McCabe, K., Hough, R. L., Dupuis, D., & Hazen, A. (2003). Racial/ethnic differences in parental endorsement of barriers to mental health services for youth. *Mental Health Services Research, 5,* 65–77.

Index

CORWIN

A SAGE Company

The Corwin logo—a raven striding across an open book—represents the union of courage and learning. Corwin is committed to improving education for all learners by publishing books and other professional development resources for those serving the field of PreK–12 education. By providing practical, hands-on materials, Corwin continues to carry out the promise of its motto: **"Helping Educators Do Their Work Better."**

CPSIA information can be obtained
at www.ICGtesting.com
Printed in the USA
FSHW020740080420
68939FS

9 781412 972734